LANCASTER COUNTY, VIRGINIA
COURT ORDERS 1775-1783

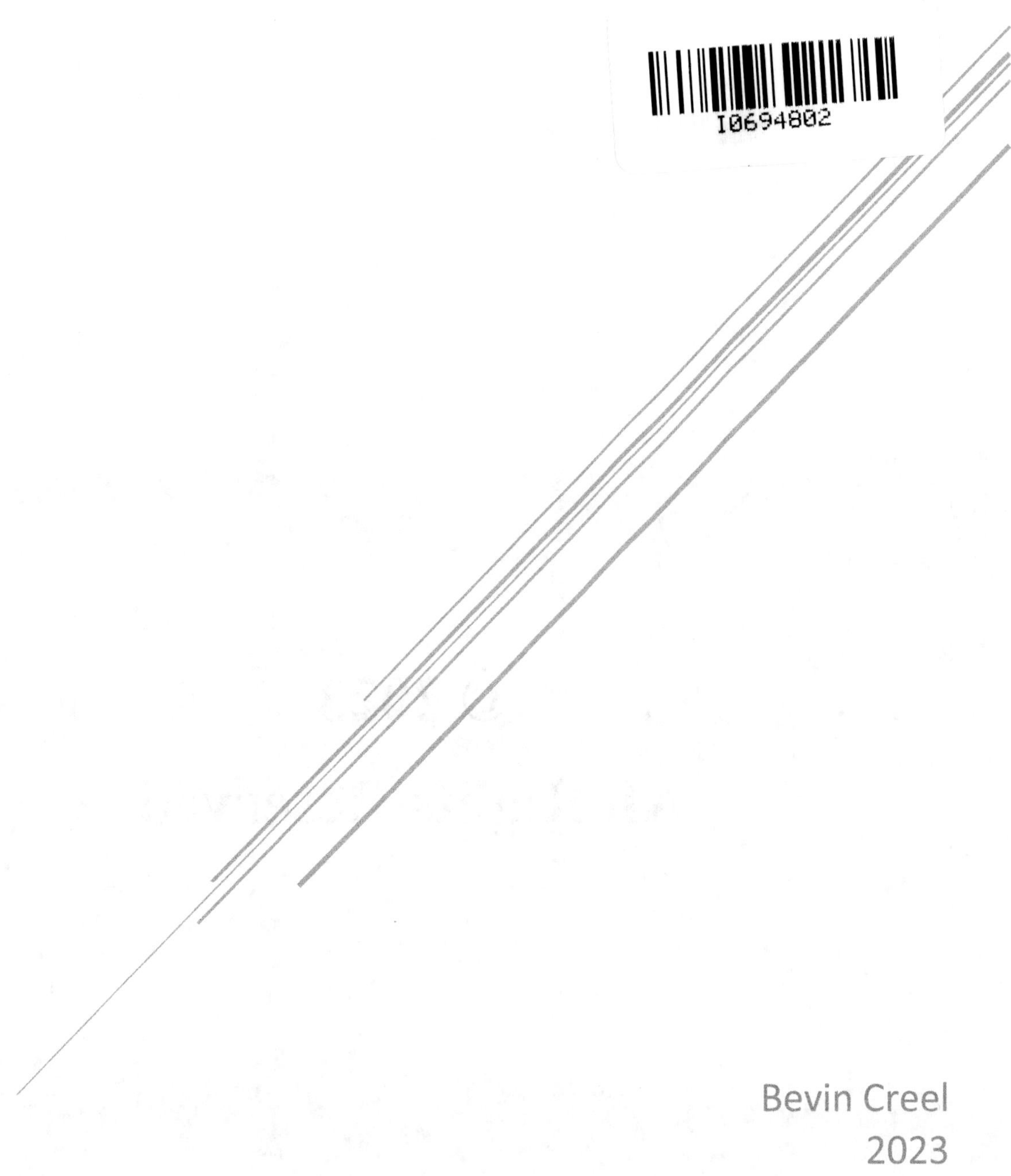

Bevin Creel

2023

Introduction

This is the sixth installment in my series of Virginia county court orders from the Revolutionary War years. My volumes for Augusta County, Richmond County, Bedford County, Brunswick County, and Halifax County are available for purchase at lulu.com. These previous volumes were approximately exact transcriptions. The present work differs, since it is my first attempt at a genealogical *abstract* of the orders, instead of a transcription. If you work long enough with these kinds of records, you will encounter much "boilerplate" language that is not genealogically relevant, and which principally serves to slow down the entire transcription process. As is the case with all works such as this, the researcher is strongly encouraged to obtain a copy of the relevant order book entry that is of particular interest to them.

This book contains abstracts of the Lancaster County court orders from 16 February 1775 to 3 January 1784, including part of Order Book 15, all of Order Book 16, and part of Order Book 17. My reading was taken from Family History Library microfilm rolls 32145 and 32146, with the exception of one illegible page. Thanks to Susan Chiarello for answering my emergency call and providing the one missing image from the Library of Virginia microfilm (Order Book 16, p 78a)! These orders cover all years of the American Revolution. The Revolution is my primary area of interest, which explains why I decline to abstract pages from these order books that fall outside of the 1775-1783 time frame.

There are no irregularities in the Lancaster orders. The Clerk's handwriting is generally good, and he has no odd quirks. There are some wartime entries that are obviously not included in the peacetime orders, such as provisions for wives, children, and parents of soldiers. As was common, the regular county court also sat as the court of claims, a court required by the Provision Law of May 1780. The proceedings of the court of claims are copied into these orders, which is standard fare for Virginia county court order books. The court also reviewed claims of losses sustained by British forces, as required by an act of the General Assembly in May 1782. Many Virginia orders contain evidence of "loyalist" activities in the county, such as men called into court for toasting His Majety's Health, or for uttering words inimical to the American cause. There were no such instances in the Lancaster orders, which is worthy of an honorable mention. If the reader is looking for examples of disaffection in the order books, I will suggest the Bedford County orders, for starters.

The Lancaster orders contain the proceedings of many Courts of Oyer and Terminer, which include the courts called to hear cases involving enslaved persons. The contents and vocabulary of many of these courts will be disturbing to some readers, and the punishments meted out were often violent and barbaric. In order to preserve the historical record as best as possible, I do not alter this content or vocabulary.

Despite my best efforts, there will be a handful of misreadings in these abstracts. This is another reason why the reader should obtain copies of orders of interest to them. The Family History Library microfilm roll number is given in the first paragraph above. The Library of Virginia holds its own microfilm. Of course, a copy might also be obtained from the Lancaster County Clerk's Office. I wish the reader luck in their research!

Bevin Creel
Washington, DC
September 2023

Lancaster County Order Book 15

[Index 1] Lancaster OB 15:400b, Feb Court 1775
Court, 16 Feb 1775, present James Ball, Dale Carter, Charles Carter, Jesse Ball, Hugh Brent, Burge Ball Gent.

[Index 2] Lancaster OB 15:401a, Feb Court 1775
On motion of Richard Payne, ordered William Mountague, Richard Ball, James Newby, Joseph Norris divide estate of George Payne decd among parties & legatees.
--Letters of administration granted to John Payne & Richard Payne on estate of Frances Payne decd. with Richard Mitchell security; and William Mountague, Richard Ball, James Newby & Joseph Norris to appraise the estate.
--George Payne orphan of William Payne decd choose Richard Payne for his guardian, Ben. Waddy security.
--Will of James Moughon decd presented by Bailie George, the named executor, and was proved by Lancelot Moore & Matthias Moughon; Hugh Brent, John Berryman, William Mason, Thomas Carter appraisers.
--Judith Payne orphan of William Payne decd chose Ben. Waddy for her guardian, security Richard Payne.
--Baker Angel bound to John Angel until age 21, to learn the Blacksmith trade.

[Index 3] Lancaster OB 15:401b, Feb Court 1775
Presentment of grand jury against Thomas Pinckard Gent for conceiling his riding chair dismissed.
--Presentment of grand jury against George Mahon for concealing thithable dismissed.
---Will of John Cundiff Sr presented by Benjamin & Richard Cundiff, the named executors, and was proved by Thomas Pitman & George Hayes.
--Ordered that late Deputy Sheriff John Bailey repay Isaac Mercer for a grand jury fine.
--William Mountague granted leave to turn road from Mrs. Ball's Mill to Northumberland by his house, also the road from Lancaster Courthouse to the "fork of the other road."
--Dedimus issued to Thomas Pollard to take deposition of John Maxwell in his suit against Bailie George.
--Report of division of estate of Elizabeth Simmons, "prevented by James Simmons from being signed & authenticated," was returned by Samuel Yop.
--Division of estate of Thomas James decd. returned.

[Index 4] Lancaster OB 15:402a, March Court 1775
Court, 16 March 1775, present Dale Carter, Jesse Ball, James Selden & John Taylor, Gent.
--Philip Smith, Burges Ball & Thomas B. Griffin granted administration on estate of Burges Smith decd, with securities Jesse Ball, James Selden & William Mountague; appraisers James Ball, Richard Mitchell, James Gordon & John Taylor.
--Alice Smith relict of Burges Smith relinquished administration, and ordered her dower be allotted after settlement of debts etc.
--George Payne orphan of William Payne bound to Martin Shearman until age 21, to learn the trade of Joiner.
--Jesse George vs John Thrall—Attachment.
--James Selden vs John Thrall—Attachment.
--John James granted administration on estate of Joan James decd, with security Richard Hutchings; appraisers William Griggs, Harry Lawson, Martin George, William Mason.

[Index 5] Lancaster OB 15:402b, April Court 1775
Court, 20 April 1775, present James Ball, Charles Carter, Dale Carter, James Selden, Hugh Brent, Thomas Lawson, Gent Justices.
William Boatment granted license to keep ordinary at the courthouse.
--Presentment of grand jury against James Ewell dismissed.
--James Packet, formerly bound to Roger Kelly, now bound to John Crowder until age 21, to learn the trade of a "good Planter."

--Jesse George vs John Thrall—Attachment. James Selden Gent was special bail for the Deft.
--Thadeus McCarty qualified as Colonel, Jesse Ball as Major, John Selden as Capt, James Ball & James Ewell as Lieutenants of militia.
--Jesse Wilder, orphan of Sarah Wilder, formerly bound to Wm. Griggs, now bound to his sd mother (Griggs relinquishing his right); she is to teach him the trade of a Weaver.

[Index 6] Lancaster OB 15:403a, April Court 1775

Richard Davis orphan of Andrew Davis bound to Bridger Haynie until age 21, being now 13, to learn the business of a Planter.
--James Selden vs John Thrall—Attachment. William Boatment was referee.

Court, 18 May 1775, present justices James Ball, Dale Carter, Charles Carter, James Selden, Hugh Brent, James Gordon.
--Division of estate of John Fendla decd was returned.
--On motion of James Mills & company, ordered the Sheriff make return on executions levied on estate of John Wormeley; slaves Nan and her child Polly, Phillis and her child Peggy were sold in said executions.
--Mungo Harvey sworn as grand jury foreman.
--Hugh Brent, Edwin Conway, Thomas Lawson, James Gordon, John Taylor, Jesse Ball & "Ball" appointed to take lists of tithables in their precincts.

[Index 7] Lancaster OB 15:403b, May Court 1775

John Bailey appointed Surveyor of Highway from the upper church to Deep Bottom & from the Cross Roads to the warf at Deep Creek Warehouse in the upper part of the county.
--Bailey George vs Maurice Wheeler—Ejectment.
--On motion of Margaret Ball, ordered Edwin Conway, James Gordon, Peter Conway & William Boatman view road between sd Ball & Martha Miller, leading to landing on Corotoman River.
--Ordered John McTire, Richard Goodridge, John Stonum, Rawleigh Hazard, Willoughby Rout, Margaret Angel, Judith Crowther appear at June court to answer grand jury presentments against them.

Court, 15 June 1775, justices James Ball, Dale Carter, Hugh Brent, John Taylor.
--Ordered Rawleigh Hazard appear at next court to answer grand juror presentment against him for retailing liquors without a license.
--Presentment of grand jury against Margaret Angel for having bastard child is continued.

[Index 8] Lancaster OB 15:404a, June Court 1775

Presentment of grand jury against Thomas Pinckard, Surveyor of highway, dismissed.
--Presentment of grand jury agaist Judith Crowther for having bastard child is dismissed, she paid fine 20 shillings.
--Will of Henry Hayes presented by Johnson Riveer, the named executor, Jesse Robinson, Thomas Dunaway, Richd. Goodridge, James Norris appointed appraisers.
--Richard Hutchings appointed Surveyor of highway from Charles Carter's great mill to Stephens ordinary.
--Presentment of grand jury against John Stonum for getting drunk, dismissed.
--Joseph Stevens, son of Richard Stephens, bound to Martin Shearman until age 21, to learn business of a Shop Joiner; his mother agreed to provide him with clothing.
--Presentment of grand jury against John McTire for swearing, discontinued, he paid 5 shillings.

[Index 9] Lancaster OB 15:404b, August Court 1775

Court 17 Aug 1775, present justices Dale Carter, Edwin Conway, James Selden, John Taylor.
--Will of John Merryman presented by John Merriman, the named executor, James Ewell, Edward Blackmore, Henry Towles, John Tuning appointed appraisers.
--Richard E. Lee admitted as attorney.
--James Ball took oath as Lieutenant in militia.

--Reuben Dogget, orphan of Reuben Dogget, formerly bound to William Weblin, now bound to Jeremiah Dogget until age 21, to learn trade of a Taylor.

[Index 10] Lancaster OB 15:405a, August Court 1775

Traverse Webb granted administration on estate of George Webb decd., with Lot Palmer his security, and Thomas Brent, Elijah Perciful, William Galloway, Edwin Conway Gent appointed appraisers.

--James Kirk Junr appointed guardian to Braxton, Catharine & John Pollard orphans of Thomas Pollard decd. in place of John Bailey their former guardian; James Selden & John Bailey were securities; ordered James Ball, Richard Mitchell & Jesse Ball Gent possess the new guardian with the estate of the sd orphans.

--On motion of Traverse Webb, ordered Thomas Brent, Elijah Perciful, Wm. Galloway & Edwin Conway divide estate of George Webb decd. among the claimants.

--On motion of John Carter Plt, against Thomas Pollard in a chancery suit, ordered depositions of Dale Carter Gent, Harry Carter & James Kirk be taken.

--On motion of John Davis, ordered the property of Davis's Warehouses, formerly taken from sd John Davis, be restored to him as proprietor thereof.

--On motion of Thomas Newton & son, ordered Maurice Wheeler be made Deft in the ejectment suit of Bailie George Plt against sd Maurice Wheeler.

[Index 11] Lancaster OB 15:405b, August Court 1775

Will of Thomas James decd formerly proved, and the widow (who qualified executrix to sd will) was since dead, and Anthony Sydnor & James Kirk (executors named in the will) having relinquished their right, Thomas James & Jonathan Wilder were granted administration; Harry Lawson, Thomas Lawson, Thomas Shearman & John Berryman appointed appraisers.

Court 18 Aug 1775, present justices Edwin Conway, James Selden, John Taylor, Thomas Lawson.
--Deed from Henry Armistead & his wife Winnefred to Burges Ball acknowledged.
--Deed of feoffment from Burges Ball & wife Mary to Henry Armistead was further proved by Winnefred Armistead, who made oath that she saw James Gordon, Ann Gordon, Jane Payne, & Sally Payne sign as witnesses.

Court 21 Sept 1775, present justices Charles Carter, Jesse Ball, Thomas Lawson, Burges Ball.
--Ordered that Sheriff collect from William Griggs the levies for two tithables for the last year.

[Index 12] Lancaster OB 15:406a, Sept Court 1775

Martha Miller granted permission to turn the road that goes to Taylors Landing through her land.

--Ordered the Sheriff pay George Bean £8 towards payment of building the prison.

--Thomas Rob granted administration on estate of Agatha Rob decd., with James Selden his security; Dale Carter, Elias Edmonds, James Kirk, & John Yerby appointed appraisers.

--Tithables belonging to Margaret Ball & Martha Miller added to clear the road from Doctor Robertsons to Taylor's Landing.

--Charles Webb orphan of George Webb choose Thomas Webb his guardian, and the court also appointed sd Thomas guardian to Jesse Webb & Lucy Webb orphans of the sd George; Lot Palmer was security; On motion of sd Thomas and Wm. Webb, ordered Edwin Conway, Thomas Brent, Elijah Perciful & Wm. Galloway divide estate of sd George Webb decd. among the claimants & possess the sd Thomas & Wm. with their parts, and also possess sd Thomas with the parts belonging to sd orphans.

--On motion of Robert Gordon, administrator of Robert Woddrop decd, execution issued against Bailie George a Sheriff of this county, for not satisfying an execution against Lawson, Dymer & Pinckard.

--Isaac Pitman granted administration on estate of Margaret Pitman decd., with Bartley James as security; Nicholas Currel, John Berryman, William Briggs, Thomas Lawson appointed appraisers.

[Index 13] Lancaster OB 15:406b, Sept Court 1775

895 pounds tobacco at Deep Creek Warehouse was sworn to by William Sydnor, Inspector.

--424 pounds tobacco at Dymer's Warehouse was sworn to by Fortunatus Sydnor, Inspector.

Court 19 Oct 1775, present justices James Ball, Charles Carter, Jesse Ball, James Selden, Burges Ball, James Gordon.
--Will of Ann Buckles proved by Elias Edmonds (a witness); Thomas Rob granted administration, with Elias Edmonds security; Dale Carter, John Yerby, James Kirk, & James Pinckard appointed appraisers.
--On motion of Daniel George, ordered Burges Ball, Henry Towles, Edward Blackmore & William Chowning divide estate of William George decd. among the heirs and possess sd Daniel with his part thereof.
--Henry Lawson appointed guardian to Sally Simmons orphan of John Simmons, with Thomas Lawson security; Ordered Nicholas Currel, Thomas Hunton & Thomas Shearman possess sd guardian with the estate of sd orphan.

[Index 14] Lancaster OB 15:407a, Oct Court 1775
Bushrod Riveer granted administration on estate of Elizabeth Riveer, with William Yerby security; Henry Lawson, Thomas Shearman, Thomas Carter, & Isaac Degge appointed appraisers.
--On motion of John James, ordered John Berryman, Thomas Shearman, Henry Lawson, & Thomas Carter divide estate of Thomas James decd.
--Account of 3366 pounds tobacco at Davis & Lowry's Warehouses sworn to by Dale Carter Gent., Inspector.

Court 16 Nov 1775, present justices John Fleet, Jesse Ball, James Selden, Thomas Lawson.
--Henry Towles granted administration on estate of John Robinson decd., with John Chowning security; Merryman Payne, William Chowning, John Chowning, & James Ewell appointed appraisers.
--Grand jury sworn, with Richard Hall as foreman.

[Index 15] Lancaster OB 15:407b, Nov Court 1775
Bushrod Riveer granted administration on estate of Mary Faulkner decd., with George Yerby security; James Kirk, Bailie George, William Yerby, & William Griggs appointed appraisers.
--John Christian (about age 14), orphan of Christopher Christian, bound to Bailie George until age 21, to learn business of a Planter.
--Thomas Mott granted administration on estate of Joseph Mott decd., with Elias Edmonds his security; Thomas Robb, James Kirk Junr, James Pinckard Junr, & George Norris appointed appraisers.

Court 17 Nov 1775, present justices Dale Carter, Jesse Ball, James Selden, James Gordon.
--Patrick Connelly having been summoned as a grand jury man, did not appear, fined 400 pounds tobacco and ordered taken.

[Index 16] Lancaster OB 15:408a, Nov Court 1775
Rawleigh Harris confessed a breach of the peace and "attempting the life of Thomas Bradshaw"; he was remanded to goal until security given.
--Bartly James assignee vs William Powell et al—Debt. Henry Currell, Henry Tapscot & John Hinton were special bail for Deft.
--John Goodridge, on presentment of grand jury, fined tens hillings as a common swearer.

Court 21 Dec 1775, present justices James Ball, Dale Carter, Jesse Ball, Edwin Conway.
--At laying of county levy, Bailie George, "S. Sheriff" was paid; David Boyd, Attorney for the King, was paid; William Boatman was paid his account; Joseph Shearman, "S. Sheriff" was paid; William Wiblin, Rebecca Robinson, Thomas Pollard, Robert Pollard, Peter Riveer, Thomas Pinckard, & Henry George were paid.

[Index 17] Lancaster OB 15:408b, Dec Court 1775
Ordered William Boatman clean the court house and furnish it with water and candles.
--Presentments of grand jury against James Ewell, John Taylor, Mungo Harvey, Thadeus McCarty, Henry Towles, John Overstreet, Frances Stephens, Joseph Parish, James Mercer, William Mugg, Peter Pool, John Bottoms, Edward Cox, Wm. Dameron, John Eustace, Wm. Mott, John Longwith, Hugh Kelly, Benjamin Garton, Wm. Schofield, & Thomas Brent are dismissed.

--Presentments against Willoughby Rout, John Hews, Luke Ashburn, Thomas Hill, & John Williams are continued.
--William Martin & Wm. Hinton ordered to pay 500 pounds tobacco for fornication.
--Presentment of grand juty against Judith Crowther for having a bastard child is discontinued, she having paid her fine.
--Rawleigh Spearman, Martin Hill, & George Brown ordered to pay 50 pounds of tobacco each for absenting themselves from divine service.
--Margaret Angel, summoned for having a bastard child, failed to appear, ordered fined 20 shillings, and "may be taken."
--Henry Towles vs John Roberts—Debt.
--Ordered Sheriff repay Thomas B. Griffin for two tithables who were exempted from last year's levy.

[Index 18] Lancaster OB 15:409a, Dec Court 1775
License granted to Rawleigh Hazard to keep an ordinary at Steptoes.
--Elizabeth Griggs orphan of Lee Griggs chose Wm. Griggs her guardian; Thomas Hubbard was his security.
--John Griggs orphan of of Lee Griggs chose Thomas Hubbard his guardian; Wm. Griggs was his security.
--Lee Griggs orphan of Lee Griggs chose Elias Edmonds his guardian; James Kirk was his security.
--Sally Yerby orphan of John Yerby chose Wm. Brent her guardian; John Yerby was his security; Ordered James Kirk, Wm. Yerby, & John Yerby possess the sd. guardian with the estate of said orphan.
--James Currell appointed guardian to Jacob Currell orphan of Jacob Currell, with William Giggs [thus] his security.
--Moses Jopes brouth before court for breach of the peace against Molly Jopes his wife, ordered he be bound to the peace and remain in custody until he shall give security.

Court 18 Jan 1776, present justices James Ball, Jesse Ball, John Taylor, Hugh Brent.
--Henry Davis appeared upon complaint of Abraham White; said Davis gave bond for his good behavior toward sd White; William Wiblin & Thomas Elliot were his securities.

[Index 19] Lancaster OB 15:409b, Jan Court 1776
Maurice Wheeler appeared upon complaint of sundry persons; said Wheeler gave bond for his good behavior; Henry Lawson, William Griggs, Charles Lee, & William Lawson were his securities.
--George Payne orphan of William Payne, formerly bound to Martin Shearman, was bound to Lowry Oliver until age 21, to learn the business of a Shop Joiner.
--On motion of Lee Griggs by Elias Edmonds his guardian, and John Griggs by Thomas Hubbard his guardian, ordered Edwin Conway, James Gordon Gent, & Thomas Brent divide estate of Lee Griggs decd among all lawful claimers.
--On motion of Job Carter, ordered Edwin Conway, James Kirk, & John Yerby divide estate of Ann Buckles decd.
--On motion of Job Carter, ordered Edwin Conway, James Kirk, & John Yerby divide estate of Agatha Robb decd.
--Bailie George vs Maurice Wheeler--Ejectment.

[Index 20] Lancaster OB 15:410a, Jan Court 1776
Ordered Richard Mitchell, John Chinn, & Richard Goodridge view road petitioned for by Joseph Norris.

Court 15 Feb 1776, present justices James Ball, Edwin Conway, Jesse Ball, Hugh Brent.
--Will of William Pasquet presented by Thomas Haydon the executor therein named, was proved by Ezekiel & John Haydon; Benjamin George, George Edwards, John Overstreet, & James Simmons appointed appraisers.
--John Eustace vs Robert Gilmour—Case.
--John Eustace vs Robert Gilmore—Attachment.
--James Gordon & Henry George granted administration on estate of Spencer Dogget, with Mathew Myars & Nicholas George as their securities; Coleman Dogget, Spencer George, John Yerby & Elias Edmonds were appointed appraisers.
--Thomas Pursley orphan of Thomas Pursley bound to Martin Shearman until age 21, to learn the business of a Shop Joiner.

[Index 21] Lancaster OB 15:410b, Feb Court 1776
William George orphan of William George bound to Lowry Oliver until age 21, to learn the business of a Shop Joiner; his mother agreed to provide him with apparel.
--Willoughby Rout fined 50 pounds of tobacco for absenting himself from divine service.
--Presentment of grand jury against Luke Ashburn & James Selden Gent dismissed.
--Bailie George appeared upon complaint of Maurice Wheeler; said George gave bond for his good behavior, with James Gordon & Richard Hall his securities.

Court 21 March 1776, present justices James Ball, Jesse Ball, James Selden, Hugh Brent, John Taylor, James Gordon.
--Will of Martha Miller presented by David Ball & John Taylor executors therein named, proved by Margaret Ball & Sarah Jones; William Mountague, Richard Ball, Edwin Conway, & James Ball Junr appointed appraisers.

[Index 22] Lancaster OB 15:411a, March Court 1776
--Will of John Campbell decd presented by Lettice Carter & Isaac Degge executors therein named, proved by Thomas Carter; Lawson Hathaway, Henry Currell, William Martin & Bartley James appointed appraisers.
--On motion of David Ball, William Mountague, Richard Ball, Edwin Conway, & James Ball Junr appointed to divide estate of Martha Miller decd.
--Travers Lunsford vs Maurice Wheeler—Slander.
--John Williams fined 50 pounds of tobacco for absenting himself from divine service.
--George Tillery vs Rawleigh Hazard—Case.
--George Chowing [thus] orphan of George Chowning bound to Lowry Oliver until age 21, to learn the trade of a Shop Joiner; his mother agreed to find him apparel.

[Index 23] Lancaster OB 15:411b, March Court 1776
John Eustace vs Robert Gilmour, Bogle & Co—Attachment.
--Anthony Sydnor vs Antho. Warwick administrator of Antho. McIntire—Attachment. Thomas Lawson, Henry Lawson, James Selden Gent, James Currell, John Gibbons, & Jesse George were garnishees.
--Lee Griggs orphan of Lee Griggs bound to Abraham White until age 21, to learn the trade of a House Joiner; his guardian Elias Edmonds agreed to find him apparel.
--On petition of James Bush, ordered Joseph Norris, James Norris, Jesse Robinson, & John Payne view road petitioned for by sd Bush.
--On motion of Isaac Degge, & with assent of John James, ordered Frances James orphan of Thomas James be brought to next court to choose a guardian.
--William Taylor petitioned for a grist mill on a run on his own land.

[Index 24] Lancaster OB 15:412a, April Court 1776
Court 18 April 1776, present justices James Ball, Jesse Ball, Thomas Lawson, James Gordon.
--On motion of Daniel George intermarried with Eliza. Reid, ordered Charles Bell, Elias Edmonds, William Edmonds, & Martin Picket of Fauquier County possess sd George with estate of the sd Reid in the hands of Eppaphroditus [thus, no last name].
--William Lawson vs John Robertson—Attachment. Thomas Hunton was garnishee.
--Ordered Henry Davis pay Thomas Elliot 50 pounds tobacco for his attendance as witness 2 days in case Abraham White against sd Davis on a breach of the peace.
--Frankey White granted administration on estate of Abraham White, with Henry Armistead & Thomas Brent her securities; Jesse Ball, Matthew Myars, Edward Carter, & John Bailie appointed appraisers.
--Bailie George vs Maurice Wheeler—Attachment.
--Spencer Wood son of Ann Wood, formerly bound to Elisha Hall & since to Thomas Lawson, ordered redelivered to sd Hall.
--John Eustace vs Robert Gilmour et al—Attachment.

[Index 25] Lancaster OB 15:412b, May Court 1776

Court 16 May 1776, present justices James Ball, John Flet [thus], Edwin Conway, Jesse Ball.
--Grand jury impanelled, with foreman Henry Tapscot.
--Jonathan Pullen petitioned for grist mill on Taffs Creek.
--William Boatman granted license to keep ordinary at Lancaster Courthouse.
--Zachariah White appointed guardian to Thomas, William, Samuel, and Maryann White orphans of Abraham White decd.; Jesse Bell was security.
--Ordered John Taylor Gent., William Sydnor, & John Bailie divide estate of Abraham White decd.
--Frankey White appointed guardian pro tempore to Presley, Sally, & Frankey White orphans of Abraham White decd. for purpose of dividing the estate.
--Anthony Sydnor appointed guardian to Elizabeth, Mary, Caty, & John King, orphans of William King decd.; Fortunatus Sydnor was security.
--Report of jury for a mill petitioned for by William Taylor was returned, continued.

[Index 26] Lancaster OB 15:413a, May Court 1776
Bushrod Riveer appointed Surveyor of highway from Kilmarnock to the lower church.
--John Hews fined 500 pounds tobacco for concealing a tithable.
--Presentments of grand jury against Burges Ball, John Overstreet, & Thos. Hill dismissed.
--Richard Mitchell Gent., Bailey George, & Joseph Shearman Sheriffs acknowledged bond to collect taxes.
--Nicholas George appointed Surveyor of highway from road opposite Merryman Paynes to Chiltons Ferry.
--Henry Tapscot appointed Surveyor of highway from Downmans Lane to the Warehouse Road, & from the fork at his house to Mitchell's shop.
--Henry Lawson appointed Surveyor from the lower church to Shearmans Ferry.
--John Wale orphan of George Wale, formerly bound to Wm. Lawson, was with consent of sd Lawson delivered back to his mother Sarah James, free from his servitude.
--Attachment granted to Bailie George against Maurice Wheeler for waste of land in controversy between them, dismissed.
--Robert Angel orphan of Samuel Angel bound to Robert Mctire until age 21, who is also allowed the profits of sd orphan's estate.
--Ordered Bailie George pay Michael Wilder 75 pounds of tobacco for three days as a witness in sd George's case against Maurice Wheeler.

[Index 27] Lancaster OB 15:413b, May Court 1776
On motion of John James, ordered dedimus issue to take depositions of Richard Hutchings, John Clayton, Harry Carter, Sarah Kirk, James Kirk, Thos. Brent & Eliza. Hubbard in a suit of John Carter vs sd John James.

Court 20 June 1776, present justices James Ball, John Fleet, Jesse Ball, Hugh Brent.
--Ordered Judith Turner pay 20 shillings for having a bastard child.
--Franky White appointed guardian to Presley, Sally, & Frankey White orphans of Abraham White decd.; William Saunders was her security; Jesse Ball Gent appointed guardian to sd orphans for purpose of receiving their parts of the estate; John Taylor Gent, William Sydnor, & John Bailey ordered to allot the widow's dower.
--Presentment of grand jury against Elizabeth Dunaway for having a bastard child discontinued, she having paid her fine.
--Petition of William Taylor to build a mill, continued.

[Index 28] Lancaster OB 15:414a; July Court 1776
Upon the establishment of the new form of government in the colony, James Ball, John Chinn, Edwin Conway, Jesse Ball, James Selden, Hugh Brent, John Taylor, Thomas Lawson, & James Gordon Gent took the oath as justices of the peace.
--Thomas B. Griffin qualified as Clerk of Court, Richard Mitchell Gent as High Sheriff, Joseph Shearman & Bailie George as Deputy Sheriffs, David Boyd, William Brown, & Richard E. Lee as Attorneys, Spencer George & Michael Wilder as Constables.

--Will of Augustine Rice presented by Nichos. George executor therein named, proved by Charles Edwards & John Harris; Charles Rogers, Rhodam Lunsford, Gavin Lowry, & Henry Carter appointed appraisers.
--Hannah Rice, widow & relict of Augustine Rice decd.. renounced all benefit from will of her sd husband, and claimed dower.

[Index 29] Lancaster OB 15:414b, August Court 1776
Court 15 Aug 1776, present justices James Ball, John Chinn, John Taylor, Thomas Lawson & James Gordon.
--Richard Mitchell Gent having resigned as Sheriff, court appointed Bailey George to proclaim sitting of the court, and recommended Edwin Conway Gent to the Governor as a proper person to be Sheriff.

Court 21 November 1776, present justices James Ball, John Chinn, Hugh Brent, John Taylor.
--Bailey George, Cryer, proclaimed court, and Edwin Conway Gent was sworn as Sheriff.
James Newby & Bailie George were sworn as Deputy Assistant Sheriffs.
--Richard Mitchell Gent was sworn as Justice.
--William Gibson petitioned for a water grist mill on a branch of Corotoman called Dick's Branch.
--Presley Neale orphan of John Neale chose Mathew Neale his guardian, with John Craine security.

[Index 30] Lancaster OB 15:415a, Nov Court 1776
Thomas Lawson Gent took oath as Vestryman.
--On motion of Nicholas George, ordered Matthew Myars, Charles Rogers & Henry Towles divide estate of Augustine Rice decd.
--Fortunatus Sydnor appointed guardian to Judith Payne Stevens and Susannah Stevens orphans of Richard Stevens decd., with Richard Mitchell Gent security.
--Richard Mitchell Gent appointed guardian to William, Joseph, & George Stephens orphans of Richard Stephens decd., with Fortunatus Sydnor security.
--Ordered James Ball, Edwin Conway Gent, William Chowning, & Henry Towls divide estate of Richard Stephens decd.

Court 19 Dec 1776, present justices James Ball, Jesse Ball, John Taylor, Thomas Lawson.
--On motion of William Steptoe, dedimus granted to take depositions of Henry Currell & Spencer Currell in a suit Justices vs John Eustace Gent.
--Daniel George acknowledged his power of attorney to Nicholas George.
--Will of Thomas Carter presented by Edward Carter & Rawleigh Carter the executors named therein, proved by Jeduthan James & William Stephens; Edwin Conway, Elias Edmonds, James Kirk Junr, & Coleman Dagget appointed appraisers.

[Index 31] Lancaster OB 15:415b, Dec Court 1776
Deed from James Waddel & Mary his wife to Elisha Hall further proved by Richard Hall.
--Deed from Thadeus McCarty & Ann his wife to John Chinn proved by Henry Tapscot & Robert Chinn.
--Will of Dale Carter Gent presented by James Carter executor therein named, proved by Spencer George & John Davis; Edwin Conway, Spencer George, Elias Edmonds, & James Kirk Junr appointed appraisers.
--John Eustace Gent petitioned to renew an order to build a mill.
--On motion of Bailie George, issued a dedimus to take deposition of Wm. Chilton in suit between sd George & Maurice Wheeler.
--Deed between William Brent & Thomas Rouand proved by Wm. Norris.
--William Griggs granted license to keep a ferry at Gilberts, also to keep an ordinary at same place.

[Index 32] Lancaster OB 15:416a, Dec Court 1776
John Selden granted administration on estate of James Selden decd., with John Taylor his security; William Mountague, Peter Conway, John Taylor, & William Boatman appointed appraisers.
--John Selden took oath as executor of the will of Richard Selden decd.

--On motion of Henry Overstreet, ordered Henry Towls, William Chowning, Wm. Arms, & John Payne divide estate of Richard Overstreet.

--On motion of Ann Davenport, ordered Jesse Ball, John Bailey, & Joseph Mason divide estate of George Davenport decd.

--William Davis granted administration on estate of Moses Davis decd., with William Gibson his security; William Gibson, Martin George, Wm. Meredith, & John Pearson appointed appraisers.

--Jeduthan Davis orphan of Moses Davis bound to William Davis until age 21, to learn trade of Carpenter.

[Index 33] Lancaster OB 15:416b, Dec Court 1776
William Sydnor the present Inspector & Joseph Shearman, assistant, recommended to the Governor as Inspectors of Tobacco at Glascocks Warehouse in Richmond County & Deep Creek Warehouse in Lancaster County.

--Charles Rogers & Gavin Lowry the present Inspectors, with John Davis & Spencer Dogget, assistants, recommended to the Governor as Inspectors of Tobacco at Davis's & Lowrys Warehouses.

--Hugh Brent & William Gibson, assistant, recommended to Governor as Inspectors of Tobacco at Indian Warehouse in Northumberland County & Dymer's in this county.

Court, 16 Jan 1777, present justices James Ball, Richard Mitchell, John Chinn, Jesse Ball.
These individuals were allowed their accounts in the laying of the county levy: William Boatman, Rawleigh Stott, Spencer George, Nicholas George, Isaac Mercer, Daniel George, Nicholas George, Lott Palmer, Wm. Webb, Benj. Palmer, Jas. Wallace, John Griggs, Jos. Fielding, Joseph Shearman (Sheriff), Bushrod Riveer, Peter Riveer, John Pinckard, Peter Riveer, Richard Riveer, John McTire, Michael Wilder, Bailie George, Johnson Riveer, Maurice Wheeler.

[Index 34] Lancaster OB 15:417a, Jan Court 1777
On motion of George Edwards heir of Richard Edwards decd., ordered Jesse Ball, John Taylor, & James Gordon allot sd George the part of negroes belonging to sd Richard by the will of William Edwards decd. in the hands of Eliza. Carter executrix of sd William Edwards.

--Deed from Thadeus McCarty & his wife Ann to John Chinn proved by Richard Mitchell Gent.

--Inventory of Robert McTire decd. was returned.

--Will of Ann Hamilton decd. presented and proved.

--Inventory of Richard Overstreet decd. recorded.

--Deed from Frances Stephens to William Sydnor proved by Fortunatus Sydnor & Gavin Lowry.

--Deed from Lowry Oliver & wife to William Brumley proved by Richard Mitchell, John Chinn, & James Newby.

--Deed George Flowers to John Flowers proved by William Lawson & James Pollard.

--On motion of Ann Wood, ordered Doctor Elisha Hall shall not remove Spencer Wood, orphan of sd. Ann, out of the county.

--James Harris & John Miller granted administration on estate of Jeriah Harris decd., with John Davis & Thomas Rob securities; James Kirk Junr., Thomas Rob, James Pinckard, & Elias Edmonds appointed appraisers.

[Index 35] Lancaster OB 15:417b, Jan Court 1777
On motion of Spencer Brown, ordered Richard Mitchell, Joseph Norris, & William Stonum settle account of John Hazard for guardianship of Rachel Newsom, and possess sd Brown with the part of sd Newsom his wife in the hands of sd Hazard.

--William Gibson's petition for a mill, continued.

--On motion of John Dogget, ordered Thomas Lawson, Nicholas Currel, & Harry Currel divide estate of John Carter, and possess sd Dogget with his part thereof.

--John Dogget granted administration on estate of Charles Lee decd., with William Gibson his security; John Carter, Henry Carter, William Saunders, & William Brown appointed appraisers.

--Will of Dale Carter Gent decd. further proved by George Carter.

--Charles Gibbs orphan of James Gibbs, formerly bound to Anthony George, now bound to Thomas Divine until age 21, to learn trade of Shoemaker.

--Mima Chilton granted administration of estate of Thomas Chilton decd., with John Pacquet & William Mitchell her securities; James Carter, William Chilton, Spencer George, & Coleman Dogget appointed appraisers.

[Index 36] Lancaster OB 15:418a, Jan Court 1777
William Gibson appointed Surveyor of highway from Carter's Great Mill to Kilmarnock in the lower part of the county.

Court 20 March 1777, present justices James Ball, John Chinn, Richard Mitchell, John Taylor.
--Rawleigh Hazard vs George Wale—Case. Abates by death of Deft.
--Richard Hutchings vs George Phillips—Case. Abates by death of Plt.
--James Selden vs John Heath—Chancery. Abates by death of Complainant.
--John Bailey guardian to Pollard's orphans vs Abraham White—Case. Abates by death of Deft.
--William Graham vs James Selden—Case. Abates by death of Deft.
--Robert Daniel et al executors of George Davis vs Burges Smith—Case. Abates by death of Deft.
--Nicholas Flood vs Robert Henning, Deft—Case. Abates by death of Plt.
--James Creswell vs James Selden—Case. Abates by death of Deft.
--Nicholas Flood vs James Ledford—Debt. Abates by death of Plt.

[Index 37] Lancaster OB 15:418b, March Court 1777
Nicholas Flood vs Charles Jones—Debt. Abates by death of Plt.
--Nicholas Flood vs Charles Jones—Debt. Abates by death of Plt.
--Nicholas Flood vs Charles Pritchard executor of Judith Housin—Debt. Abates by death of Plt.
--Nicholas Flood vs Charles Pritchard executor of Judith Housin—Debt. Abates by death of Plt.
--Report of division of land of Thomas Sharp decd. between Burges Ball & William Chowning was returned.
--Will of James Kirk presented by Wm. Kirk, William Gibson, Lawson Hathaway, & Thomas Hathaway executors named therein, proved by William Yerby & John Hutchings; Richard Mitchell, Thomas Lawson Gent, John Berryman, & William Yerby appointed appraisers.
--Burges Ball acknowledged his deed of gift to Henry Armistead.
--Burges Ball acknowledged power of attorney to Henry Armistead, Thomas B. Griffin, & James Gordon to dispose of lands in Lancaster County.
--Burges Ball acknowledged power of attorney to Henry Armistead, Thomas B. Griffin, & James Gordon to dispose of certain slaves.

[Index 38] Lancaster OB 15:419a, March Court 1777
On motion of William Boatman, the court set liquor rates.
--Rawleigh Hazard granted license to keep ordinary at Kilmarnock.
--Inventory of Jeriah Harris decd. returned.
--William Sydnor sworn Inspector at Deep Creek Warehouse, and at Glascocks in Richmond County, Gawin Lowry & Charles [thus] sworn Inspectors at Lowry's & Davis's Houses.
--Inventory of estate of Dale Carter Gent decd. returned.
Griffin Thomas vs James Armstrong—Attachment. Garnishees were Bailie George executor of James Maughon, and Henry Armistead "for Burges Ball."
---James Carter granted administration on estate of Charles Chilton decd., with John Davis his security; Stephen Chilton, Spencer George, Stephen Chilton Junr., & Coleman Dogget appointed appraisers.
--Inventory of estate of Thomas Chilton decd. returned.

[Index 39] Lancaster OB 15:419b, March Court 1777
Jesse Denny granted administration on estate of Nicholas Hill decd., with Lawson Hathaway his security; Thomas Yerby, Charles Coppedge, John Selden, & William Pitman appointed appraisers.
--James Kirk orphan of James Kirk decd. chose James Kirk his guardian; James Gordon security.

--On motion of William Gibson, ordered Richard Mitchell, Thomas Lawson Gent, John Berryman, & William Yerby divide negroes left by their grandmother Elizabeth Yerby among the children of James Kirk decd., agreeable to the will of sd Elizabeth.

--Inventory of estate of Thomas Carter decd. returned.

--John Pasquet & Molly his wife acknowledged their deed to Meredith Mahanes.

--Jesse Ball Gent recommended to the Governor as militia Colonel, in place of Thadeus MacCarty, who has removed.

--Thomas B. Griffin recommended as Lieutenant Colonel, in place of Col Jesse Ball.

--John Taylor Gent recommended as Major in place of James Selden Gent decd.

[Index 40] Lancaster OB 15:420a, April Court 1777

Court 17 April 1777, present justices James Ball, Richard Mitchell, John Chinn, John Taylor.

--Thomas B. Griffin acknowledged his deed to Cyrus Griffin, and it was proved by Thomas Edwards, James Newby, & Joseph Shearman.

--Jesse Denny vs Elisha Hall—Justices Attachment.

--Division of estate of Richard Overstreet decd. returned.

--Division of estate of Richard Stephens decd. & allotment of dower in sd estate was returned.

--Division of slaves & estate of George Payne decd. returned.

--Joseph Shearman sworn as Inspector at Deep Creek Warehouse.

--Settlement of guardian accounts of John Hazard with Rachel Newsom returned.

--Mary Kirk widow of James Kirk renounced all benefit from his will.

--Will of Edward Blackmore decd. presented by Jemima Blackmore & Henry Towles executors therein named, proved by Henry Towles & John Chowning; William Chowning, John Chowning, Jesse Chilton, & James Ewell appointed appraisers.

[Index 41] Lancaster OB 15:420b, April Court 1777

On motion of Mary Kirk, ordered Richard Mitchell, John Berryman, Thomas Lawson, & William [no name shown] allot dower of sd Mary in estate of her late husband James Kirk decd.

--Report of possessing John Dogget with the estate of John Carter was returned.

--Leanna Hutchings granted administration on estate of Richard Hutchings decd., with Coleman Dogget & John Dogget her securities; John Berryman, Wm. Yerby, Wm. Gibson & Elmor Dogget appointed appraisers.

Court 18 April 1777, present justices James Ball, John Chinn, Jesse Ball, James Gordon.

--Will of William Wale presented in court and proved, and the handwriting of the witnesses Elmore Dogget, Thomas West & Isaac Currell "who are now in the army at the northward" was also proved.

--Inventory of estate of Charles Lee decd. returned.

--Inventory of estate of Nicholas Hill decd. returned.

--John Flowers granted administration n estate of George Flowers decd., with Thomas Lawson & Thomas Carter his securities; William Gibson, John Parrot, John Berryman, & James Brent appointed administrators.

[Index 42] Lancaster OB 15:421a, April Court 1777

Sarah[? Obscured] Lee appointed guardian to her two children Susannah & Winny Lee orphans of   Lee, with John Dogget her security.

--Henry Tapstot vs John Rogers—Chancery.

--On complaint of Spencer Currell for sureties of the peace against William Hinton, ordered sd Hinton give bond, with Thomas Carter & John Dogget his securities.

--Present justices Richard Mitchell, Thomas Lawson, John Taylor Gent.

--The complaint of Fleet Hinton against Henry Fleet for sureties of the peace, dismissed.

--On complaint of Edward Carter against Henry Davis for sureties of the peace, ordered sd Davis give bond, with John Selden & Moses Chilton his securities.

--Anthony Sydnor allowed execution against the garnishees in his suit against Anthony Warwick.

--Ordered William Hinton pay William Griggs for three days' attendance as witness on Spencer Currel's complaint against sd Hinton.

[Index 43] Lancaster OB 15:421b, April Court 1777

Thomas Pollard petitioned for a water grist mill on Carter's Creek, adjoining land of Rawleigh Shearman.
--Johnson Riveer sworn as Constable.
--Ordered Spencer Currell pay Martin Shearman Junr. for three days' attendance as witness on sd Currell's complaint against Wm. Hinton.
--Henry Tapscot, John Berryman, Henry Towles, William Yerby, Peter Conway, & James Ball Junr. recommended to the Governor as Justices.
--Lazarus George vs Jeriah Harris—Case. Abates by death of Deft.
--William Brumley appointed Overseer of highway from Rawleigh Downman's gate to the Cross Road, in place of Thadeus McCarty.
--Thomas Carter recommended as militia Captain in place of Henry Lawson, who resigned, and Isaac Degges as Lieutenant in place of sd Carter.

Court 15 May 1777, present James Ball, John Chinn, Jesse Ball, John Taylor.
--Grand jury impannelled, with Matthew Myars foreman.

[Index 44] Lancaster OB 15:422a, May Court 1777

Inventory of estate of George Flowers decd. returned.
--Inventory of estate of Richard Hutchings decd. returned.
--Will of Joseph Mason decd. presented by John Bailey & Rawleigh Davenport executors named therein, proved by Rawleigh Davenport & John Mason; Jesse Ball, Ozwell Newby, Thomas Flint, & Moses Chilton appointed appraisers.
--Deed Jeremiah Dogget & his wife Molly to James Ewell, acknowledged.
--Inventory of estate of Charles Chilton decd., returned.
--Mungo Harvey appointed Overseer of highway from Jesse Ball's mill to the road leading to Mahon's Bridge.
--James Norris appointed Surveyor from the cross road at Peter Riveer's to the cross road at John Chinn's mill.
--Ozwell Newby appointed Surveyor from Northumberland County to the road leading to Mungo Harvey's.
--On motion of Leanna Hutchings against John James for counter security, Wm. Brent gave security for sd James's guardianship of Frances James orphan of Thomas James decd.

[Index 45] Lancaster OB 15:422b, May Court 1777

Ordered Coleman Dogget, James Kirk, & James Carter divide estate of George Purcel decd.
--William Hendren granted administration on estate of William Oldham decd., with John Taylor Gent his security; Jesse Ball, John Bailey, William Wiblin, & Nicholas George appointed to divide the estate.
--Deed of gift for land from Elmor Dogget to his son John Dogget was proved by Rawleigh Hazard & William Griggs.
--Ordered James Alverson, Thomas Howard, James Howard, & Charles Doby appraise estate of William Oldham decd.
--Ordered William Chilton Junr. be summoned to answer complaint of David Boyd Gent for a breach of the peace.
--New Commission of the Peace dated 6 May 1777 was read in court, and James Ball, Henry Fleet, John Chinn, Jesse Ball, John Taylor, Thomas Lawson, Henry Tapscot, John Berryman, Henry Towles, & James Ball Junr. qualified as Justices of the Peace.
--On motion of Ann Davis, ordered John Berryman, William Gibson, & Martin George allot her dower in land of her late husband Moses Davis; William Davis appointed guardian to Jeduthan Davis son of Moses decd.

[Index 46] Lancaster OB 15:423a, May Court 1777

Thomas Gaskins orphan of Charles Gaskins bound to Thomas Perkins until age 21, to learn the occupation of Sailor or Seaman.
--Jesse Ball Gent sworn as Colonel of militia, Thomas B. Griffin as Lieutenant Colonel, John Taylor Gent as Major.

--Will of John Yerby decd. presented by John Yerby & William [no last name], executors therein named, and was proved by William Brent & William Schofield; Elias Edmonds, John Meredith, James Kirk, & Thomas Schofield appointed appraisers.
--William Mountague & Henry Lawson recommended to Governor as proper persons to be added to the Commission of the Peace.
--Martin George paid fine five shillings for not attending divine service.
--William Yopp paid fine five shillings for getting drunk.
--Fleet Hinton paid fine five shillings for not attending divine service.

[Index 47] Lancaster OB 15:423b, May Court 1777
John Wormley paid fine twenty shillings for being a common swearer.
--Henry Fleet ordered to give security for the peace; John Fleet Gent was security for his appearance, if required.
--John McTire paid fine twenty shillings for being a common swearer.
--Mungo Harvey vs Augustine Carter—Attachment. James Carter was garnishee.
--Ordered George Bean be paid for moving the prison house to the most convenient place.

Court 19 June 1777, present justices James Ball, Henry Tapscot, Henry Towles, John Berryman.
--William Hinton fined 500 pounds tobacco for fornication & keeping a house of bad fame.
--Eppa Lawson paid fine 5 shillings for being drunk.

[Index 48] Lancaster OB 15:424a, June Court 1777
Robert Nicken being presented by grand jury for adultery, imparlance granted him to next court.
--Mary Wilkerson paid fine 20 shillings for having a bastard child.
--Thomas Lawson paid fine 5 shillings for being drunk.
--Inventory of estate of John Yerby decd. returned.
--William Brown petitioned for grist mill.
--Deed of gift for land from Elmor Dogget to his son John Dogget was further proved by Charles Lee & John Parrot.
--Deed in trust from Frances Stephens to William Sydnor further proved by Rev David Currie.
--Deed of lease from William Brent to Thomas Rouand, acknowledged.
--Inventory of estate of Joseph Mason decd. returned.
--Report of the persons appointed to value the land for William Gibson to build a water grist mill was returned, which was opposed by John Eustace Gent, but was ordered to be recorded.

[Index 49] Lancaster OB 15:424b, June Court 1777
Hugh Brent Gent qualified Inspector of tobacco at Dymers Warehouse & Indian [Warehouse?] in Northumberland.
--On complaint of William Lawson Junr. against Henry Fleet for sureties of the peace, John Fleet Gent gave security for sd Henry to keep the peace.
--John Voy vs Richard E. Lee—Attachment.
--Jeduthan Pinckard vs Charles Purcell—Attachment.
--Petition of William Taylor for a mill, continued.
--Petition of Thomas Pollard for a mill, continued.
--Petition of Jonathan Pullen for a mill, continued.
--John Eustace vs Robert Gilmour—Attachment.
--John Rogers & Wm. Mitchell granted administration on estate of Richard Rogers decd., with Wm. Carpenter & Mungo Harvey their securities; Henry Tapscot, Thomas Stott, Richard Mitchell, & John Chinn appointed appraisers.
--James Hudnal qualified as executor to the will of Wm. Wale, formerly proved in court; John Parrot, Wm. Brent, James Brent, & John Flowers appointed appraisers.

[Index 50] Lancaster OB 15:425a, July Court 1777
Court 17 July 1777, present justices James Ball, John Taylor, John Berryman, James Ball Junr.
--Inventory of estate of Richard Rogers decd. returned.
--Deed of gift from John Rogers to Betty Rogers, acknowledged.

--Ordered Willoughby Rout pay 5 shillings or 50 pounds tobacco for absenting himself from divine service.

--Inventory of estate of William Wale decd. returned.

--John Fleet, James Gordon, Thomas Lawson, & John Berryman Gent were appointed to tender the oath of allegiance in the lower part of the county, and John Taylor Gent in Wiccomico Parish, and Henry Tapscot, Henry Towles, & James Ball Junr. in the upper part of the county.

--Deed from John Chinn & his wife Sarah was acknowledged.

--Mungo Harvey vs Augustine Carter—Attachment. James Carter was garnishee.

--Henry Tapscot vs Lowry Oliver—Attachment.

[Index 51] Lancaster OB 15:425b, July Court 1777

Elizabeth Flood et al vs Richard Hall—Attachment.

--Elizabeth Flood et al vs Meredith Nellums—Attachment.

--Ordered Bailie George provide provisions for wives & children of Moses Dameron & Thomas Cottrell agreeable to direction of last Assembly.

--Presentment of grand jury against Rawleigh Hazard for keeping a tipling house, continued.

--Jesse Chilton vs Charles Nelson—Attachment.

--Petition of Jonathan Pullen to build a water grist mill, continued.

--Deed from George Flowers to John Flowers was further proved by Thomas Hathaway.

--Richard Mitchell & James Gordon Gent were sworn as Justices of the Peace.

--Petition of William Taylor to build a water grist mill, continued.

--John Eustace vs Charles Alexander—Case.

--On motion of Henry Fleet, dedimus issued to take depositions of Edwin Conway, Sarah C. Conway, & Walker Conway in a suit Richard E. Lee vs sd Fleet.

[Index 52] Lancaster OB 15:426a, August Court 1777

Court 21 August 1777, present justices James Ball, John Fleet, Jesse Ball, John Taylor, & James Gordon.

--John Clayton vs Christopher Millar.

--Deeds of lease & release & bond from Burges Ball to Robert Gilmour were acknowledged by Henry Armistead, Thomas B. Griffin, & James Gordon, attorneys for sd Ball.

--Inventory of estate of Wm. Oldham decd. lying in Lancaster Co, also of his estate in Richmond, were returned.

--Account of profits of the estate of Sally Simmons orphan of John Simmons decd. was returned.

--Thomas Downing, assignee vs Peter Conway et al.

--Will of Marget Rob decd. presented by Job Carter, executor therein named, and was proved by Edwin Conway & John Millar.

--Elizabeth Flood et al vs John Leland—Case. Referees were Richard Mitchell, Andrew Robertson & Cyrus Griffin Gent.

--The complaint of Judith Crowther against Judith Turner for sureties of the peace was dismissed.

--Judith Turner ordered to pay Rachel Hill for her attendance, 1 day, as witness on the complaint of Judith Crowther.

--Elizabeth Flood et al vs Richard Hall—Attachment. James Gordon Gent was special bail for the Deft.

[Index 53] Lancaster OB 15:426b, August Court 1777

Elizabeth Flood et al vs Burges Ball—Case. Referees were Richard Mitchell, Andrew Robertson, & Cyrus Griffin Gent.

--Elizabeth Flood et al vs Henry Armistead—Case. Referees were Richard Mitchell, Andrew Robertson, & Cyrus Griffin Gent.

--Elizabeth Flood et al vs Merideth Nellums—Attachment. Garnishees were Bailie George, Thomas Lawson Gent & Thomas Edwards.

--Hugh Brent & Wm. Yerby Gent sworn as Justices of the Peace.

--John McTire appointed Surveyor of highway from the sign post near Doctor Robertsons to Maj John Taylor's landing in the upper part of the county.

--Isaac Pitman appointed Overseer of highway from the lower church to Charles Carter Esq's new mill in the lower part of the county.

--William Chowning, James Ewell, Bailie George, Thomas Hathaway, & Richard Selden were recommended to the Governor as militia Lieutenants, and William Gibson & Elias Edmonds as Ensigns.

[Index 54] Lancaster OB 15:427a, Sept Court 1777
Court 18 September 1777, present justices James Ball, Jesse Ball, Henry Tapscot, Henry Towles.
--Philip Smith et al, administrators of Burges Smith vs Richard Hall—Attachment. Sheriff returned one negro, who was ordered to be sold.
--Philip Smith et al, administrators of Burges Smith vs Lowry Oliver—Attachment. James Ball Gent & William Newton were garnishees. Said Newton was inpartnership with Richard Mitchell Gent.
--Jesse Bailey, orphan of John Bailey, chose John Bailey as his guardian, with William Chowning security; Ordered Henry Towles, John Chowning, & John Payne possess the guardian with sd orphan's estate.
--Reuben Dogget orphan of Reuben Dogget chose William Wiblin as his guardian, with Jesse Ball his security; Ordered Henry Towles Gent possess sd guardian with sd orphan's estate.

[Index 55] Lancaster OB 15:427b, Sept Court 1777
Richard Nutt granted administration on estate of James Newby decd., with John Goodridge his security; John Mactire, Thomas Flint, Elijah Robinson, & Rawleigh Davenport were appointed appraisers.
--James Ewell, William Chowning, & Bailie George sworn as militia Lieutenants, and Elias Edmonds & William Gibson as Ensigns.
--Thomas Hubbard granted administration on estate of James Hubbard decd., with John Yerby his security; William Gibson, William Brent, William Yerby, & John Meredith were appointed appraisers.
--Sam, a negro man slave belonging to the estate of Richard Hutchings decd., having been taken up in Chesapeake Bay going to the enemies of the state, being brought before court, ordered conveyed to jail.
--Inventory of estate of Augustine Rice decd. returned.

[Index 56] Lancaster OB 15:428a, Oct Court 1777
Court 16 October 1777, present justices James Ball, James Gordon, Henry Towles, John Berryman.
--Allotment of dower to Ann Davis, widow of Moses Davis decd., returned.
--Moses Sutton, Plt vs John Webb Junr—Attachment. Richard Riveer Junr. was garnishee.
--Inventory of estate of Margaret Robb decd. returned.
--Catherine McDaniel vs. Richard Hall—Attachment.
--On motion of William Griggs, ordered Sarah James be summoned to give security for guardianship of her children.
--Thomas Carter sworn as militia Captain, also Isaac Deggs, Richd. Selden, & Thomas Hathaway as Lieutenants, and John Chowning as Ensign.
--Jesse Chilton vs Charles Nelson—Attachment. James Ball & Thomas B. Griffin Gent, as executors of LeRoy Griffin Gent decd. were garnishees.
--Jemima Mason granted administration on estate of John Mason decd., with Thomas Garner & Benj. George her securities; John Nichols, James Kirk, John Dogget, & William Dogget appointed appraisers.

Index 57] Lancaster OB 15:428b, October Court 1777
Petition of Jonathan Pullen for a mill on Corotomon, discontinued.
--Petition of William Taylor for a mill, continued.
--Henry Tapscot vs Lowry Oliver—Attachment.
--On motion of John Connelly, next friend to Patrick Connelly, ordered Henry Tapscot, Henry Towles, & James Ball Junr. Gent examine into the state of mind & sense of the sd Patrick, also into the circumstances & direction of his estate.
--Eliza. Flood et al, administrators of Nicholas Flood vs John Leland guardian of Molly Lee—Case. Referees were Cyrus Griffin, Richard Mitchell, & Andrew Robertson Gent.
--Account of profits of the estate of orphans of Thos. Pollard decd. was returned.by the guardian.
--Edwin Conway, Jesse Ball, & Hugh Brent Gent were recommended to the Governor for the office of High Sheriff.

[Index 58] Lancaster OB 15:429a, October Court 1777

Edwin Conway Gent granted permission to turn the road thro' his land leading to Scotland mill, by the side of John Cundiff's fence.

--Profits of the estate of Ezekiel Hester, an orphan, was returned, and on oath of Frances White administratrix of Abraham White decd. his late guardian, was recorded.

[The Clerk's handwriting changes at this point]
Court 20 November 1777, present justices Richard Mitchell, John Taylor, Thomas Lawson, James Ball, & Henry Towles.

--William Sydnor returned account of tobacco at Deep Creek Warehouse.

--Jacob Currell orphan of Jacob Currell decd. chose William Sullivant as his guardian.

--Frances Bond orphan of John Bond decd. chose Charles Rogers as her guardian.

--Caty Bond orphan of John Bond decd. chose Elias Edmonds as her guardian.

--Charles Rogers returned account of tobacco at Davis's & Lowrys Warehouses.

--On motion of Sarah Bond, appointed Jesse Ball, John Taylor, & Henry Towles Gent to divide the estate of John Bond decd.

--Jemima Mason appointed guardian to Molly & Betty Mason orphans of John Mason decd.

--Edwin Conway sworn as Sheriff.

--James Newby & Bailie George sworn as Deputy Sheriffs.

--Moses Chilton granted administration on estate of Ann Chilton decd.

[Index 59] Lancaster OB 15:429b, November Court 1777
Jesse Ball Gent, James Newby, Coleman Dogget, & James Carter appointed to appraise estate of Ann Chilton decd.

--Moses Chilton granted administration on estate of Stephen Chilton decd.

--Jesse Ball Gent., James Newby, Coleman Dogget, & James Carter appointed to appraise estate of Stephen Chilton decd.

--Charles Lee granted administration on estate of John Eustace Beale decd.

--Rawleigh Shearman, James Pollard, John James, & Thomas Hathaway appointed to appraise estate of John Eustace Beale decd.

--James Kirk was foreman of grand jury.

--Rawleigh Hazard vs Vincent Brent—Trespass, Assault & Battery.

--On complaint of Bailie George for sureties of the peace against Maurice Wheeler, ordered sd Wheeler give bond, with Charles Lee, William Griggs, & John Clayton his securities.

[Index 60] Lancaster OB 15:430a, November Court 1777
--On complaint of Maurice Wheeler for sureties of the peace against Bailie George, ordered sd George be discharged.

--Presentment of grand jury against Henry Davis, continued.

--At laying of the county levy, William Boatman allowed his account, as well as the following [only those given by name]: Samuel Hunt, Bailie George (Sub Sheriff), James Newby (Sub Sheriff), Spencer George, Michael Wilder, William Carpenter, Tarpley Thomas, Edward Bailey, John Carpenter, William Gibson, William Kirk, James Harris, William Dogget. The following individuals were charged sums in the levy: Patrick Connelly, William Hinton, Fleet Hinton for warrant against H. Fleet, Maurice Wheeler for warrant against Bailie George, Henry Davis, James Newby. Also ordered Bailie George's account be certified to the Treasurer for finding sundry persons provisions.

--Edwin Conway sworn as Vestryman.

[Index 61] Lancaster OB 15:430b, November Court 1777
Coleman Dogget appointed guardian to Lucy Mason orphan of John Mason decd.

--John Edwards appointed guardian to Sarah Mason orphan of John Mason decd.

--Deed from Elisha Hall to Edwin Conway was proved by Richard Mitchell, James Gordon, & Henry Towles.

--William Griggs appointed guardian to John & Lawson Wale orphans of George Wale decd.

--On motion of Zachariah Barr & James Hudnall, Sarah James summoned to next court to make up her administration account on the estate of her first husband George Wale decd.

Court 19 February 1778, present justices James Ball, John Fleet, Richard Mitchell, John Chinn, Jesse Ball, Thomas Lawson, James Gordon, Henry Tapscott, & Henry Towles.
--The Clerk of Court, Thomas B. Griffin being long confined by sickness & unable to attend court, LeRoy Peachey appointed Clerk Pro Tempore.
--Deed from Henry Newby & his wife Mary and Mary Newby to Thomas B. Griffin was proved by James Newby & Rawleigh Coats.
--Margaret Ball vs Samuel Dunaway & al—Trespass. Ordered a dedimus issue to take deposition of Richard Mitchell Gent.

[Index 62] Lancaster OB 15:431a, February Court 1778
Ordered Michael Wilder receive from the Treasurer 10 pounds for support of Martha Cotterill wife of Thomas Cotterill a Mariner in the service of the state.
--Report of the settlement of Nicholas Reads estate to Nicholas George attorney for Daniel George was returned.
--Inventory of the estate of Edward Blakemore decd. returned.
--Catharine Brent orphan of Hugh Brent Gent decd. chose Joseph Shearman as her guardian, with Henry Tapscott his security
--William Chowning appointed guardian to Chatwin Chowning orphan of Chatwin Chowning decd., with Charles Rogers his security.
--Jesse Ball, Henry Towles Gent, & Matthew Myars appointed to allot unto Sarah Bond her dower in lands of her former husband Thomas Sharp decd.
--Henry Towles Gent, Jesse Chilton, Matthew Myars, & James Ewell appointed to divide the estate of Chattin Chowning decd. agreeable to his will.
--Christopher Christian orphan of Christopher Christian decd. bound to William Wiblin until age 21.
--Inventory of the estate of Ann Chilton decd. returned.
--Will of John Norris decd. was presented by Judith Norris, George Norris, & William Norris, executors therein named, and was proved by Edwin Conway Gent & John Miller.

[Index 63] Lancaster OB 15:431b, Feb Court 1778
Edwin Conway Gent, Elias Edmonds, James Pinckard, & William Schofield appointed to appraise the estate of John Norris decd.
--Elias Edmonds, James Kirk, Jonathan Pullen, & Thomas Schofield appointed to divide the estate of John Yerby decd. according to his will, and to possess Eliza Percifull with his wife's part thereof.
--Inventory of the estate of Stephen Chilton decd. was returned.
--Will of Hugh Brent Gent decd. presented by James Brent & Edwin Conway, executors therein named.
--Thomas Lawson Gent, Henry Lawson, James Kirk, & William Gibson appointed to appraise the estate of Hugh Brent Gent decd.
--Report respecting the insanity of Patrick Connolly was returned, and ordered he be conveyed to the Hospital at Williamsburg and be allowed 12 pounds out of his estate for his support.
--Anthony Sydnor vs Anthony Warrick administrator of Anthony McIntire [McQutrac?] decd.—Attachment.
--Will of Elizabeth Lawson decd. presented by William Lawson, and was proved by Ann Lawson & John Flowers.
--Thomas Lawson, James Currell, Lawson Hathaway, & Thomas Hathaway appointed to appraise the estate of Elizabeth Lawson decd.

[Index 64] Lancaster OB 15:432a, Feb Court 1778
The complaint of Jesse Chilton against John Arms for sureties of the peace was continued.

Court 19 March 1778, present justices James Ball, Thomas Lawson, Henry Tapscott, James Ball Junr.
--Elizabeth James granted administration on estate of Bartlett James decd.
--John Fleet Gent, Harry Currell, Thomas Hunton, & Nicholas Currell appointed to appraise the estate of Bartlett James decd.
--Inventory of the estate of Hugh Brent Gent decd. was returned.

--Nuncupative will of Hugh Kelly decd. presented in court by Hugh Kelly, and was certified by Thomas Lawson Gent, and proved by Harry Currell & Gilbert Currell, and sd Hugh Kelly was granted administration.

--Thomas Lawson Gent, Thomas Carter, Isaac Degge, & Lawson Hathaway appointed to appraise estate of Hugh Kelly decd.

--Will of Isaac Weaver was presented in court by Thomas Nicken, and sd Nicken was granted administration.

--Elmore Dogget, John Nichols, William Gibson, & William Dogget appointed to appraise the estate of Isaac Weaver decd.

[Index 65] Lancaster OB 15:432b, March Court 1778

William Boatman vs Thomas Hubbard—Case. Ordered a dedimus issue to take deposition of Samuel Hunt.

--Present Jesse Ball, Gent.

--Will of Moses Chilton decd. presented by Jesse Ball Gent & James Newby executors therein named.

--Coleman Dogget, James Carter, Rawleigh Davenport, & John Pasquet appointed to appraise the estate of Moses Chilton decd.

--Deed of feoffment from Mary Neasom to Ozwald Newby was proved by 3 of the witnesses.

--Jesse Chilton vs Charles Nelson—Attachment.

--John McTire's account of his guardianship of Milly & Lewis Hening orphans of Robert Hening decd. was recorded.

--Will of Thomas West decd. presented by Betty West the executrix therein named.

--William Gibson sworn as Inspector of tobacco at Indian creek & Dymer's Warehouses.

--Henry Towles Gent appointed guardian to Braxton, Katharine, & John Pollard, orphans of Thomas Pollard decd.

[Index 66] Lancaster OB 15:433a, March Court 1778

Will of George Brent decd. was presented by Thomas Brent & Samuel Yop two of the executors therein named.

--Edwin Conway, James Gordon Gent, John Nichols, & Richard Lock appointed to appraise the estate of George Brent decd.

--Inventory of the estate of John E. Beale was returned.

--Will of Sarah Kirk decd. presented by John Yerby & Elias Edmonds, the executors therein named.

--James Gordon Gent, William Edwards, George Norris, & Thomas Robb appointed to appraise estate of Sarah Kirk decd.

--Job Carter granted license to keep Ordinary at the court house.

--The complaint of Jesse Chilton against John Arms for sureties of the peace, dismissed.

--Ordered Jesse Chilton pay William Luckham 75 pounds of tobacco for 3 days attendance in sd Chilton's suit against John Arms.

--Will of Thomas Kirk decd. presented by Edwin Conway Gent, and he was granted administration.

--John Taylor, James Gordon Gent, Thomas Brent, & George Norris appointed to appraise the estate of Thomas Kirk decd.

[Index 67] Lancaster OB 15:433b, March Court 1778

Edwin Conway Gent granted administration on estate of James Kirk decd.

--John Taylor, James Gordon Gent, Thomas Brent, & George Norris appointed to appraise estate of James Kirk decd.

--Richard Mitchell, James Ball, & Henry Towles Gent appointed Tax Commissioners for ensuing year.

--Gawen Lowry granted administration on estate of Hannah Garner decd.

--George Carter, Henry Carter, Rodham Lunsford, & John Harris appointed to appraise estate of Hannah Garner decd.

--James Gordon Gent, Elias Edmonds, & James Carter appointed to view road petitioned for by Coleman Dogget.

--Richard Mitchell, Edwin Conway, James Ball, John Chinn, Nicholas Currell, Henry Towles, John Taylor, James Newby, & Thomas Lawson Gent sworn as Vestrymen for Christ Church Parish.

Court 16 April 1778, present justices Richard Mitchell, John Chinn, John Taylor, Henry Tapscott, & Henry Towles.

[Index 68] Lancaster OB 15:434a, April Court 1778
Thomas Shearman appointed Clerk of Court.
--Richard Mitchell, John Chinn, & Henry Tapscott Gent appointed to inspect the records of the Clerk's office, and to deliver the records to Thomas Shearman the present Clerk.
--John Chinn & Henry Tapscott appointed to try the weights & scales at Deep Creek Warehouse, James Gordon & Henry Towles Gent at Davis's and Lowry's, and Thomas Lawson & John Berryman at Dymers.
--Inventory of the estate of Moses Chilton decd. returned.
--James Brent vs Isaac Mercer—Attachment.
--John Thrall vs Bushrod Riveer—Attachment.
--John James vs Bushrod Riveer—Detinue.
--Henry Tapscott Gent, Joseph Shearman, & John Bailey appointed to settle Richard Payne's guardianship of the estate of George Payne orphan of William Payne decd., and possess John Payne therewith.
--William Griggs resigned keeping ferry at Gilberts.

[Index 69] Lancaster OB 15:434b, May Court 1778
Court 21 May 1778, present justices James Ball, John Fleet, Richard Mitchell, John Chinn, Thomas Lawson, James Gordon, Henry Tapscott, & John Berryman.
--Ordered that the Clerk of Court certify (to the Treasurer) Richd. Mitchell Junr's account against Sarah Williams wife of John Williams, a Mariner in the service of the state.
--Deed from John Connolly & wife Mary to Jesse Harrison was acknowledged.
--Deed of feoffment from Rawleigh Carter to Edward Carter was proved by Nicholas George, John Payne, & William Chowning.
--Deed of bargain & sale from James Blackerby & wife Ann to Henry Tapscott was proved by James Newby, William Stonum, & George Cammell, & the receipt thereon indorsed was proved by George Scurlock.
--A writing purported as the nuncupative will of Charles Chilton decd. was presented by William Chilton, and ordered to lie until the witnesses attend.
--Will of Thomas B. Griffin Esq decd. presented by William Griffin, the executor therein named, and was proved by Samuel Brumley & William Brent.
--James Ball, John Chinn, Henry Tapscott, & William Sydnor appointed to appraise the estate of Thomas B. Griffin Esq decd.
--Inventory of the estate of George Brent decd. was returned.
--Inventory of the estate of Hugh Kelly decd. was returned.

[Index 70] Lancaster OB 15:435a, May Court 1778
Deed of trust from Richard Hall & his wife Mary to Elisha Hall was proved by John Fleet, Thomas Lawson, & Richard E. Lee.
--Will of Ellinor Horton decd. was presented by John Hutchings, the executor therein named, who was granted administration; William Norris by his attorney moved to enter a caveat, and was refused.
--James Brent, John Parrott, Thomas Rouand, & William Kelly appointed to appraise estate of Ellinor Horton decd.
--Inventory of estate of John Norris decd. was returned.
--Report of settlement of Richard Payne's guardianship of the estate of George Payne orphan of William Payne decd. was returned.
--Betty West qualified as executrix of the will of Thomas West decd.
--William Sanders, Richard Lock, John Bean, & John Carter appointed to appraise estate of Thomas West decd.
--William Gibson granted administration on estate of William Davis decd.
--Martin George, William Merrideth, John Pearson, & John Flower appointed to appraise estate of William Davis decd.
--Caty Hinton & Henry Hinton granted administration on estate of Fleet Hinton decd.
--Thomas Lawson Gent, Nicholas Currell, Thomas Hunton, & Thomas Ingram appointed to appraise estate of Fleet Hinton decd.

[Index 71] Lancaster OB 15:435b, May Court 1778

William Gibson appointed guardian to Jeduthan Davis orphan of Moses Davis decd.
--Sarah Angell orphan of Samuel Angell decd. bound to Zachariah Alfurd & Margaret his wife until age 18, to learn to "read, sew, knit, and spin."
--Elizabeth James appointed guardian to Bartlet, Mary, & Elizabeth James orphans of Bartlet James decd.
--Ann James orphan of Bartlet James decd. chose Lawson Hathaway her guardian.
--Spencer George appointed guardian to John James orphan of Bartlet James decd.
--John Fleet Gent, Harry Currall, Thomas Hunton, & Nicholas Currell appointed to divide estate of Bartlet James decd. & possess the widow & legal representatives with their part.
--Richard E. Lee vs John Parrott—Petition. Referees were Henry Lawson & Thomas Rouand.
--Bethel Cornelious orphan of William Cornelious bound to Rawleigh Coatstill "until he arrives" to age 21.
--John McTire granted administration on estate of William Cornelious decd.
--Oswald Newby, Thomas Flint, Jesse Robinson, & Elijah Robinson appointed to appraise estate of William Cornelious decd.

[Index 72] Lancaster OB 15:436a, May Court 1778
John Payne granted administration on estate of George Payne decd.
--Andrew Robertson, Ozwald Newby, Thomas Flint, & Peter Riveer appointed to appraise estate of George Payne decd.
--John Berryman qualified as executor of the will of Hugh Brent Gent decd.
--Charles Norris granted administration on estate of Thomas & Peter Norris decd., with Rawleigh Stott his security
--Homer Webb, Alexander Hunton, John Kirk, & George Hunt appointed to appraise estate of Thomas & Peter Norris decd.
--Robert Chinn was foreman of grand jury.
--William Schofield Junr. paid fine 5 shillings for not attending divine service.
--John McTire paid fine 20 shillings for being a common swearer.
--Samuel Dunaway paid fine 20 shillings for being a common swearer.
--Henry Tapscott fine 15 shillings for not keeping the road in repair whereof he was Surveyor.

[Index 73] Lancaster OB 15:436b, May Court 1778
Rawleigh Shearman paid fine 5 shillings for not attending divine service.
--Rawleigh Hazard granted license to keep ordinary at his house.
--Thomas Dunaway appointed Surveyor of road in place of Ozwald Newby.
--Deed from Richard Payne & Alice his wife to Joseph Sampson was proved by Thomas Davis & John Davis.
--Ozwald Newby moved for counter security from Rawleigh Davenport for his guardianship of the estate of Andrew Chilton; John Bailey became security.
--William Sydnor & Henry Lawson sworn as Vestryman of Christ Church Parish.
--Absent James Ball Gent.
--Jesse Chilton resigned keeping ferry at Smiths, & John Chowning was appointed in his place.
--Edwin Conway Gent Sheriff acknowledged bond to collect taxes.
--Charles Lee assignee of R. E. Lee vs John E. Beale—Debt. By consent of the administrator, "this suit not to abate by the Deft's death."
--Charles Lee vs John E. Beale—Case. By consent of the administrator, "this suit not to abate by the Deft's death."

[Index 74] Lancaster OB 15:437a, May Court 1778
John Thrall vs Bushrod Riveer—Attachment.
--Thomas Crowder vs Peter Garton—Trespass, assault, & battery.
--Thomas Crowder vs Benjamin Garton Junr.—Trespass, assault, & battery.
--Benjamin Garton Junr. vs Thomas Crowder—Petition.
--Aaron Dameron & Moses Dameron vs Thomas Cottrel—Trespass, assault, & battery.
--Katharine McDaniel vs Richard Hall—Attachment.
--Richard Ball guardian of Sally Edwards vs John Dale—Case.

[Index 75] Lancaster OB 15:437b, May Court 1778

John James vs Bushrod Riveer—Detinue. Benjamin Cundiff was special bail for the Deft.

--Jeremiah Pullen vs Thomas Smither—Scire Facias.

--John Sebree vs John Goodridge—Trespass, assault, & battery.

--John Goodridge vs John Sebree—Slander.

--Joshua Hubbard appointed Surveyor of road in place of George Norris.

--Richard Stott appointed Surveyor of road in place of Henry Tapscott Gent.

--Coleman Dogget "about road" continued until next court.

[Index 76] Lancaster OB 15:438a, June Court 1778

Court 18 June 1778, present justices James Ball, Richard Mitchell, John Chinn, Thomas Lawson, Henry Tapscott, & John Berryman.

--George Kelly vs John Moughon—Petition.

--Elisha Hall vs James Ball—Petition.

--Elisha Hall vs John Davis—Petition.

--William Brown[?] vs Richard Ball—Petition.

--Inventory of Ellinor Horton decd. returned.

--Will of Epaphroditus Lawson decd. presented by Mary Lawson the executrix therein named, and was proved by Henry Lawson & Richard E. Lee.

--Nicholas Currell, Richard Hall, Richard E. Lee, & Thomas Hunton appointed to appraise estate of Epaphroditus Lawson decd.

--Will of Elizabeth Brady decd. presented by Betty Brady, the executrix therein named, and was proved by the oaths of Mary Pollard & Elizabeth Clayton.

[Index 77] Lancaster OB 15:438b, June Court 1778

Edney Tapscott, John Nichols, William Gibson, & Rawleigh Hazard appointed to appraise estate of Elizabeth Brady decd.

--Inventory of estate of Thomas West decd. was returned.

--Deed from Enoch George & wife to Charles Williams, and bond, was proved by William Brown.

--William Griggs vs William Steptoe—Debt.

--John Fleet, Thomas Lawson, James Gordon Gent appointed to take list of tithables in lower part of the county, Henry Tapscott & Henry Towles in upper part, and John Taylor in Wiccomoco Parish.

--Inventory of estate of William Cornelious decd. returned.

--John Eustace vs Robert Gilmour—Attachment. Garnishees were Thomas Lawson, Henry Lawson, & William Steptoe.

--Jemima Chilton appointed guardian to Edward, Lucy, & Molly Chilton orphans of Thomas Chilton decd.

--James Newby, Coleman Dogget, & Spencer George appointed to settle estate of Thomas Chilton decd. in the hands of James Carter administrator & possess Jemima Chilton guardian to Edward, Lucy, & Molly Chilton orphans of the sd decd. therewith.

[Index 78] Lancaster OB 15:439a, June Court 1778

Report of road petitioned for by Coleman Dogget returned.

--Presentments of grand jury against Lazarus George, George Currell, James Findly, John Davis, William Carter, Abraham Fitchal, Willoughby Routt, Thomas Pinckard, William Edwards, William Riveer Junr., Thomas Bell, John Selden, James Ewell, Joseph Shearman, & Henry Tapscott are dismissed.

--Presentments of grand jury against Thomas Rouand, Robert Nicken, Richard Hall, Judith Yerby, & Peter Conway continued until next court.

--John Sullivant paid fine shillings for being a common swearer.

William Chilton paid fine 2 shillings for getting drunk.

--James Pinckard appointed Surveyor of road in place of William Edwards.

--Anthony Warrick administrator of Anthony McIntire[?] decd. vs William Garner administrator of Robert Ramsey decd.—Scire Facias. Abates by death of Deft.

--William Griggs vs Jesse George—Petition.
--William Griggs vs Thomas Hubbard—Petition.

[Index 79] Lancaster OB 15:439b, June Court 1778
William Dogget vs William Steptoe & Joanna his wife—Case.
--William Griggs vs Charles Jones—Petition.
--William Griggs vs Joseph Sullivan & Craven Everitt—Debt. Conditional judgment against Deft Sullivan and Bailie George Sub Sheriff; John Taylor Gent was security for Deft Everitt.
--William Griggs vs Bridgar Haynie & Thomas Hubbard—Debt.
--William Griggs vs Thomas Brent & Craven Everitt—Debt.
--William Griggs vs Spencer Dogget & Harry George—Debt. Abates by death of Deft Dogget; Conditional judgment against Deft George & Bailie George Sub Sheriff.

[Index 80] Lancaster OB 15:440a, June Court 1778
William Griggs vs James Selden & Edwin Conway—Debt.
--William Griggs vs George Phillips & James Waddy—Debt.
--William Griggs vs John Boyd & James Selden—Debt.
--William Griggs vs Thomas Pollard & James Pollard—Debt. Conditional judgment against Deft Thomas Pollard & Bailie George Sub Sheriff; Jonathan Wilder was special bail for Deft James Pollard.
--George Yerby executor of Elizabeth Yerby decd. vs Thomas Ellit [thus]—Case.
--Nicholas George assignee of George Norris vs John Garlington—Debt.

[Index 81] Lancaster OB 15:440b, June Court 1778
Nicholas Pope administrator of Elizabeth Martin decd. vs William Martin—Chancery. Abates by death of Plt.
--Moses George vs Spencer Dogget—Debt. Abates by death of Deft.
--Ambrose Wake vs Harry Currell—Debt. Richard E. Lee was special bail for Deft.
--John McTire vs George Norris—Petition.
--Nicholas George vs John Taylor—Case.
--Nicholas George assignee of James Selden vs John Taylor—Debt.
--Fleet Hinton vs Thomas Cane—Petition. Abates by death of Plt.

[Index 82] Lancaster OB 15:441a, July Court 1778
Court 16 July 1778, present justices James Ball, John Chinn, James Gordon, James Ball Junr., & William Yerby.
--Commission for privy examination of Sarah Chinn to a deed from John Chinn & sd Sarah his wife to Henry Tapscott was returned.
--Petition of Henry Lawson against Thomas Bridgford dismissed.
--Presentment of grand jury against Thomas Shepherd dismissed.
--Inventory of estate of Epaphroditus Lawson decd. returned.
--Will of James Webb decd. presented by James Ball Junr. Gent one of the executors therein named, and was proved by James Ball & James Ball Junr. Gent.
--William Mitchell, Richard Mitchell Junr., Rawleigh Davenport, & Thomas Flint appointed to appraise estate of James Webb decd.
--Deed of feoffment from Enoch George & Mary his wife to Charles Williams was proved by Charles Hammonds & Nicholas Lawson George.
--Bond from Enoch George to Charles Williams proved by oaths of Charles Hammonds & Nicholas Lawson George.
--Motion of John Eustace for leave to build a water grist mill, dismissed.
--Will of Susanna Moughon decd. proved by oath of Bailie George.
--Inventory of the estate of John Mason decd. returned.
--On motion of William Yerby Gent respecting tobacco & salt saved of a French scow[?], ordered Sheriff make sale thereof.

[Index 83] Lancaster OB 15:441b, July 1778
Judith Edwards granted administration on estate of Thomas Edwards decd.
--Endwin [thus] Conway Gent, Elias Edmonds, John Cundiff, & William Schofield appointed to appraise estate of Thomas Edwards decd.
--Richard Glascock vs Robert Gilmour—Chancery.
--Petition of Rachel Taylor administratrix against Phillip Brooks was continued.
--Petition of John McTire against Merryman Payne was continued.
--Spencer M. Ball & al, justices of Northumberland vs Martin Shearman & Joseph Ball—Debt. Dismissed, Defts being no inhabitants of the county.
--Edwin Fielding vs William Nutt—Debt.
--Joseph Batchelder vs Isaac & James Currell—Debt.
--Thomas Newton & son vs Maurice Wheeler—Chancery.
--Thomas Pollard vs John Goodridge—Trespass, assault, & battery.
--Present Richard Mitchell Gent.

[Index 84] Lancaster OB 15:442a, July Court 1778
Samuel Yopp vs James Simmons—Chancery.
--Sarah Wilder vs Traverse Lunsford—Trespass, assault, & battery.
--Mary Leach orphan of Anthony Leach decd. bound to Edwin Conway Gent until age 18, to learn to "read, sew, knit, and spin."
--Margaret Leach orphan of Anthony Leach decd. bound to Judith Brent until age 18, to learn to "read, sew, knit, and spin."
--David Boyd vs William Wise—Detinue.
--James Muse vs Charles Carter—Debt. Abates by death of Deft.
--Henry Tapscott vs John Rogers—Chancery.
--Hudson Muse assignee of James Muse vs Spencer Dogget—Debt.
--Jesse George vs John Thrall—Attachment.

[Index 85] Lancaster OB 15:442b, July Court 1778
Elisha Hall Plt vs John Eustace Gent—Case.
--Ordered the church wardens of Christ Church Parish bind out the orphans of John Williams decd.
--Edward Degge vs William Powell—Debt. Abates by death of Deft.
--The King vs Rawleigh Hazard—Summons.
--James Wallace vs Elijah Perciful—Case.
--Presentment of grand jury against Richard Hall & Elizabeth Yerby dismissed.
--The King vs James Robinson, Jesse Robinson, & Nicholas Pope—Debt.
--William Allason vs Rober [thus] Clark—Case.
--Traverse Lunsford vs Maurice Wheeler—Scandal.

[Index 86] Lancaster OB 15:443a, July Court 1778
Bartley James assignee of William Brown attorney for Anthony Warrick administrator of Anthony McQutrac [?] decd. vs William Powell & Thomas Copedge—Abates by death of Plt.
--Bartley James assignee of William Brown attorney for Anthony Warrick administrator of Anthony McQutrac[?] Decd. vs Thomas Copedge & William Powell—Debt. Abates by death of Plt.
--Jesse George vs John Clayton—Trespass, assault, & battery.
--Thomas Pollard vs Bailie George—Scandal.
--Maurice Wheeler vs Bailie George—Scandal.
--Maurice Wheeler vs Bailie George—Trespass, assault, & battery.
--David Boyd vs James Pinckard—Petition.

[Index 87] Lancaster OB 15:443b, July Court 1778
David Boyd vs Elihu Hall & wife—Chancery.

--David Boyd vs Elihu Hall—Detinue. Thomas Pinckard was security for Deft.
--John Adams vs Richard Sheardock—Trespass, assault, & battery.
--Jonathan Pullen vs James Pinckard—Case.
--Thomas Pinckard vs John Taylor—Petition.
--Inventory of estate of Moses Davis decd. returned.
--Inventory of estate of William Davis decd. returned.
--Inventory of estate of Elizabeth Brady decd. returned.
--John Fleet vs Anthony George—Debt. Judgment against Deft & Bailie George Sub Sheriff.

[Index 88] Lancaster OB 15:444a, July Court 1778
On petition of Elias Edmonds to build a water grist mill on Graces Run, ordered the Sheriff summon a jury to view the land
--Goodright vs Holdfast—Ejectment.
--Thomas B. Griffin vs James Armstrong—Attachment. Abates by death of Plt.
--Mungo Harvey vs Augustine Carter—Attachment. James Carter was garnishee.
--William Peachey administrator of Nichs. Flood vs Thomas B. Griffin & al, administrators of Burges Smith—Case.
--William Peachey administrator of Nicholas Flood vs Henry Armistead—Case.
--Elizabeth Pope vs Fleet Hinton—Case. Abates by death of Deft.

[Index 89] Lancaster OB 15:444b, July Court 1778
Richard E. Lee vs Henry Fleet—Case.
--William Lawson Junr. vs Henry Fleet—Case.
--Sarah Wilder vs Charles Lee—Trespass, assault, & battery.
--William Peachey one of the administrators of Nicholas Flood decd. vs Richard Hall—Attachment.
--Justices of Lancaster vs Judith Brent & Thomas Pinckard—Debt.
--Vincent Brent assignee &c vs Fortunatus Sydnor—Debt.

[Index 90] Lancaster OB 15:445a, July Court 1778
Phillip Smith, Burges Ball, & Thos. B. Griffin administrators of Burges Smith vs Lowry Oliver—Attachment.
--Elizabeth McTire vs William Lewis—Case.
--William Norris appointed Surveyor of road in place of Hugh Brent Gent decd.
--James Brent vs Isaac Mercer—Attachment. Sheriff returned attachment on one negro girl named Sarah.
--Ordered James Brent pay Edward Carter for 4 days attendance for sd Brent vs Isaac Mercer.
--Thomas Brent & Samuel Yobb executors of George Brent decd. vs Bailie George—Case.
--James Wallace vs Rawleigh Davenport—Scire Facias.

[Index 91] Lancaster OB 15:445b, July Court 1778
Elisha Hall vs Elias Edmonds—Case.
--Petition of Elisha Hall against George Bean, continued.
--Petition of Elisha Hall against William Gibson administrator &c, continued.
--Petition of Thomas George against Edward Carter, continued.
--William Norris vs John Hutchings executor of Ellinor Horton decd.—Case.
--Petition of William Blackerby against John Sebree, continued.
--Jeduthan James vs James Ewell—Case.
--Robert Coleman assignee vs George Robertson—Debt. Samuel Denny security for Deft.
--George Kelly vs John Clayton—Petition.
--Lott Palmer appointed guardian to Hannah, Nancy, & Jemima Webb orphans of Traverse Webb decd.

[Index 92] Lancaster OB 15:446a, July Court 1778
On motion of Rachel Webb, Thomas Brent, James Wallace, & William Galloway appointed to allot to sd Rachel her dower in lands of her decd. husband Traverse Webb.

Court 17 July 1778, present justices James Ball, Richard Mitchell, John Chinn, James Gardner, Henry Tapscott, & James Ball Junr.
--John Roane et als vs Sarah Jones—Chancery.
--David Galloway vs David Boyd—Chancery.
--Petition of Richard Ball for a mill, continued.
--John Fleet & wife vs David Boyd executor of Newton Keene—Chancery.
--LeRoy Peachey vs Luke Williams Junr.—Chancery.
--Justices of Northumberland vs John Leland administrator of John Williams decd.—Debt. Abates by death of Deft.

[Index 93] Lancaster OB 15:446b, July Court 1778
John Wormeley vs Elias Hull—Chancery.
--James Hathaway et al vs John Hathaway—Chancery.
--Rawleigh Downman Junr. vs William Palmer—Injunction.
--William Glascock Junr. vs William Glascock executor of Judith Glascock—Case. Abates by death of Deft.
--John Brown [or Brenon] vs John Read—Case.
--John Wormeley vs Stephen Hull—Injunction.
--Richard Hill vs John Wormeley—Injunction.
--Mungo Harvey & wife vs Richard Ball—Chancery.

[Index 94] Lancaster OB 15:447a, July Court 1778
Spencer Dogget vs John Connolly—Chancery. Abates by death of Plt.
--Thomas Carter vs Benjamin Williams—Case.
--John Heath vs Thomas Crowther—Case.
--Justices of Lancaster vs John Eustace—Debt.
--Thomas Pollard administrator of Saml. Angell vs Fortunatus Sydnor administrator of Wm. King—Case.
--John Carter vs Thomas Pollard et al—Chancery.
--Spencer George vs Thomas, Alexander, and John Hunton—Chancery.
--Margaret Ball vs Samuel Dunaway & George Goodridge—Case.

[Index 95] Lancaster OB 15:447b, July Court 1778
John McTire vs Thomas Pinckard—Case.
--John Yerby administrator of John Woodbridge vs John Leland & al administrators of John Williams—Chancery. Abates by death of Plt.
--Matthew Myars vs John Wormeley—Case.
--Richard Ball vs Mungo Harvey—Injunction.
--William Battin vs John Bailey—Detinue.
--Thomas Pollard vs Fortunatus Sydnor administrator—Debt.
--Craven Everitt vs Ruth Everitt administratrix—Case.

[Index 96] Lancaster OB 15:448a, July Court 1778
Traverse Lunceford vs Maurice Brent—Case.
--Benjamin Garton vs William Martin—Case.
--William Steptoe vs Thomas Pollard—Trespass, assault, & battery.
--William Powell vs William Steptoe—Chancery. Abates by death of Plt.
--George Yerby vs Judith Brent—Case.
--Robert C. Jacobs vs Thomas Pollard et al—Debt. William Montague was special bail for the Deft.
--Robert C. Jacobs vs Thomas Pollard et al—Debt. William Montague special bail for Deft.
--William Nutt assignee vs Thomas & James Pollard—Debt.

[Index 97] Lancaster OB 15:448b, July Court 1778
Thomas Myars vs John Wormeley—Case.
--James Mills vs George Conner—Case.

--The report of Elijah Perciful's wife's part of her decd. father John Yerby's estate was returned.

--On petition of William Montague for a water grist mill on McHans Run, ordered the Sheriff summon a jury to view the land.

--James Muse vs William Perciful—Attachment.

--Thomas Griggs vs Elias Edmonds—Debt.

[Index 98] Lancaster OB 15:449a, July Court 1778

John Garlington vs George Norris—Slander.

--Jesse George vs Spencer Dogget & Harry George—Debt.

--Joseph Hubbard assignee vs Maurice Wheeler—Debt.

--John Irby administrator of John Woodbridge vs James Montague—Debt. Abates by death of Plt.

--John Turbervile vs John Hunton—Debt.

--Joseph Hubbard assignee vs Maurice Wheeler—Debt.

--George Reynolds vs Thomas B. Griffin—Debt. Abates by the death of the parties.

--George Yerby executor vs Thomas Elliott—Case.

[Index 99] Lancaster OB 15:449b, July Court 1778

James Muse vs John Kirk—Debt.

--James Newby executor vs Henry Tapscott administrator—Case.

--Jeremiah Adderton vs Richard Ball—Debt.

--George Glascock vs William Glascock Jr—Case. Abates by death of Deft.

--Daniel Muse vs Thomas Smithder—Deft. Bailie George special bail for the Deft.

--William Griggs vs John E. Beale—Case. Abates by death of Deft.

--John Thrall vs Anthony George—Trespass, assault, & battery. Judgment against Deft & Bailie George Sub Sheriff.

[Index 100] Lancaster OB 15:450a, July Court 1778

Robert Edmonds vs John Goodridge—Trespass, assault, & battery.

--Henry Tapscott vs Lowry Oliver administrator—Case.

--Henry Tapscott vs James Newby executor—Case.

--Henry Tapscott vs Elias Edmonds—Case.

--Thomas Pollard vs Rawleigh Shearman—Case.

--Petition of Rebecca Craine against John Wormeley, continued.

--Petition of Elmore Dogget Junr. against John Hewes abates by death of Plt.

--Richard E. Lee vs Maurice Wheeler—Case. Michael Wilder security for Deft.

[Index 101] Lancaster OB 15:450b, July Court 1778

John Flower vs Lott Palmer—Case.

--Henry Tapscott Junr. vs Rawleigh Stott—Case.

--John Eustace vs Richard Hall—Debt. Judgment against Deft & Bailie George Sub Sheriff.

--William Boatman vs Thomas Hubbard—Case.

--John Ramey vs Monceiure Collins—Case.

--Spencer George vs John McTire—Trespass, assault, & battery.

--Zachariah Barr & al vs Sarah James—Summons.

[Index 102] Lancaster OB 15:451, July Court 1778

Petition of Isaac Gaskins administrator of John Gaskins decd. against Thomas Pinckard, continued.

--Petition of William Griggs against James Waddy, discontinued.

--Moses Sutton vs David Boyd—Chancery.

--Petition of William Brown against Elizabeth Griggs administrator, discontinued.

--John McTire vs James Pinckard—Attachment.

--William Downling vs John Ramey & Rodham Lunsford—Trespass, assault, & battery.

--James Gordon Junr. vs George Carter—Case.

--Betty Robinson vs Richard Goodridge—Detinue.

[End]

Lancaster County Order Book 16

[Index 103] Lancaster OB 16:1, Called Courts
Court of Oyer & Terminer 20 Sept 1770 for trial of Davey a negro man slave belonging to Martha Carter, on suspicion of felony, present justices Thomas Pinckard, George Heale, William Dymer, James Ball, Martin Shearman, & Richard Mitchell; Joseph Norris & his slave Richard were witnesses for the King; Deft found not guilty, but it appearing to court that sd. Davey was "guilty of other felonies," and David Boyd Gent Attorney for the King having prepared another indictment for breaking into a store house belonging to William Sydnor, Deft was found guilty, and ordered he be burnt in the hand at the bar, and that he receive 39 lashes on his bare back at the public whipping post.

Court of Oyer and Terminer 19 Oct 1770 for trial of Will a negro man slave belonging to George Heale Gent on suspicion of felony, present justices James Ball, John Chinn, Edwin Conway, James Selden, James Ewell, & Jesse Ball; Robert Davis & Daniel a slave belonging to Robert Belvard were witnesses; Deft found not guilty.

[Index 104] Lancaster OB 15:2a, Called Courts
Court 26 Nov 1770 for examination of Lambert Rouse, charged with stealing a hide of leather from Peter Miller, present justices James Ball, George Heale, Richard Mitchell, James Selden, & Jesse Ball; John Miller, William King, & Joshua Hubbard were witnesses; Deft found guilty of a misdeameanor.

Court of Oyer & Terminer 9 Feb 1771 for trial of James a negro man slave belonging to Margaret Davis, also Intry a negro man slave belonging to Edward Carter, on suspicion of felony, present justices Dale Carter, Richard Mitchell, John Chinn, Edwin Conway, & James Selden; William Watson & Benjamin Night were witnesses for the King; Deft James acquitted; Deft Intry having confessed to taking "some meal," ordered he receive 39 lashes on his bare back at the public whipping post.

[Index 105] Lancaster OB 15:2b, Called Courts
Court of Oyer & Terminer 11 July 1771 for trial of Toby a negro man slave belonging to Simon Degge, also Jerry & Fanny belonging to the estate of Samuel Hinton decd., accused of poisoning and taking away the lives of Nell & Hannah belonging to John Fleet Gent, and Will belonging to James Kirk, present justices Thomas Pinckard, James Ball, Dale Carter, Edwin Conway, James Selden, & Hugh Brent; Jerry & Fanny were acquitted; Toby was found guilty of "administereing medicine," and ordered he be burnt in the hand at the bar and receive 25 lashes on his bare back at the public whipping post.

Court of Oyer & Terminer 8 Aug 1771 for trial of Daniel & Anthony two negro man slaves belonging to the estate of William Dymer Gent decd. (William Nutt was his administrator), present justices James Ball, Dale Carter, John Fleet, John Chinn, Edwin Conway, Hugh Brent, John Taylor, & Burges Smith; David Boyd Gent was attorney for the King; Defts were accused of breaking into the house of William Hathaway of Christ Church Parish on the night of 2 Aug 1771 and stealing bacon; Daniel confessed the sd fact; Anthony pled not guilty; Both were found guilty, and ordered they be hanged by the neck until dead, on Monday the 19th; Defts were valued at £75 each.

[Index 106] Lancaster OB 16:3a, Called Courts
Court of Oyer & Terminer 7 May 1772 for trial of Davie a negro man slave belonging to Martha Carter on suspicion of felony, present justices James Ball, Richard Mitchell, John Chinn, & Burges Smith; David Boyd Gent was attorney for the King; Deft was accused of breaking into the house of James Riveer of Christ Church Parish on 2

May 1772 and stealing fish hooks, sundry goods & silver work; Deft pleaded not guilty; He was found guilty, and ordered to be hanged by the neck until dead, on Monday the 18th; Deft valued at £60.

[Index 107] Lancaster OB 16:3b, Called Courts
Court 25 June 1772 for examination of Mary alias Molly Carter, charged with taking 45 shillings out of the house of John McTire, present justices James Ball, John Chinn, Jesse Ball, & Burges Smith; Witnesses were William Brumley & John McTire; Deft was referred to the General Court in Williamsburg to be tried.

[Index 108] Lancaster OB 16:4a, Called Courts
Court 29 June 1772 for examination of William Nicken, charged with breaking into the house of John Mason and stealing "sundry meal," present justices Dale Carter, Edwin Conway, James Selden, Hugh Brent, & John Taylor; Deft found not guilty and discharged.

Court of Oyer & Terminer 7 Aug 1772 for trial of Daniel a negro man slave belonging to the estate of James Tapscott decd. of Northumberland County, on suspicion of felony, present justices Dale Carter, Edwin Conway, James Selden, John Taylor; David Boyd was attorney for the King; Daniel, a slave belonging to Ann Tapscott of Northumberland County, was accused of breaking into Catpoint tobacco warehouse in Lunenburg Parish, Richmond County on 30 June 1772, and stealing a hogshead of tobacco; Deft pleaded not guilty; He was found guilty, and ordered he be burnt in the hand at the bar; John Eidson & Philip Soleleather entered their attendance one day each as witnesses against the prisoner, and traveling 30 miles each.

[Index 109] Lancaster OB 16:4b, Called Courts
Court of Oyer & Terminer 18 Sept 1772 for trial of Ned, negro man slave belonging to James Ball Gent, on suspicion of felony, present justices Thomas Pinckard, Dale Carter, Richard Mitchell, Edwin Conway, Hugh Brent, & Burges Smith; David Boyd was attorney for the king; Deft was accused of stealing sheep the property of Thomas Flint on 1 Sept 1772; Deft pleaded not guilty; He was found guilty, and ordered he be burnt in the hand at the bar.

[Index 110] Lancaster OB 16:5a, Called Courts
Court of Oyer & Terminer 10 Oct 1772, for trial of Sam a negro man slave belonging to Burges Ball, Jeffery belonging to Elizabeth Towles, & James belonging to James Brent, for stealing 2 sheep belonging to James Ewell Gent, present justices James Ball, Dale Carter, Richard Mitchell, Edwin Conway, Jesse Ball, James Selden, John Taylor, & Burges Smith; The Defts pleaded not guilty; They were found guilty, and ordered they be burnt in the hand at the bar, and receive 35 lashes on their bare backs at the public whipping post.

[Index 111] Lancaster OB 16:5a, Called Courts
Court 22 Jan 1773 for examination of John Hutchingson & Frances Sullivan, charged with stealing a small silver can and one silver spoon of Thomas Pinckard Gent, present justices Richard Mitchell, Edwin Conway, James Selden, James Ewell, & John Taylor; Deft Hutchingson found not guilty and discharged; Deft Sullivan referred to the General Court in Williamsburg for trial; Thomas Pinckard Gent, Michael Wilder, & Thomas Pollard posted bond for their appearance as witnesses for the King at the trial.

[Index 112] Lancaster OB 16:5b, Called Courts
Court 22 Jan 1773 for examination of William Nicken, charged with breaking into the store house of Anthony McQutrac and stealing £30, present justices Richard Mitchell, Edwin Conway, James Selden, James Ewell, & John Taylor; Deft was referred to the General Court in Williamsburg for trial; Thomas Pollard, Thomas Hubbard, Richard Hutchings, Robert Nicken, John Yerby, & Anthony McQutrac posted bond for their appearance as witnesses for the King at the trial.

[Index 113] Lancaster OB 16:6a, Called Courts
Court of Oyer & Terminer 22 Jan 1773 for trial of James a negro man slave belonging to John Clayton, present justices Dale Carter, Richard Mitchell, Edwin Conway, Jesse Ball, James Selden, James Ewell, Hugh Brent, & John Taylor; David Boyd was attorney for the King; Deft charged with breaking into the storehouse of Anthony

McQutrac, Merchant, of Christ Church Parish on 8 Aug 1772 and stealing £30; Deft pleaded not guilty; He was found guilty, and ordered to be hanged by the neck until dead on 2 February; He was valued at £100.

[Index 114] Lancaster OB 16:6b, Called Courts
Court 4 Feb 1773 for examination of Robin Pinn, charged with stealing a great coat belonging to Bailie George, present justices James Ball, Dale Carter, Richard Mitchell, James Selden, & Burges Smith; Deft was found guilty of a "great misdemeanor," and ordered he receive 39 lashes on his bare back at the public whipping post; Joseph Dale was allowed for his attendance one day as witness for the King, and traveling 12 miles.

[Index 115] Lancaster OB 16:7a, Called Courts
Court of Oyer & Terminer 3 March 1773 for trial of Charles a negro man slave belonging to Joseph Shearman, on suspicion of breaking open the corn house of Burges Smith Gent and stealing half a barrel of corn, present justices James Ball, Dale Carter, Jesse Ball, & John Taylor; Deft pleaded not guilty; He was found guilty, and ordered he be burnt in the hand at the bar.

[the handwriting of the Clerk changes at this point]

Court of Oyer & Terminer 3 Jan 1774 for trial of Fielding a negro man slave belonging to John Wormeley, on suspicion of breaking open the house of Samuel Dunaway in the night time and stealing goods to the value of £3, present justices James Ball, Dale Carter, Edwin Conway, Jesse Ball, Burges Smith, Burges Ball, Thomas Lawson & James Gordon; Deft pleaded not guilty; He was found not guilty of the burglary, but was guilty of stealing sd goods; Ordered he be burnt in the hand at the bar and receive 29 lashes on his bare back at the public whipping post.

[Index 116] Lancaster OB 16:7b, Called Courts
Court of Oyer & Terminer 3 Oct 1774 for trial of Will a negro man slave belonging to James Gordon Gent, and Duke a negro man slave belonging to John Wormeley Gent, on suspicion of burglary, present justices James Ball, Dale Carter, Richd. Mitchell, John Fleet, Jesse Ball, & Burges Ball; Deft was charged with entering the house of William Boatman and stealing rum valued at 20 shillings in the night time of 23 Sept; Deft pleaded not guilty; He was found guilty; Ordered he be burnt in the hand at the bar.

Court of Oyer & Terminer 6 Sept 1775 for trial of Natt a negro man slave the property of Walter James, on suspicion of raping Sarah James, present justices James Ball, Charles Carter, Edwin Conway, James Selden, John Taylor, Hugh Brent, Thomas Lawson, Burges Ball, & James Gordon; He was charged with raping sd Sarah Janes on 21 August; He pleaded guilty; Sary James, Lawson Hathaway, Thos. Bridgford, & James Currell were witnesses; Deft was found guilty, and ordered he be hanged by the neck until dead on the 18th; Deft was valued at£80.

[Index 117] Lancaster OB 16:8a, Called Courts
Court of Oyer & Terminer 14 Sept 1775 for trial of Tom a negro man slave the property of Nancy Darmeron of Northumberland County, on suspicion of raping Cloe Carter of Lancaster County, present John Fleet, Edwin Conway, James Selden, John Taylor, Burges Ball, & James Gordon; Deft charged with raping sd Cloe Carter on 21 August; He pleaded not guilty; Cloe Carter, Abraham Fitchett, & "sundry negro witnesses" gave testimony; Deft was found guilty, and ordered he have "each of his ears nailed to the pillory, & then cut out," and that he be branded on the cheek with a hot iron, and receive 39 lashes on his bare back at the public whipping post, and ordered the Sheriff execute the same "while this court is sitting."

[Index 118] Lancaster OB 16:8b, Called Courts
Court 19 Oct 1775, complaint being made against Charles a negro man slave belonging to George Heale Gent of Fauquier County, for hog stealing; Deft denied the fact; He was found guilty, and ordered he receive 39 lashes on his bare back.

Court of Oyer & Terminer 21 Dec 1775 for trial of James a negro man slave the property of James Gordon Gent on suspicion of felony, present justices Dale Carter, Jesse Ball, Edwin Conway, & John Taylor; Deft charged with stealing & killing one sheep in November last; Deft pleaded not guilty; He was found guilty, and ordered that he be burned in the hand in presence of the court.

Court of Oyer & Terminer 3 April 1776 for trial of Will a negro man slave the property of James Ball Gent, on suspicion of attempting to take the life of Jeriah Harris, present justices John Fleet, Edwin Conway, James Selden, & James Gordon; Deft charged with attempting the life of the sd Harris by stabbing him with a knife; Deft pleaded not guilty; He was found guilty of a "great misdemeanor," and ordered he receive 39 lashes on his bare back at the public whipping post.

[Index 119] Lancaster OB 16:9a, Called Courts
Court of Oyer & Terminer 17 Feb 1777 for trial of Daniel a negro man slave the property of Sally Simmons orphan of John Simmons decd., on suspicion of felony, present justices James Ball, John Fleet, Jesse Ball, & Thomas Lawson; Deft charged with breaking into the house of James Currell in the night time and stealing sundry goods valued at 10/-; Deft pleaded guilty, ordered he be burnt in the hand at the bar, and receive 39 lashes on his bare back.

Court of Oyer & Terminer 21 Aug 1777 for trial of Daniel a negro man slave the property of Sally Simmons orphan of John Simmons decd., for felony, present justices James Ball, John Fleet, Richd. Mitchell, John Taylor, James Gordon, Henry Tapscot, Henry Towles, & John Berryman; Deft charged with breaking into the house of Jesse Carter in the night of 20 August and stealing 12 yards of Virginia cloth; Deft pleaded guilty, and ordered he be hanged by the neck until dead on 10 September next; Deft was valued at £ 120.

[Index 120] Lancaster OB 16:9b, Called Courts
Court 19 Feb 1778 for examination of William Yerby on suspicion of "has having furnished the enemies of this state with provision and other necessarys and particularly by delivering up a French vessel and cargo to two British ships of war," present justices James Ball, John Fleet, Richard Mitchell, John Chinn, James Gordon, & Henry Towles. Court adjourned until tomorrow.

[Index 121] Lancaster OB 16:10a, Called Courts
Court 20 Feb 1778, continued from the 19th for examination of William Yerby, present justices James Ball, John Fleet, Richard Mitchell, John Chinn, Jesse Ball, John Taylor, James Gordon, & Henry Towles; William Brown was attorney for Deft; Deft found guilty, and ordered he be sent to the next General Court in Williamsburg for trial. Henry Tapscott Junr., Nicholas George, John Chowning, John McTire, Henry Overstreet, Samuel Dunaway, William Carpenter, John Carpenter, Henry Lawson, James Currell, Nicholas Currell Junr., & Henry Fleet to be witnesses in behalf of the Commonwealth at sd trial.

Court of Oyer & Terminer 21 Feb 1778 for trial of Nick a negro man slave belonging to Rev David Currie, and Billy a negro man slave belonging to Charles Carter Esq, under suspicion of burglary and felony, present justices James Ball, Richard Mitchell, James Gordon, & Henry Towles; The Defts pleaded not guilty, and they were found not guilty.

[Index 122] Lancaster OB 16:10b, Called Courts
Copy of certificate given by Capt Ben. Caldwell of His Majesty's ship Emerald to William Yerby was recorded, and sent to the General Court for trial of Capt Yerby. Summary of certificate: Capt Caldwell would not receive any negroes on board his ship, or stop the ferries passing in the river, given on board ship off Carter's Creek in Rappahannock River 6 Jan 1778.

Court of Oyer & Terminer 10 Aug 1778 for trial of Will a negro man slave belonging to John Pearson, on suspicion of breaking into the house of Elizabeth McGrigor and stealing 4 pounds 12 shillings cash and a quantity of bacon, present justices James Ball, Richard Mitchell, John Chinn, Thomas Lawson, John Taylor, & William Yerby; Deft pleaded guilty, and ordered he be burnt in the hand at the bar, and receive 39 lashes on his bare back.

[Index 123] Lancaster OB 16:11a, August Court 1778

Court 20 Aug 1778, present justices James Ball, John Fleet, Richard Mitchell, John Chinn, John Taylor, Thomas Lawson, James Gordon, Henry Tapscott, Henry Towles, and James Ball Junr.
--Inventory of the estate of Fleet Hinton decd. was returned.
--Thadeus McCarty vs John Kirk & George Edwards—Debt. Discontinued, the Defts being no inhabitants.
--Katharine McDonald vs John Selden administrator of James Selden—Case.
--William Barber vs Joseph Hubbard—Case.
--Matthias James vs Edwin Conway & Jesse George—Debt. Nicholas George was special bail for Deft.
--John Boswell vs William Griggs—Case.
--Thomas Hunton vs Benjamin Barton Junr.—Case.

[Index 124] Lancaster OB 16:11b, August Court 1778

Jonathan Pullen vs James Pinckard—Case.
--William Allason vs Robert Clark—Case.
--Summons of Zachariah Bar and James Hudnall against Sarah James abates by death of sd James.
--John Clutton vs Thomas Davis—Case.
--On motion of William Griffin executor of Thomas B. Griffin Esq decd., William Peachey, LeRoy Peachey, Hudson Muse, William Miskel, William Colston, Charles McCarty, James Ball, Richard Mitchell, John Chinn, Henry Tapscott, & William Sydnor Gent were appointed to settled sd Thomas B. Griffin's administration account of Burges Smith Gent decd's estate.
--John Turberville vs John Hunton—Debt.
--William Griggs returned his guardianship account of the estate of John & Lawson Wale orphans of George Wale decd.
--Inventory of estate of Thomas B. Griffin Esq decd. returned.
--Allotment of Rachel Webb's dower in land of her decd. husband Traverse Webb returned.

[Index 125] Lancaster OB 16:12a, August Court 1778

William Merrideth is recommended to the Governor as an Assistant Inspector of tobacco at Dymer's Warehouse, and Indian Creek Warehouse in Northumberland County.
--John Taylor Gent recommended to the Governor as County Lieutenant, Edwin Conway Gent as Colonel, James Gordon Gent as Lieutenant Colonel, James Ball Junr. Gent as Major, John Bailey as Capt in place of James Ball Junr., Isaac Deedge [thus] as Capt in place of William Yerby, and Lawson Hathaway as Second Lieutenant in Capt Thomas Carter's company.
--Charles Ball, Henry Lawson, & John Selden Gent recommended to the Governor to be added to Commission of the Peace.
--Male tithables of William Ball, Thomas & Matthew Myars, and Sampson Demovil were exempted from clearing the ferry road, but that they keep the road from the sign post to the sd Ball's gate in repair.
--Will of Jesse Ball Gent decd. presented by James Ball Junr. & Peter Conway executors therein named, and was proved by James Ball, James Ball Junr. Gent, & James Newby.
--John Taylor Gent, William Montague, Richard Ball, & John Bailey appointed to appraise estate of Jesse Ball Gent.
--Fortunatus Sydnor granted administration on estate of Elizabeth Sydnor decd.
--Sarah Ellen Carter & Ann Pynes Carter orphans of Joseph Carter decd. chose William Sydnor for their guardian.
--Matthew Myars appointed guardian to Joseph Carter orphan of Joseph Carter decd.
--Rodham Lunceford appointed guardian to Polly Page Carter orphan of Joseph Carter decd.
--James Gordon, Henry Towles Gent, & Charles Rogers appointed to divide estate of Joseph Carter decd. agreeable to his will.
--Henry Lawson returned guardianship account of the estate of Sally Simmons orphan of John Simmons decd.

[Index 126] Lancaster OB 16:12b, August Court 1778

Report of the jury about a mill petitioned for by Elias Edmonds was returned.
--Report of jury about mill petitioned for by Richard Ball was returned.
--Report of jury about mill petitioned for by William Montague was returned.

--On motion of George Carter by his attorney, ordered dedimus issue to take deposition of William Stephens at the suit of James Gordon Junr.

--On motion of John McTire, Edwin Conway, John Taylor, & Charles Ball Gent appointed to divide land of Robert Hening decd. agreeable to his will.

--Petition of Rebecka Craine against John Wormeley, continued.

--Petition of Richard E. Lee against John Parrott, dismissed.

--On motion of William Griggs who intermarried with Ruth Everitt widow of Thomas Everitt decd., Edwin Conway, James Gordon, & Charles Ball Gent appointed to divide sd Everitt's estate, and possess sd Griggs with one third part in right of his wife, also the other two thirds as guardian to sd Everitt's orphans.

--William Griggs appointed guardian to Charles & John Denny Everitt orphans of Thomas Everitt decd.

--On motion of David Boyd, dedimus issued to take deposition of William Stewart Pasquet (an infirm person) in his suit against Elihu Hall; William Brown was attorney for sd Hall.

--Petition of Rachel Taylor administrator &c against Phillip Brooks, continued.

--Petition of John McTire vs Merryman Payne.

--Petition of Isaac Gaskins vs Thomas Pinckard.

--Petition of Elisha Hall against George Bean.

--Petition of Elisha Hall against William Gibson.

--Petition of Thomas George against Edward Carter.

[Index 127] Lancaster OB 16:13a, August Court 1778

Leanna Cornelius summoned to next court to show cause why her children should not be bound.

--Joseph Dobbs appointed guardian to James Dogget orphan of Spencer Dogget decd., with Spencer George his security.

--Richard Lee executors vs Maurice Wheeler—Case. Michael Wilson was security for Deft.

--Petition of William Blackerby against John Sebree.

--Inventory of estate of Thomas Edwards decd. returned.

Court 17 Sept 1778, present justices James Ball, Richard Mitchell, Thomas Lawson, Henry Tapscott, William Yerby, & James Ball Junr.

--John Eustace vs Richard Hall—Debt.

--Mary Schofield granted administration on estate of Thomas Schofield decd.

--John Merrideth, Elias Edmonds, James Findla, & Jonathan Pullen appointed to appraise estate of Thomas Schofield decd.

--John James returned his guardianship account of estate of Frances James orphan of Thomas James decd.

--James Ball Junr. Gent appointed Surveyor of road in place of John Bailey.

[Index 128] Lancaster OB 16:13b, Sept Court 1778

William Wiblin appointed Surveyor of road from the church to Mrs. Agatha Ball's mill.

--John Adams vs Bennit Bush—Trespass, assault, & battery.

--Job Carter vs Richard Hall—Debt. Judgment against Deft & Edwin Conway Gent Sheriff.

--Job Carter vs Richard Hill—Case; Judgment against Deft & Edwin Conway Gent Sheriff.

--Job Carter assignee of John Wormeley, who was assignee of Jesse Denny vs Richard Hall—Debt; Judgment against Deft & Edwin Conway Gent Sheriff.

--Benjamin Smith & Elizabeth his wife & Robert Sydnor, executors of Robert Porteus Downman decd. vs John Galloway—Debt. William Galloway was special bail for Deft.

[Index 129] Lancaster OB 16:14a, Sept Court 1778

Jeremiah Adderton vs Richard Ball—Debt.

--Frances Bond by Charles Rogers her guardian vs William Lewis—Detinue. Samuel Denny & William Betts were securities for Deft.

--Petition of Thomas Pinckard against John Eustace executor of Hancock Eustace, continued.

--Petition of Charles Lee administrator of John E. Beale, continued.

--Jonathan Pullen vs James Pinckard—Case.

--Petition of Daniel Rich against William Mitchell, dismissed.

--Leroy Peachey vs John Kirk—Scire Facias.

--William Schofield vs Thomas Pollard administrator of Samuel Angell decd.—Scire Facias.

--Deed from Peter Conway & Frances his wife to Job Carter was acknowledged.

[Index 130] Lancaster OB 16:14b, Sept Court 1778
Coleman Dogget vs Spencer George for sureties of the peace, dismissed.

--Spencer George vs Coleman Dogget for sureties of the peace, dismissed.

--Deed from Job Carter & Judith his wife to James Gordon Gent was acknowledged.

--Petition of Rebecka Craine vs John Wormeley, continued.

--Petition of Rachel Taylor administrator &c vs Phillip Brooke, continued.

--Petition of Isaac Gaskins administrator &c vs Thomas Pinckard, continued.

--Present James Gordon Gent.

--Petition of Thomas George vs Edward Carter.

--Ordered Edward Carter pay Dennis Conway for attendance as witness in sd Carter's suit vs Thomas George, & for traveling 45 miles.

--Ordered Edward Carter pay Willoughby Rout for attendance as witness in sd Carter's suit vs Thomas George, & for traveling 25 miles.

--William Sydnor produced an account of tobacco at Deep Creek Warehouse.

--Present John Taylor & Henry Towles Gent.

--William Griggs granted administration on estate of Sarah James decd.

--John James, William Mason, Thomas Hathaway, & Lawson Hathaway appointed to appraise estate of Sarah James decd.

--Leanna Hutchings appointed guardian to William Hutchings orphan of Richard Hutchings.

--Petition of Leanna Hutchings administratrix of Richard Hutchings decd. vs John James; same vs William Gibson; both continued.

[Index 131] Lancaster OB 16:15a, Sept Court 1778
Petition of William Blackerby vs John Sebree.

--Petition of Elisha Hall vs George Bean.

--Petition of Elisha Hall vs William Gibson administrator of William Davis decd.

--Petition of Charles Lee vs Richard E. Lee.

--Ordered John Sebree pay John Cornish for attendance as witness in sd Sebree's suit vs William Blackerby, and for traveling 32 miles.

--Job Carter appointed guardian to Charlotte Harris orphan of Jeriah Harris decd.

--Edwin Conway, John Taylor, & James Gordon Gent appointed to divide the estate of Jeriah Harris decd.

Court 15 Oct 1778, present justices James Ball, John Taylor, Thos. Lawson, Jas. Gordon, John Berryman, James Ball Junr., & William Yerby.

--Inventory of estate of Elizabeth Lawson decd. returned.

--Inventory & division of estate of Bartlet James decd. returned.

--Inventory of estate of Jesse Ball Gent returned.

--John Webb son of Leanna Cornelius bound to Tarpley Thomas until age 21, to learn the trade of Wheelwright.

[Index 132] Lancaster OB 16:15b, Oct Court 1778
Sally Angell orphan of Samuel Angell, with consent of her former master, was bound to Abner Palmer until age 18.

--John Taylor Gent sworn as County Lieutenant, Edwin Conway as Colonel, James Gordon Gent as Lieutenant Colonel, James Ball Junr. as Major, Isaac Degge as Captain 3rd company, John Bailey as Captain 4th company, John Chowning as Second Lieutenant to Capt Bailey, Edward Blakemore as Ensign to Capt Bailey, & Lawson Hathaway as Second Lieutenant to Capt Carter in the county militia.

--Mungo Harvy & wife vs Richard Ball—Chancery. James Ball, William Montague, & James Ball Junr. Gent were referees.

--Richard Ball vs Mungo Harvey—Injunction; James Ball, William Montague, & James Ball Junr. Gent were referees.

--Charles Rogers produced account of tobacco in Davis's & Lowry's warehouses.

--John Harris vs John Miller & James Harris administrators—Detinue.

--Richard Hall vs Rawleigh Hazard—Case.

[Index 133] Lancaster OB 16:16a, October Court 1778

William Doggett Junr. vs Thomas Pinckard—Case.

--Spencer Currell vs William Hinton—Assault & Battery.

--Bushrod Riveer vs Bailie George—Case.

--Inventory of estate of Sarah Kirk decd. returned.

--Deed of bargain& sale from William Schofield & Betty his wife to William Schofield Junr., acknowledged.

--Bill of sale from Thomas Cottrell to Michael Wilder was proved by Bailie George.

--Inventory of estate of Thomas Norris & Peter Norris decd. was returned.

--James Hudnall vs George Pitman—Petition.

[Index 134] Lancaster OB 16:16b, October Court 1778

Isaac Gaskins vs Thomas Pinckard—Petition.

--Petition of Thomas Pinckard vs John Eustace executor &c.

--Thomas Pinckard vs Charles Lee administrator &c—Petition.

--John Taylor, Thomas Lawson, & James Gordon Gent. recommended to the Governor as property persons to act as Sheriff.

--William Griggs vs Joseph Sullivant &   Everitt—Debt.

--William Griggs vs Henry George—Debt.

[Index 135] Lancaster OB 16:17a, October Court 1778

Leanna Hutchings administratrix &c vs John James—Petition.

--Leanna Hutchings administratrix &c vs William Gibson—Petition.

--Thomas Griggs appointed guardian to his daughter Sarah Griggs; James Gordon Gent, Thomas Rob, & John McTire appointed to possess sd Griggs with the sd Sarah's estate.

--Settlement of James Carter's administration of estate of Charles Chilton was returned.

--Richard E. Lee granted administration on estate of William Mason decd.

--Henry Lawson, William Lawson, Nicholas Currell, & Thomas Hunton appointed to appraise estate of William Mason decd.

--Deed from Thomas Rouand & Mary his wife to Thad. McCarty was proved by oaths of William Yerby, Richard E. Lee, & John Fleet Gent.

--James Ewell recommended to the Governor as Captain of militia in place of Capt Robert Chinn, who resigned; and recommended Rawleigh Tapscott as Second Lieutenant in sd company.

[Index 136] Lancaster OB 16:17b, Oct Court 1778

Nicholas George vs John Garlington—Debt.

--James Gordon Gent appointed Tax Commissioner in place of Richard Mitchell Gent, who is "in a state of inability."

--Matthew Myars vs John Wormley—Case.

--John McTyre vs Thomas Pincard—Case.

--James Ball, John Chinn, Henry Tapscott, William Sydnor, & Richard Mitchell Gent appointed to divide estate of Thomas B. Griffin Gent decd.

--Ordered Leanna Hutchings pay John Doggett as witness in her suit vs John James.

--Ordered Leanna Hutchings pay Elmore Doggett as witness in her suit against William Gibson.

[Index 137] Lancaster OB 16:18a, Oct Court 1778
Court 16 Oct 1778, present justices James Ball, John Taylor, Thos. Lawson, James Gordon, & James Ball Junr.
--John McTyre vs Thomas Pinckard—Case. A jury came, with John Clutton foreman.
--Thomas Pinckard ordered to pay Robert C. Jacobs as witness in his suit vs McTyre.
--John Roun &c vs Elizabeth Jones &c—Chancery; Abates by death of Plt.
--John Fleet vs Anthony George—Debt.

[Index 138] Lancaster OB 16:18b, Oct Court 1778
Goodright vs Holdfast—Ejectment.
--John Davis vs John Harvey—Assault & Battery. Discontinued, the Deft being no inhabitant.
--James Kirk Junr. vs Richard Ball—Debt; Abates by death of Plt.
--William Chilton &c vs Fleet Hinton—Assault & Battery; Abates by death of Deft.
--Moses Davis vs John Hutchings—Case; Abates by death of Plt.
--Robert Coleman assignee &c vs George Robertson—Debt. Samuel Denny was security for Deft.
--Jones vs Jones—Chancery. [in margin]

[Index 139] Lancaster OB 16:19a, Oct Court 1778
Job Carter vs Richard Hall—Debt.
--Job Carter vs Richard Hall—Case.
--Job Carter assignee &c vs Richard Hall—Debt.
--Frances Bond by Chas. Rogers her guardian vs William Lewis—Detinue. John Taylor Gent was special bail for Deft.
--Richard E. Lee vs Maurice Wheeler—Case. A jury came, John Clutton foreman.

[Index 140] Lancaster OB 16:19b, Nov Court 1778
Court 19 Nov 1778, present justices James Ball, Richard Mitchell, Henry Tapscott, Henry Towles, & John Berryman.
--Richard E. Lee sworn as Clerk pro tempore.
--John Taylor Gent sworn as Sheriff.
--James Newby & John Bailey qualified as Under Sheriffs.
--Travis Lunceford vs Maurice Wheeler.
--Inventory of estate of Thomas Schofield decd. was returned.

[Index 141] Lancaster OB 16:20a, Nov Court 1778
Nancy Webb bound to William Wiblin & his wife Hannah until age 18.
--Fortunatus Sydnor petitioned for a water grist mill on "a run."
--Margaret Brent, widow of George Brent decd., petitioned for her dower; Ordered Edwin Conway, John Taylor, & Elias Edmonds lay off sd dower.
--Margaret Brent widow of George Brent relinquished her legacy under the will of her decd. husband.
--Margaret Brent orphan of George Brent chose Thomas Brent as her guardian.
--Thomas Brent & Samuel Yop appointed guardians to George Brent, Charles Brent, & Saryann Brent orphans of George Brent decd.
--Edwin Conway, John Taylor, & John Edmonds appointed to divide estate of George Brent decd.
--Deed from Richard Lock & Winifred his wife to Stephen Lock[?, page damaged] was proved.

[Index 142] Lancaster OB 16:20b, Nov Court 1778
Johnson Reveer granted administration on estate of Richard Reveer decd.
--Peter Reveer, William Reveer Junr., Richard Goodridge, & Jesse Robins appointed to appraise estate of Richard Reveer decd.
--Lawson Wale chose Zachariah Barr as his guardian; John Berryman, William Yerby Gent, Bailee George, & John James appointed to possess sd Barr with the estate of sd Lawson which is now in hands of William Griggs.
--Henry Lawson appointed to purchase corn for use of Rachel Hill, widow of Martin Hill decd.

--Mathew Miars appointed foreman of grand jury.

--Rawleigh Shearman, presented by grand jury, paid his fine.

--James Ewell sworn as militia Captain.

--Margaret Christian orphan of Christopher Christian bound to William Wiblin & Hannah his wife until age 18.

--Report possessing Thomas Griggs with the estate of Sarah Griggs his daughter was returned.

[Index 143] Lancaster OB 16:21a, Nov Court 1778

Richard Selden & William Gibson recommended to the Governor as militia Captains, Elias Edmonds & Lott Palmer as Lieutenants, & James Pollard as Ensign.

--Rawleigh Davenport appointed Surveyor of road in place of Mungo Harvey.

-On motion of Doctr. Andrew Robertson, Thomas Flint, Ozwald Newby, Johnson Reveer, & John McTyre were appointed to view the road leading by sd Robertsons.

--Jesse Robinson appointed Surveyor of road from Col John Taylors landing to the sign post opposite Doctr. Andrew Robertsons, in place of John McTyre.

--George Edwards appointed Surveyor of road in place of Thomas Hammonds.

--John Taylor Gent appointed guardian to Milly & Lewis Henning orphans of Robert Henning decd.; William Montague, Peter Conway, & Richard Bell appointed to settle account relative to sd orphan's estate.

--Sally Hill orphan of William Hill chose Spencer George her guardian; John Yerby, Elias Edmonds, & James Carter appointed to possess sd George with sd Hill's estate.

--William Griggs vs Maurice Wheeler.

[Index 144] Lancaster OB 16:21b, Dec Court 1778

Court 17 Dec 1778, present justices James Ball, Richard Mitchell, John Chinn, Henry Tapscott, John Berryman, Henry Towles, William Yerby, & James Ball Junr.

--Thaddeus McCarty took oath as Clerk.

--The county levy was laid. The following individuals were allowed their accounts: The representatives of Thos. Shearman decd. the late Clerk, James Newby, Edwin Conway Gent, George Beane, John Pinckard, Abner Palmer, James Ball Junr. Gent, Spencer George, Johnson Reveer, William Webb, Rawleigh Stott, Nicholas Currell, John McTyre, Michael Wilder, & Bailie George.

--Windfield Robinson son of Windfield Robinson was bound to John Langsdale until age 21, to learn the trade of Shoemaker.

[Index 145] Lancaster OB 16:22a, Dec Court 1778

Thomas George, on account of ill health, exempted from paying levy in future.

--Division of estate of Edward Blakemore decd. returned.

--Deed from Elmore Doggett to Rawleigh Hazard proved.

--Inventory of estate of Richard Reveer decd. returned.

--William Sullivan, presented by grand jury, paid his fine to Henry Lawson.

--John Mctyre, presented by grand jury, paid his fine to Henry Towles Gent.

--Robert Chinn, presented by grand jury, paid his fine to Henry Towles Gent.

--James Newby appointed guardian to Newman Chilton orphan of Moses Chilton decd.

--On motion of Jonathan Pullen, who intermarried with the widow of Moses Chilton decd., Richard Mitchell, James Ball Junr. Gent, William Sydnor, & Rawleigh Davenport were appointed to divide estate of sd deceased & possess sd Pullen with his wife's part.

--John Berryman & William Yerby Gent appointed to examine the state of the records.

--Isaac Currell &c vs John Hathway [thus], dismissed.

--On motion of Isabel Kent, widow of Jesse Kent, who died in the service of the state, ordered the Treasurer pay £50 to John Berryman Gent for the support of sd Kent's family.

[Index 146] Lancaster OB 16:22b, Dec Court 1778

On motion of Hannah Thatcher, whose husband died in the service of the state, ordered the Treasurer pay £30 to John Berryman Gent for the support of her family.

--Ordered depositions of Rawleigh Shearman & William Sullivan be taken in the suit of George vs Wheeler for ejectment.
--On motion of Milly Galloway whose husband died in the service of the Continent, ordered the Treasurer pay £30 to Richard Mitchell Gent for her use.
--On motion of Fortunatus Sydnor, ordered William Brown Gent lay off an acre of land petitioned for last court for a mill, the County Surveyor being dead.

Court 18 Feb 1779, present justices James Ball, Richard Mitchell, John Berryman, James Gordon, Henry Towles, & James Bally Jnr.
--Inventory of estate of James Webb decd. returned.
--Division of estate of Chatten Chowning decd. returned.
--Division of estate of John Bond decd. returned.
--Inventory of estate of Frances Payn decd. returned.

[Index 147] Lancaster OB 16:23a, Feb Court 1779

George Scurlock, James Alderson, George Cammel, John Dale, William Kelly, James Kelly, Mich[a]el Wilder, Simon Laughlin, & William Griggs having entered into a recognizance, and the same being a criminal matter, it was dismissed.
--John Taylor Gent, William Montague, John Wormeley, & Richard Ball appointed to divide estate of George Payne decd., & possess Thomas Haydon (who intermarried with Judith the daughter of sd decd.) with his wife's part.
--Will of Walter James decd. presented by Eliza James the widow of sd deceased, who was granted administration.
--Will of John Nichols decd. presented by Benjamin George & Thomas Bell two of the executors therein named; They were granted administration; Mary Nichols, widow of the deceased, dissented.
--William Brown, William Yerby, Edwin Conway Gent & Fortunatus Sydnor appointed to appraise estate of John Nichols & allot to the widow Mary Nichols her dower.
--James Ball, Richard Mitchell, John Chinn, & James Ball Junr. Gent appointed to settle accounts of the orphans of Thomas Pollard decd., and possess Thomas Chinn their present guardian with their estates.
--George Currell appointed guardian to Elizabeth Purkins orphan of Thomas Purkins.

[Index 148] Lancaster OB 16:23b, Feb Court 1779

Zachariah Barr appointed guardian to Lawson Wale orphan of George Wale decd.; John James, William Mason, & Thomas Carter appointed to possess sd Barr with sd orphan's estate which is now in the hands of William Griggs.
--John Adams vs Richard Shearleock—Assault & Battery; Dedimus granted the Deft to take deposition of Edward Bailey.
--Deed from Richard Hall & Mary his wife to Peter Conway was proved by James Gordon, Henry Tapscott, & Edwin Conway Gent.
--Deed of gift from Ann Shearman to Joseph Shearman proved by oaths of Richard Mitchell Gent & Thomas Stott.
--Commission for privy examination of Ann Blackerby wife of James Blackerby, respecting a deed from sd James to Henry Tapscott Gent, was returned.
--John Clayton petitioned for a water grist mill on the great swamp.
--George Chitwood granted leave (on the information of Henry Towles Gent) to alter the road from the courthouse to Chowning's ferry.

[Index 149] Lancaster OB 16:24a, Feb Court 1779

John Berryman Gent sworn as Vestryman in Christ Church Parish.
--The county levy was laid. These men were paid as patrollers: John Carpenter, Edwd. Bailey, Tarpley Thomas, LeRoy Newby, & William Carpenter; The following were also allowed their accounts: Thomas B. Griffin Gent decd., the estate of Thomas Shearman decd., Col Edwin Conway, Bailie George, David Boyd Gent (attorney); James Newby and Bailie George were debtors in the levy.
--Charles Reveer orphan of Richard Reveer decd. bound to John Reveer Junr. until age 21 (he being 7 years of age on 11 April 1778).

[Index 150] Lancaster OB 16:24b, Feb Court 1779
Thomas May orphan of Henry May bound to James Bush, he being 16 years of age on 7 Dec 1778, to learn the trade of Shoemaker.
--Benjamin Garton vs William Martin—Case. Plt granted a dedimus to take depositions of Benjamin Garton Jr. & Anthony Garton.
--William Meredith sworn as Inspector of tobacco at Dymer's & Indian Warehouses.
--David Boyd vs Elihu Hall—Detinue.
--Deed from Thomas Dunaway & Susanna his wife, and Edwin Gaskins & Sarah his wife to William Doggett, also a bond for performance of covenants, were acknowledged.

[Index 151] Lancaster OB 16:25a, Called Court
Court of enquiry 25 Feb 1779 for examination of Simon Laughlin, William Kelly, James Kelly, George Cammell & George Scurlock, charged with breaking into the house of George Yerby of Richmond County and taking a negro man slave Ben, valued at £500, present justices James Ball, James Gordon, John Berryman, Henry Tapscott, & James Ball Junr.; Ordered the Defts post bond for their appearance at the next grand jury court; Richard E. Lee was security for William Kelly, Bailie George was security for James Kelly, Joseph Norris was security for George Cammell, Joseph Norris was security for George Scurlock.

[Index 152] Lancaster OB 16:25b, Called Court
James Alderson entered his attendance as evidence on behalf of the Commonweath.

Court 18 March 1779, present justices James Ball, Richd. Mitchell, John Berryman, & James Ball Junr.
--Report of the jury about a mill petitioned for by Fortunatus Sydnor was returned.
--Report of the juty about a mill petitioned for by John Clayton was returned.
--On petition of Jane Burn whose husband died in the service of this state, ordered the Treasurer pay John Berryman Gent £30 for her use.
--Jesse Chilton orphan of Jesse Chilton chose William Chilton as his guardian.
--On petition of Leannah Overstreet whose husband died in the service of this state, ordered the Treasurer pay John Berryman Gent £50 for her use.
--Rachell Hill, widow of Martin Hill decd., granted administration on his estate.
--John Fleet Gent, Nicholas Currell, William Martin, & Thomas Hunton Senr. appointed to appraise estate of Martin Hill decd.
--Viewers report about a road petitioned for by Andrew Robertson was returned.

[Index 153] OB 16:26a, March Court 1779
Division of estate of Moses Chilton decd. returned.
--Inventory of estate of Sarah James decd. returned.
--Richard Hall vs Rawleigh Hazard, dismissed.
--Deed from Edwin Conway & Sarah his wife to Charles Bell acknowledged.
--Deed from Edwin Conway & Sarah his wife to John Cundiff acknowledged.
--Edwin Conway Gent appointed guardian to Charles & John Denny Everitte orphans of Thomas Everitte decd.; James Gordon, John Taylor, & Charles Bell Gent appointed to possess sd guardian with the estates of sd orphans which is in the hands of William Griggs their former guardian.
--Report of division of estate of Thomas Everitte deceased was returned.
--Grand Jury vs John Goodridge, dismissed.
--Petition of Rebeca Craine vs John Wormeley.
--John Craine a witness for Rebecca Craine against John Wormeley entered his attendance for the Plt, traveling 12 miles.

[Index 154] OB 16:26b, March Court 1779
Petition of John Angell against William Riley.
--Present Henry Tapscott Gent.

--Division of estate of George Payne decd. returned.
--On petition of Bushrod Riveer, ordered Henry Lawson, Thomas Carter, Isaac Degge, & Thomas Hathway view the road petitioned for by sd Riveer.
--On motion of John Carter by his attorney, ordered a dedimus issue to take deposition of Edward Carter in the suit Pollard vs Carter.

Court 15 April 1779.
John Taylor Gent Sheriff produced a Commission of the Peace from the Deputy Governor, and James Ball Gent (being the eldest in the sd commission) took that oath, and then John Fleet, James Gordon, John Berryman, William Yerby, Charles Bell, Henry Lawson, & John Selden Gent. Present said justices.

[Index 155] OB 16:27a, April Court 1779
Ordered the Clerk certify to the Governor that James Ball Junr. Gent is left out of the Commission of the Peace by mistake, that Jesse Ball & Hugh Brent are dead, and that John Chinn & Peter Conway refuse to qualify
--Job Carter granted license to keep ordinary.
--Job Carter granted leave to turn the road by the court house.
--Grand Jury vs William Chilton &c is dismissed, the jury being thought illegal.
--Inventory of estate of Walter James decd. returned.
--Deed of gift from William Chilton to William Chilton proved by Matthew Myars & Gawen Lowry.
--Richard Mitchell, Henry Towles, & Henry Tapscott Gent sworn as Justices of the Peace.
--Report about a road petition for by Bushrod Riveer was returned.
--Deed of gift from Robert Chinn to his children was proved.
--Inventory of estate of Isaac Weaver decd. returned.
--William Sydnor, Fortunatus Sydnor, Gawen Lowry, Charles Rogers, & William Gibson were sworn as Inspectors of tobacco

[Index 156] OB 16:27b, April Court 1779
Henry Tapscott & Richard Mitchell Gent appointed to test the weights at Deep Creek Warehouse, James Gordon & Henry Towles Gent at Lowry's and Davises, & John Berryman & Wm. Yerby Gent at Dymers.
--William Gibson & Richard Selden qualified as militia Captains, John Chowning sworn as Lieutenant, & James Pollard as Ensign.
--William Kirk appointed Ensign to 3rd militia company.
--Male tithables belonging to James Tapscott & Job Carter ordered to clear road from Capt Selden's mill to the post below Col Edwin Conway's gate.
--Ferriages from Chownings to Urbanna rated 9 shillings for man & horse each, and 18 pence for man & horse at Lowry's on Corotomon.
--Jonathan Pullen appointed Surveyor of road from John Mason's old field to the church road, and to the new mill.
--Ordered the Collector pay Bailie George his account.
--Settlement of Thomas B. Griffin's administration account of the estate of Burges Smith decd. was returned.
--William Kirk sworn Ensign in the 3rd militia company.
--Chloe Evans widow of William Evans decd. was granted administration on his estate; William Gibson, John Flowers, James Brent, & John Parrott appointed to appraise the estate.

[Index 157] OB 16:28a, May Court 1779
Court 20 May 1779, present justices James Ball, John Berryman, Willm. Yerby, Henry Lawson, & John Selden.
--Amos Thomas son of James Thomas bound Tarpley Thomas, to learn the trade of Wheelwright.
--Molly Riveer daughter of Richard Riveer bound to Thomas Davis.
--Rawleigh Hazard granted license to keep ordinary at his house at Kilmarnick.
--The county's standard weights & measures ordered to be lodged in hands of Job Carter.
--Grand jury impannelled: Elias Edmonds (foreman), Coleman Doggett, John Yerby, John James, William Mason, James Brent, James Carter, John Cundiff, John Hutchings, Edwin Kent, James Ewell, Joseph Norris, John Clutton, John Rogers, Jesse Robinson Junr., Ozwald Newby, Richard Mitchell Junr., & John Harris.

--Grand jury offenders were summoned to next court, except Dolly Davis who paid her fine to Henry Lawson Gent, and Molly Taylor who paid her fine to William Davenport Gent of Northumberland County; also Samuel Dunaway, William Montague, Henry Fleet, John Goodridge, John Hutchings, Maurice Wheeler, John Maughan, William Schofield Junr., John Selden, John McTyre, & Henry Currell, who came into court and paid their fines.

[Index 158] OB 16:28b, May Court 1779
Lott Palmer was sworn as Lieutenant in the 5th militia company, and Edward Blakemore as Ensign in the 4th company.
--Ordered the Treasurer pay Henry Lawson Gent £50 for the support of Rachel Hill whose husband died in the Navy service of this state.
--William Carpenter sworn as Constable.
--Division of George Payn's estate referred back to the persons who were formerly appointed to divide, to make another division of sd estate of the negroes in three equal parts, and possess Richard Housing Payne with two parts of the same that were devised by George Payne the elder to George Payne the younger, and the personal estate to divide equally.
--William Lawson Junr. vs Henry Fleet—Assault & Battery.
--David Boyd vs William Montague—Case.
--Petition of John McTyre vs William Newton.
--William Griggs vs Maurice Wheeler—Peace Warrant.
--George Yerby vs Simon Laughlin &c—Detinue.
--Mary Lawson vs Charles Rogers &c—Chancery.

[Index 159] OB 16:29a, May Court 1779
George Brent vs William Garlington—Assault & Battery.
--William Sanders vs Thomas Hubbard—Case.
--Hugh Harris assignee of John Gordon vs Richard Hall—Debt.
--John Selden vs Richard Hall—Chancery.
--John Taylor vs Richard Hall—Case.
--Maurice Wheeler by his attorney was granted a dedimus to take deposition of Thomas Lawson Gent in sd Wheeler's case vs William Griggs.
--Thomas Walls vs Travers Lunceford—Case.
--James Connelly vs Maurice Wheeler—Slander.

[Index 160] OB 16:29b, May Court 1779
Petition of Nicholas Currell &c vs James Connelly.
--Petition of John Newby vs T. B. Griffin's executor.
--John Harris vs John Miller &c administrator &c—Detinue. Referees were James Ball, John Taylor, & James Gordon Gent.
--Richard Stott vs T. B. Griffin's executor—Case.
--Joseph McAdam vs Thomas Pollard—Case.
--Richard Ball vs George Beane—Debt.
--Elijah Percifull vs John Galloway &c—Debt. LeRoy Pope was special bail for Deft.
--Rachel Hill administrator &c vs William Hinton—Case.

[Index 161] OB 16:30a, May Court 1779
Edwin Kent &c vs Moses Chilton's executor—Debt.
--Thomas West vs Henry Fleet—Assault & Battery.
--John Hammond &c vs Stephen Chilton—Petition.
--Edwin Fielding vs William Nutt—Sci. Fa.

Court of Enquiry 8 June 1779 for examination of William Steptoe, charged with stealing a barrel of tar from Rawleigh Hazard, present justices James Ball, Henry Tapscott, John Berryman, Charles Bell, Henry Lawson, & John Selden. The Deft was discharged from the prosecution.

[Index 162] OB 16:30b, June Court 1779
John Taylor Gent Sheriff presented a Commission of the Peace from the Governor, James Ball, Richard Mitchell, Thomas Lawson, James Gordon, Henry Towles, William Yerby, James Ball Junr., Henry Lawson, & John Selden Gent were sworn Justices of the Peace.
--Richard Mitchell & Henry Lawson Gent appointed Coroners.
--William Yerby & Henry Lawson Gent appointed to take list of tithables below Carter's mill, James Gordon Gent between sd Mill & Selden's mill, John Selden Gent for Wiccomoco Parish, Richd. Mitchell, James Ball Junr., & Henry Towles Gent in the upper part of the county.
--Joseph Dobs ordered to pay 20 shillings for being a common swearer.
--John Wormeley ordered to pay 20 shillings for being a common swearer.

[Index 163] OB 16:31a, June Court 1779
Richard Ball ordered to pay £5 for gaming.
--Henry Tapscott & Charles Bell Gent sworn as Justices of the Peace.
--John Harris appointed Surveyor of road from the main road down to Lowry's Warehouse.
--John Davis appointed Surveyor of road from the main road down to Davis's Warehouse.
--Elijah Percifull sworn as militia Ensign.
--Rawleigh Hazard vs William Steptoe—Case. William Yerby, Benjamin George, & William Gibson were referees.
--William Steptoe vs Rawleigh Harzard—Case. William Yerby, Benjamin George & William Gibson were referees.

Court 15 July 1779, present justices Richard Mitchell, Thomas Lawson, Henry Lawson, & John Selden.

[Index 164] OB16:31b, July Court 1779
John Berryman Gent sworn as Justice of the Peace.
--Appraisement and division of the estate of James Kirk decd. was returned.
--Appraisement and division of the estate of Elizabeth Yerby decd. was returned.
--Martin Hill Garton, son of Rachel Hill, about 12 years of age, bound to George Foard until age 21, to learn the art of navigation.
--Mary Mecolly orphan of James Mecolly bound to Elizabeth James the elder.
--Lucyann Wood daughter of Ann Wood bound to Elizabeth James the younger.
--John McTyre petitioned for a water grist mill on Straytons run.
--John Longweth appointed Suveyor of road from Carters mill to Killmarnock in place of William Gibson who resigned.
--Present Jas. Gordon, Henry Tapscott, John Berryman & Jas. Ball Junr. Gent.

[Index 165] Lancaster OB 16:32a, July Court 1779
Settlement of Bailie George's executorship of estate of James Maughan decd. was recorded.
--On motion of Chloe Evans, ordered the Clerk certify to the Auditors that her husband William Evans died in the Navy service of the state.
--Deed of gift from Richard Ball to his son James Wallace Ball was acknowledged.
--Will of Thomas Shearman decd. presented by Ann Shearman the widow; she was granted administration.
--John Berryman, Henry Lawson, Nicholas Currell, & James Pollard appointed to appraise estate of Thos. Shearman decd.
--William Barber vs Joseph Hubbard—Case. Richard Mitchell & William Yerby were referees.
--John Harris vs John Miller & James Harris administrators of Jeriah Harris decd.—Detinue. The referees James Ball, James Gordon, & John Taylor returned their report regarding the negro slave Richard, who was detained by the Defts: they found that John Harris promised to give sd negro, at his death, to his granddaughter Charlotte, daughter of the sd Jeriah Harris; Judgment for Plt.

[Index 166] Lancaster OB 16:32b, July Court 1779
Petition of John Davis &c vs Harry Everett.
--Jonathan Goodright vs Ferdinando Holdfast—Ejectment. Rachel Webb admitted as Deft for one third of the premises, and Hannah, Nancy, & Jemima Webb infants for the rest, by Lott Palmer their guardian.
--Ordered that William Ball pay 20 shillings for being a common swearer.
--On motion of Rachel Webb & Lott Palmer, by David Boyd their attorney, ordered a dedimus issue to take deposition of William Galloway.
--On motion of Charles Bell Gent, James Pinkard appointed Surveyor of road from Mrs. Robb's to the cross roads that divide Elias Edmonds, John Yerby & the sd Charles Bell.

[Index 167] Lancaster OB 16:33a, July Court 1779
Richard Stott vs William Griffin executor of T.B. Griffin decd.—Case. Referees were James Gordon, Edwin Conway, & John Berryman Gent. Judgment for Plt.
--Coleman Doggett vs John McTyre—Case.
--John McTyre vs Coleman Doggett—Case.
--Rawleigh Hazard vs Thomas Divine—Case. William Yerby, William Gibson, & Benjamin George were referees.
--John Fleet & Edwin Conway sworn as Justices of the Peace.
--Charles Lee vs Elisha Hall—Case.
--Giles Robinson vs Elijah Robinson—Detinue.

[Index 168] Lancaster OB 16:33b, July Court 1779
John & Richd. Payne administrators of Frans. Payne decd. vs Thomas Rout & John Calloway—Debt.
--Reuben Allen &c vs George Davis & Tarpley Thomas—Petition.
--Reuben Allen &c vs George Davis—Petition.
--Petition of John Edwards &c vs William Doggett.
--Andrew Robertson vs James Montague & wife—Debt.
--John Humphries vs John Wormeley—Case. A jury came, Robt. Chinn foreman; Judgment for Plt.

[Index 169] Lancaster OB 16:34a, July Court 1779
Ordered John Humphries pay Isaac Rice for attendance as witness in sd Humphries's suit vs John Wormeley.
--James Pollard vs George Phillips—Case.

Court 19 August 1779, present justices Edwin Conway, James Gordon, Henry Tapscott, William Yerby, Henry Lawson, & John Selden Gent.
--Report possession Margaret Brent with her dower in husband Geo. Brent's estate, returned.
--Allotment & account of sales of Newman Chilton's part of his father Moses Chilton's estate, returned.
--Account of Henry Lawson Gent, guardian to Saryann Simmons, recorded.
--Deed of bargain & sale from John Payne & wife Elenor to Moses Lunceford, acknowledged.

[Index 170] Lancaster OB 16:34b, August Court 1779
Report of jury about a mill petitioned for by John McTyre returned, dismissed; sd John petitioned for another jury.
--Richard Mitchell Gent appointed Tax Commissioner in place of James Ball Gent during sd Ball's inability.
--Deed of bargain & sale from John Hathaway &al to Lawson Hathaway was proved.
--Matthias James vs Jesse George & [no first name] Conway—Debt.
--William West vs John James—Petition.
--John Newby vs William Griffin executor of T. B. Griffin decd.—Petition.
--On motion of John McTyre, Henry Tapscott Gent appointed to lay off an acre of land petitioned for by sd McTyre about a mill, the county Surveyor being dead.
--Rawleigh Tapscott sworn as militia Lieutenant.
--Edward Carter appointed guardian to Anthony, Mary, & Catherine Kirk orphans of James Kirk decd.
--Robert C. Jacobs vs Thomas Pollard &c—Debt.

--Robert C. Jacobs vs Thomas Pollard &c—Debt.

[Index 171] Lancaster OB 16:35a, August Court 1779
John Taylor, James Gordon, William Yerby Gent, & Elias Edmonds appointed to settle administration account of estate of James Kirk decd., also the estate of Thomas Kirk decd., & possess Edward Carter (guardian of orphans of sd James) with their parts of sd estate.
--Giles Robinson vs Elijah Robinson—Detinue.
--William Chownings account as guardian to Chatten Chowning orphan of Geo. Chowning decd. was presented.
--William Griggs administrator &c vs Thomas Pollard &c—Debt.
--Walter Jones executor of Wm. Flood decd. vs John Richardson—Debt.
--Ordered James Pollard pay James Newby as witness for sd Pollard in his suit against Geo. Phillips.
--Elijah Percifull vs James Ledford—Petition.
--On motion of Thomas Chinn, ordered Richard Mitchell, James Gordon, Charles Bell Gent, & James Tapscott settle accounts of the orphans of Thomas Pollard decd. with Edwin Conway Gent as administrator of James Kirk decd. who was guardian to sd orphans.
--On motion of James Simmonds, ordered a dedimus issue for deposition of Edney Tapscott an aged person in the suit Yopp vs Simmons, in Chancery.

[Index 172] Lancaster OB 16:35b, Sept Court 1779
Court 16 Sept 1779, present justices James Ball, Richard Mitchell, Thomas Lawson, James Ball Junr. & Henry Lawson.
--Inquisition for Commonwealth vs estate of Robert Biglow[?] Esq, returned.
--Inventory of estate of Thomas Searman [thus] deceased, returned.
--Deed from William Grayham & others to William Montague assigned to Rev Mr John Leland by the sd Montague, which assignment was acknowledged.
--Richard Mitchell Gent granted administration on estate of William Stevens decd.
--Henry Towles, William Chewning, John Chewning, & Nicholas George appointed to appraise estate of William Stevens decd.
--William Chewning orphan of George Chewning decd. chose William Chewning as his guardian.
--Present Edwin Conway Gent.
--Charles Rogers appointed guardian to Jane Chewning orphan of George Chewning decd.
--John Chewning appointed guardian to Lorrimer Chewning orphan of George Chewning decd.
--Present John Berryman Gent.
--James Gordon, John Taylor, Charles Bell, & William Yerby Gent appointed to settled with executors of Hugh Brent decd. who was guardian to Thomas Kirk decd. & possess Edwin Conway Gent administrator of sd Kirk with his estate.
--Harry Currell vs Edward Cox—Assault & Battery.
--John Taylor, James Gordon, William Yerby Gent. & Elias Edmonds appointed to settle estate of Sarah Kirk decd. & possess Edward Carter with the sd estate which is now in the hands of Edwin Conway Gent.

[Index 173] Lancaster OB 16:36a, Sept Court 1779
James Newby's account as guardian to Newman Chilton, recorded.
--Jonathan Pullen vs James Pinckard—Case. Ordered dedimus issue to take deposition of Thomas Pollard, who is in the service of this state.
--John Davis &c vs Harry Currell—Debt.
--Elijah Percifull vs James Ledford—Petition.
--Jury's report about mill petitioned for by John McTyre was returned, Ozwald Newby contested it.
--John Edwars [thus] &c vs William Doggett—Petition.
--Richard Mitchell & Edwin Conway Gent appointed to settle Richard Nutt's[?] administration account of estate of James Newby Junr. decd.
--A paper believed by the court to be the will of Daniel Payne was presented by Nicholas Payne.

--William Chewning, John Chewning, James Ewell, & Nicholas George appointed to appraise estate of Daniel Payne decd.

--Settlement of Richard Nutt's administration account of the estate of James Newby Junr. decd. was returned.

[Index 174] Lancaster Ob 16:36b, Oct Court 1779

Court 21 Oct 1779, present justices James Ball, Richd. Mitchell, Thomas Lawson, William Yerby, James Ball Junr., & Henry Lawson.

--Deed of bargain & sale from George Heale Gent & Sarah his wife to William Warren, acknowledged.

--Deed of bargain & sale from William Montague & Lucy his wife to Rev John Leland acknowledged.

--Report possession Sarah Bond with her dower of her former husband Thomas Sharp's land, returned.

--Report possession John Bailey with the estate of Jesse Bailey orphan of John Bailey decd., returned.

--Richard Mitchell & Henry Lawson Gent sworn as Coroners.

--Deed of bargain & sale from John Eustace & Alice Corbin his wife to Elmour Doggett was proved.

--Deed of bargain & sale from John Berryman Gent & Sarah his wife to Henry George was proved.

--Inventory of estate of William Stephens decd. returned.

--Inventory of estate of Daniel Payne decd. returned.

--On petition of Amny [thus] Laws, ordered Rev John Leland Clk be summoned to next court to show cause why sd Amny, who he claims as a servant, may not be set free.

--Present John Fleet Gent.

[Index 175] Lancaster OB 16:37a, Oct Court 1779

On motion of Thomas Bell, ordered the executors of John Nichols decd. be summoned to shew cause why the inventory of sd Nichols's estate is not returned.

--Deed of bargain & sale from Spencer Hinton to Thomas Lawson Gent acknowledged.

--Deed of bargain & sale from Thomas Lawson Gent & Lettice his wife to William Lawson acknowledged.

--List of tobacco in Lowry's & Davis's warehouses was returned by Charles Rogers, Inspector.

--List of tobacco in Dymer's warehouse returned by Wm. Gibson, Inspector.

--William Meredith recommended to the Governor as a proper person to act as Inspector at Dymer's Warehouse, & William Kirk as Assistant Inspector.

--John Taylor Gent recommended to the Governor as a proper person to act as Sheriff.

--On motion of Edward Carter, ordered James Gordon Gent, James Carter, & William Stephens view road petitioned for by sd Carter.

--Henry Chilton granted administration on estate of John Chilton decd.; Henry Lawson Gent, Thomas Carter, Lawson Hathaway, & Isaac Deggs appointed appraisers.

--Thomas Pinckard vs Robert C. Jacob—Case.

[Index 176] Lancaster OB 16:37b, Oct Court 1779

Smith & Gatewood vs Thomas West—Debt.

--Alexander Davis vs John McTyre—Assault & Battery.

--Edwin Hull vs Jeduthen Brent—Assault & Battery.

--Sarah Hammonds vs Peter Poole—Case. Deft was returned "not to be found."

--James Ewell vs William Buckan—Case.

--Sarah Hinton vs Henry Fleet—Case.

--William Biven vs Henry Fleet—Case.

--Rawleigh Shearman vs William Griggs—Case.

--Rawleigh Hazard vs Thomas West—Case.

[Index 177] Lancaster OB 16:38a, Oct Court 1779

James Brent vs Moses Hester—Petition.

--Lawson Hathaway vs Richd. E. Lee—Petition.

--William Griggs vs George Phillips—Case.

--Fortunatus Sydnor appointed guardian to Elizabeth, Mary, Catharine, & John King orphans of William King decd.

--Margaret Ball vs Samuel Dunaway &c—Case.
--List of tobacco in Deep Creek warehouse returned by Willm. Sydnor, Inspector.
--List of transfer tobacco in Deep Creek warehouse returned by William Sydnor.
--Deed of bargain & sale from Mary Schofield to John Hutchenson acknowledged.
--Deed of gift from Elmour Doggett to his son William Doggett was proved.
--Rawleigh Hazard vs William Steptoe—Case.
--William Steptoe vs Rawleigh Hazard—Case.
--Rawleigh Hazard vs Thomas Divine—Case.
--Rawl. Hazard ordered to pay Thomas Brent of his attendance as witness for sd Hazard in his case vs William Steptoe, and for travelling 12 miles each day from his place of residence.

[Index 178] Lancaster OB 16:38b, Oct Court 1779

Ordered Rawl. Hazard pay John Edward for his attendance as witness for sd Hazard in his suit vs Thos. Divine.
--On petition of William Horton, convict servant, against John Wormeley for his freedom, ordered sd Horton return to his master and serve his full time according to his conviction.
--Moses Sutton vs John Webb—Attachment.

Court 22 Oct 1779, present justices James Ball, John Fleet, Thomas Lawson, & Henry Lawson.
--Bailee George vs Maurice Wheeler—Ejectment. A jury came, to wit. Richard Ball, Thomas Robb, Lott Palmer, Eleazer Robinson, Giles Robinson, Peter Conway, John Wormeley, Jesse Robinson Junr., Richd. Goodridge, William Montague, Jas. Tapscott, & Johnson Riveer; Judgment for Plt.
--Deed of bargain & sale from James Tapscott & Elizabeth his wife to William Sydnor, acknowledged.
--Present Edwin Conway, Henry Tapscott, & John Selden Gent.

[Index 179] Lancaster OB 16:39a, Oct Court 1779

James Gordon executor &c vs Joseph Sullivant &c—Case.
--Commonwealth vs James Robinson &c—Debt.
--John Fleet & wife vs Keenes executors—Chancery.
--Craven Everett vs Ruth Everett administratrix—Case.
--Bailee George ordered to pay William Schofield for his attendance as witness for sd George in his case vs Maurice Wheeler.
--Samuel Dunaway ordered to pay James Warrick for his attendance as witness for sd Dunaway in his case vs Margaret Ball.
--Bailee George ordered to pay Michael Wilder for his attendance as witness for sd George in his cast vs Maurice Wheeler.
--Edwin Conway & James Gordon Gent appointed Commissioners for carrying into execution an act of Assembly for laying a tax payable in certain enumerated commodities.
--Benjamin Garton vs William Martin—Case.

[Index 180] Lancaster OB 16:39b, Oct Court 1779

Male labouring tithables of Thomas Brent, Elijah Percifull, & Mrs. Agatha Ball ordered to assist in clearing road from the White Stone to the Coach Road.
--Bailee George ordered to pay Jonathan Wilder for his attendance as witnesss for sd George in his case vs Maurice Wheeler.
--Thomas Myars vs John Wormeley—Case.
--James Mills vs George Conner—Case. Abates by death of Deft.
--Elijah Percifull appointed Surveyor of road from the White Stone to the Coach Road.
--Daniel Muse vs Thomas Smither—Case.
--Job Carter vs Richard Hall—Case. A jury came, George Norris foreman & others.
--Charles Bell, James Ball Junr. & James Tapscott Gent appointed Inspectors of the paper currency.

[Index 181] Lancaster OB 16:40a, Oct Court 1779

David Boyd vs Elihu Hall—Detinue. A jury came, to wit. Richard Ball & others.

--Ordered Bailee George pay John Fleet Gent for his attendance as witness for sd George in his case vs Maurice Wheeler.

--Ordered that David Boyd Gent pay Presly Cockrell for his attendance as witness for sd Boyd in his case vs Elihu Hall, & for travelling 9 miles each day from his place of residence.

--Hathaway vs Ritchie—Ordered a dedimus issue to take deposition of Sarah Currell an aged person for the Plt.

Court 18 November 1779, present justices James Ball, John Fleet, Richd. Mitchell, Thos. Lawson, Henry Tapscott, & John Selden.

--John Sullivant appointed Surveyor of road from Norris's Hill to the plantation of Anthony Sydnors in place of George Edwards.

--Grand jury impannelled, with Robert Chinn as foreman, Robert Gilmoure, and others.

[Index 182] Lancaster OB 16:40b, Nov Court 1779

Deed from John Hathaway &c to Thomas Hathaway proved by John Cook.

--Elizabeth & William Hinton granted administration on estate of Richard Hinton decd.

--John Fleet, Thomas Lawson, Henry Lawson Gent. & Thomas Hunton appointed to appraise estate of Richard Hinton decd.

--Amny Laws vs John Leland—Petition for her freedom; Ordered she be discharged from her servitude.

--Bailee George vs Maurice Wheeler—Case.

--James Tapscott vs Stephen Pouquett—Attachment. Henry Tapscott Junr. was garnishee.

--Thomas Crouther vs Peter Garton—Assault & Battery.

--Thomas West vs Joseph Sullivant—Case.

--Sarah Hammonds vs Peter Poole—Case.

--Justices vs Thos. Bell & Ben. George executors of John Nichols decd.—Summons.

[Index 183] Lancaster OB 16:41a, Nov Court 1779

William Shirk qualified as Assistant Inspector at Dymer's warehouse.

--James Tapscott appointed Surveyor of road from Selden's mill to the post below Col Edwin Conway's gate in place of sd Conway.

--Ordered Sheriff give notice to William Boatman who was formerly in care of the court house, to furnish the court with the body of the laws.

--Ordered Amny Laws pay Ozwald Newby for his attendance as witness for sd Laws against Rev John Leland Clk. The court laid the county levy; The following individuals were allowed their claims [only those given by name]: David Boyd Gent Attorney for the Commonwealth, John Bailey Sub Sheriff, James Newby Sub Sheriff, Thads. McCarty Clerk of Court, Job Carter, Michael Wilder, Thomas Davis for patroling, John Hazard for patroling, Henry Davis for patroling, Tarpley Thomas for patroling, Charles Dodson for patroling, Michael Wilder for patroling, David Garland for patroling, John Sullivant for patroling, Nicholas George for attending called court on Willm. Yerby, Henry Fleet for same, George Ford for same.

[Index 184] Lancaster OB 16:41b, Called Court

Court of Oyer & Terminer 10 Dec 1779 for trial of negro man slave Harry belonging to Corbin Griffin Esq of York Town, and Judy a negro woman belonging to Mrs. Ann Chinn, charged with having broken into the house of Capt Robert Chinn & stealing cotton, present justices James Ball, Richard Mitchell, James Gordon, Henry Tapscott, James Ball Junr. & Henry Lawson; Defts found not guilty and ordered discharged.

[Index 185] Lancaster OB 16:42a, Jan Court 1780

Court 20 Jan 1780, present justices Edwin Conway, William Yerby, Henry Lawson, & John Selden.

--William Merideth sworn Inspector at Dymer's and Indian Warehouses.

--Report about a road petitioned for by Edward Carter was returned.

--Inventory of estate of Richard Hinton decd. returned.

--John Berryman & Henry Lawson Gent appointed to try the weights at Dymer's warehouses, and James Gordon & Henry Towles Gent at Davis's & Lowrys Warehouses, and Richd. Mitchell & James Ball Junr. at Deep Creek.
--Sally Mayes orphan of Henry Mayes decd. chose Johnson Riveer as her guardian.
--On motion of Elizabeth Hill widow of James Hill decd., ordered James Gordon, Charles Bell, William Yerby Gent, & Elias Edmonds divide estate of the decd. & allot the widow her dower.
--On motion of John James, ordered dedimus issue to take deposition of John Roberts in his suit against Bushrod Riveer.
--On motion of Bailee George, ordered dedimus issue to take deposition of John Roberts at the suit of Bushrod Riveer.
--Bailee George vs Maurice Wheeler—Case.
--Richard Goodridge, Jesse Robinson, James Norris, & Peter Riveer appointed to divide land of Henry Mayes decd.

[Index 186] Lancaster OB 16:42b, January Court 1780
Thomas Pollard vs Bailie George—Ordered dedimus issue to take depositions of John Currell & James Pinkard for the Plt.

Court February 17 Feb 1780, present justices James Ball, James Gordon, Henry Tapscott, John Berryman, James Ball Junr., Henry Lawson.
--Mortgage deed from John Hall to Thomas Pinckard Gent proved by Christopher Miller & Peter Conway.
--Inventory of estate of Hannah Garner decd. returned.
--Ordered the Sheriff pay out of the public tobacco in his hands the following individuals: Thads. McCarty, Rawleigh Davenport, Thomas Dunaway, John Bailey, & Molly Carter.
--Anthony Sydnor son of Anthony Sydnor decd. bound to William Lawson for 3 years, to learn trade of a Joyner.
--John Wormely came into court and acknowledged William Houghton, who was formerly his servant, to be clear of his servitude.
--Deed from John Hunton to William Boatman proved.
--Samuel Mahanes exempted from paying levy.
--Henry Carter exempted from paying levy.

[Index 187] Lancaster OB 16:43a, Feb Court 1780
Henry Hinton appointed guardian to Lucy & Katharine Hinton orphans of Fleet Hinton decd.
--Thomas Lawson Gent, Thomas Ingram, Thomas Hunton, & John Edwards appointed to divide estate of Fleet Hinton decd. & allot the widow her dower, also possess Henry Hinton guardian to the orphans with their parts.
--William Mason who intermarried with a daughter of Henry Mayes decd. allowed to remove a house builty by him upon the part of land, according to the division, belonging to him.
--Edwin Conway Gent petitioned for water grist mill on Cabbin Run.
The following individuals were returned by the grand jury, and their cases were dismissed upon their paying costs: John Wormely, William Chilton (younger), Joseph Hubbard, John Edwards, John Mahone, Mary Webb, Daniel Rich, John Hazard, Hannah Price, William Stanton, & John McTyre.
--Commonwealth vs Elijah Percifull—Indictment.
--Division of land of Henry Mayes decd. returned.

[Index 188] Lancaster OB 16:43b, Feb Court 1780
Commonwealth vs Robert Jones—For sureties of the peace. John McTyre was security for the Deft.
--Deed from John Arms & wife to James Ewill was proved.
--Aminadab Seekright vs Maurice Wheeler—Case.
--Sukey Riveer orphan of Richard Riveer bound to Thomas Beverly[?].
--Ordered the Commonwealth pay William Rains & James Bush for their attendance as evidence for the Commonwealth vs Robert Jones.
--George Norris vs Joseph Hubbard—Case.
--Rawleigh Hazard vs John Parrott—Case. Deft returned not found.
--Present John Fleet Gent.

--On motion of John Sullivant, James Gordon, William Yerby Gent, Thos. Brent, & Elias Edmonds appointed to divide land of John Nichols decd., and allot to Mary the widow her dower.

[Index 189] Lancaster OB 16:44a, Feb Court 1780

On petition of William Montague & Richard Ball, ordered Richd. Mitchell, Edwin Conway, & James Gordon Gent divide land held by sd Montague & Ball according to the will of Capt Richd. Ball decd.

--Commonwealth vs Thomas Cottrill—Sureties of Peace. Bailie George & William Griggs were security for Deft.

--Ordered Commonwealth pay John Mahone & Elizabeth Roberts for attendance as evidence for the Commonwealth vs Thomas Cottrell.

--Deed of feoffment from John Selden & Ann his wife to Peter Conway acknowledged.

--Elizabeth Robinson vs Richard Goodridge—Detinue; A jury came, to wit. John Newby, John Clayton, John Sullivant, James Wallace, John Hill, Bailie George, Richard Cundiff, John Parrott, James Brent, Elijah Percifull, Newton Brent, & Coleman Doggett.

[Index 190] Lancaster OB 16:44b, Feb Court 1780

Court 18 Feb 1780, present justices James Ball, John Fleet, Richd. Mitchell, James Gordon, & Henry Tapscott.

--Commonwealth vs Maurice Wheeler—Sureties of the Peace. Deft ordered to post bond, with John James & Job Carter his securities.

--James Brent vs Moses Hester—Petition.

--William Robinson vs John McTyre—Trespass, Assault, & Battery.

--Elizabeth Robinson vs Richard Goodridge—Detinue; The jury sworn yesterday returned verdict for Plt, ordered she recover against the Deft one negro woman called Cumbo.

--Spencer Brown granted administration on estate of George Neasome decd.; Richard Mitchell Gent, Wm. Sydnor, Robert Chinn, & William Burnley to appraise the estate and possess sd administrator with the same after settling account with Wm. Stott the guardian of the decd.

[Index 191] Lancaster OB 16:45a, Feb Court 1780

Thomas Cottrell vs Maurice Wheeler—Slander.

--Maurice Wheeler vs Thomas Cottrell—Trespass, Assault, & Battery.

--Maurice Wheeler vs David Garland—Case.

--Justices vs John Nichols's executors—Summons.

--John Edwards vs William Doggett—Petition.

--Commonwealth vs Maurice Wheeler—Peace Warrant.

--John Hutchings petitioned for water grist mill.

--Ordered Elizabeth Robinson pay Eleazer Robinson for attendance as witness for sd Robinson vs Richard Goodridge.

[Index 192] Lancaster OB 16:45b, April Court 1780

Court 20 April 1780, present justices James Ball, Thomas Lawson, William Yerby, Henry Towles, John Berryman, & Henry Lawson.

--Division of land of John Nichols decd. returned.

--Jury's report concerning a mill petitioned for by Edwin Conway Gent was returned.

--On motion of Isaac Degge, ordered the division of the estate of Simon Degge decd. be recorded.

--The plat of an acre of land laid off for Fortunatus Sydnor's mill was returned.

--Deed of bargain & sale from George Kelly to John Parrott proved, and the receipt thereon was acknowledged by Richard E. Lee Gent.

--Charles Carter Esq petitioned for a water grist mill on New Mill Swamp.

--Will of Merryman Payne Junr. decd. presented by Nicholas Payne executor therein named.

[Index 193] Lancaster OB 16:46a, April Court 1780

John Chowning, Matthew Myars, Nicholas George, & Thomas Carter appointed to appraise estate of Merryman Payne decd.

--Deed of bargain & sale from John Arms & Judith his wife to James Ewell was further proved by Henry Towles Gent.
--Deed of bargain & sale from George Heale Gent to John McTyre, Richard Cundiff, & Richard Mitchell Junr. was proved.
--Inventory of estate of George Neasom decd. returned.
--Present Richard Mitchell & Charles Bell Gent.
--Ordered the Clerk certify to the Auditors that Jesse Kent died about May 1778 in the Navy service of the state, and has left a widow and five children.
--William Smith who is now in the service of the state, having a wife and 3 children, they were allowed corn and pork for their support.
--Ordered the Clerk certify to the Auditors that William Thatcher died about March 1776 in the Navy service of the state, and left a widow and 2 children.
--Kester Toon appointed guardian to William Oliver orphan of William Oliver decd.

[Index 194] Lancaster OB 16:46b, April Court 1780
Mungo Harvey & wife vs Richard Ball—Chancery; Richard Mitchell, John Chinn, Edwin Conway, & James Gordon Gent were referees.
--Richard Ball vs Mungo Harvey—Injunction; Referred to Richard Mitchell, John Chinn, Edwin Conway, & James Gordon Gent.
--Spencer George vs Thomas Hunton &c—Chancery.
--LeRoy Peachey vs Luke Williams—Chancery.
--John Edwards vs William Doggett—Petition.
--Thomas Pinckard Gent vs John Eustace Gent—Petition.
--John Riveer, Thomas Bradshaw, & James Findla exempted from paying publick dues.

[Index 195] Lancaster OB 16:47a, April Court 1780
Will of William Sanders decd. presented by Betty Sanders widow and executrix therein named; Thomas Garner, John Bean, Stephen Lock, & William Brown appointed to appraise estate of the decd.
--Thomas Pinckard vs Robert C. Jacob—Case; Ordered dedimus issue to take deposition of Richard E. Lee.
--Moses Lunceford granted administration on estate of George Payne decd. (the former administration being repealed); Edny Tapscott, Benjamin George, John Sullivant, & George Edwards appointed to appraise the estate.
--Jury report concerning a mill petitioned for by John McTyre was returned.
--Executors of R. P. Downman decd. vs James Montague—Petition.
--Maurice Wheeler vs Thomas Cottrell—Petition.
--Appearing to the court that the former division of the estate of John Nichols decd. was improperly done, on motion of Thomas Bell one of the executors and legatees in the will of sd decd., ordered sd division be referred back to the former persons appointed for that purpose.
--Sarah Wilder vs Travers Lunceford—Assault & Battery.
--John Davis sworn as assistant Inspector at Davis's & Lowry's warehouses.

[Index 196] Lancaster OB 16:47b, April Court 1780
Court 21 April 1780, present justices James Ball, Richard Mitchell, Henry Tapscott, & Henry Lawson.
--John James vs Bushrod Riveer—Detinue.
--Job Carter granted license to keep Ordinary at Lancaster courthouse.
--Fortunatus Sydnor &c vs Sarah Bond &c—Chancery. Ball [no first name shown] was a co-Defendant.
--Richard Mitchell Gent appointed Surveyor of road from Morattico Mill to Deep Bottom.
--Richard Goodridge vs James Robinson—Case; LeRoy Pope was security for the Deft.
--Ordered Sheriff pay William Carpenter out of the depositum in his hands.

[Index 197] Lancaster OB 16:48a, April Court 1780
Spencer M. Ball vs John Eustace—Trespass.
--Edwin Gaskins vs Jonathan Pullen—Petition.

--John Fleet vs William Biscoe—Slander.
--Judith Griggs vs Anthony Kirk &c—Chancery. The Defts appeared by Edward Carter their guardian.
--Rawleigh Hazard vs John Parrott—Case.
--Tait's executors vs Taylor's executors—Sci fa.; Abates by death of Rodham Kenner Gent.
--Tait's executors vs Taylor's executors—Sci. fa.; Abates by death of Rodham Kenner Gent.
--William Griggs vs Maurice Wheeler—Sureties of the Peace.

[Index 198] Lancaster OB 16:48b, April Court 1780
Thomas Pollard vs Bailie George—Case.
--William Scofield vs Thomas Pollard—Case.
--Thomas Pollard vs John Carter—Case.
--Thomas Pollard assignee &c vs William Boatman &c—Debt.
--James Montague & wife vs William Hunt—Debt.
--Elizabeth Hinton vs Thomas Pollard &c—Debt.
--Henry Tapscott vs Newton Keen's executors—Case.
--Thomas Pinkard vs Robert Gilmoure—Case.
--Thomas Newton & son vs Thomas Pollard—Chancery.

[Index 199] Lancaster OB 16:49a, April Court 1780
William Griggs vs James Selden & Edwin Conway—Debt.
--Traverse Lunceford vs Maurice Brent—Case.
--Benjamin Garton vs William Martin—Case; A jury came, to wit. John Yerby, William Mitchell, William Luckham, Maurice Wheeler, James Tapscott, Spencer Brown, Lott Palmer, William Scofield, Traverse Lunceford, Jesse Robinson, James Norris, & Bushrod Riveer; Judgment for Plt.
--Ordered John Sullivant pay Mildred Findla for her attendance as witness for him vs Thomas Bell.
--Richard Glascock vs Robert Gilmoure—Chancery.

[Index 200] Lancaster OB 16:49b, April Court 1780
David Boyd vs William Montague—Case.
--George Yerby vs Simon Laughlin—Detinue.
--Geroge Brent vs William Garlington—Trespass, Assault, & Battery.
--William Sanders vs Thomas Hubbard—Case; Abates by death of Plt.
--Hugh Harris assignee &c vs Richard Hall—Debt.
--John Selden vs Richard Hall—Chancery.
--James Connelly vs Maurice Wheeler—Slander.

[Index 201] Lancaster OB 16:50a, April Court 1780
Elijah Percifull vs John Galloway—In debt.
--Rachel Hill administratrix &c vs William Hinton—Case.
--Edwin Kent & wife vs Moses Chilton's executors—Debt.
--Thomas West vs Henry Fleet—Trespass, Assault, & Battery.
--Charles Lee executor &c vs Elisha Hall—Case.
--Giles Robinson vs Elijah Robinson—Detinue.
--William Biscoe vs Henry Fleet—Case.
--Sarah Hinton vs Henry Fleet—Case.

[Index 202] Lancaster OB 16:50b, April Court 1780
Thomas Pinckard vs Robert C. Jacob—Case.
--Rawleigh Shearman vs William Griggs—Case.
--Merriwether Smith & P. Gatwood vs Thomas West—Debt.
--Sarah Hammonds vs Peter Poole—Case.
--Seekright vs Maurice Wheeler—Trespass.

--Maurice Wheeler vs Thomas Cottrill—Trespass, Assault, & Battery.

[Index 203] Lancaster OB 16:51a, April Court 1780
Thomas Cottrell vs Maurice Wheeler—Slander.
--Maurice Wheeler vs David Garland—Case.
--George Norris vs Joseph Hubbard—Case.
--Commonwealth vs Elijah Percifull—Summons.

[Index 204] Lancaster OB 16:51b, May Court 1780
Court 18 May 1780, present justices James Ball, Richard Mitchell, Thomas Lawson, Henry Tapscott, Henry Towles, & William Yerby.
--John Taylor Gent and Henry Tapscott Gent returned results of the election for Commisioners of the Tax.
--Inventory of estate of Merryman Payne decd. returned.
--Deed of bargain & sale from John Hathaway &c to Thomas Hathaway was acknowledged by Lawson Hathaway, proved as to Isaac Currell by John Fleet & Thomas Lawson, and proved by Thomas Carter as to Hathaway, and was recorded, "together with the commission for the privy examination of Sarah, Joannah, Judith, Mary, and Dolly."
--Robert Chinn was grand jury foreman.
--Grand jury offenders summoned to next court, except Henry Fleet & John McTyre, who paid their fines to John Berryman Gent, the church warden.
--Thomas Pinckard vs Robert Gilmoure.
--William Mitchell appointed Surveyor of road from Mrs. Aggatha Balls mill to the main road the leads down to Col John Taylors, in place of Rawh. Davenport.
--Eleazer Robinson appointed [Surveyor] from the sign post at Doctor Robertsons to Col Taylors landing over Mahones Bridge in place of Jesse Robinson Senr.; John Clutton is appointed from Richd. Mitchells shop to Rawh. Downmans lane and down to William Sydnors gate in place of Richd. Stott; William Yopp from the post below Col Conways gate to the coach road in place of Thomas Garner; John Mason from the county line to the crossroads between Mrs. Margarett and Mrs. Aggatha Balls mills in place of Thomas Dunaway; and Thomas Carter from the fork of the road by James Pollards to Mr Eustaces little mill and down to Dymers warehouse.

[Index 205] Lancaster OB 16:52a, May Court 1780
John Riveer Junr. & William Allen exempted from paying levy, being infirm.
--Indenture of bargain & sale from Thomas Edwards & Betty his wife to John Sullivant, acknowledged.
--Indenture of bargain & sale from Richard Cundiff & Susannah his wife to Bartholomew Dameron was acknowledged.
--John Chinn Gent petitioned for a water grist mill at the place called Morattico old mill, James Ball Gent adjacent property holder.
--Indenture of bargain & sale from Bartholomew Dameron & Mary his wife to Richard Cundiff was acknowledged.
--Deed of bargain & sale from Richard Hall & Mary his wife to John Selden Gent was proved, that the deed was "executed on the ninth day of Mary 1780" notwithstanding the date thereof which was by mistake.
--Indenture of bargain & sale from Peter Conway & Frances his wife to James Tapscott was proved by Richard Mitchell, John Selden, & William Sydnor.

[Index 206] Lancaster OB 16:52b, May Court 1780
Due proof made by Thomas Gaskins Gent that Hancock Eustace late of Northumberland County decd. was Capt in the 2nd Virginia Regt commanded by William Byrd Esq in 1759, and John Eustace Gent claiming as heir at law to sd Eustace, made oath that he had never received bounty land under the proclamation of 1763.
--Bill of sale from James Connolly to Maurice Wheeler proved.
--John Flowers appointed guardian to John Flowers orphan of George Flowers decd.
--John Berryman Gent, James Brent, William Gibson, & George Carter appointed to allot the widow of George Flowers decd. her dower, and divide the estate.
--John McAdam vs George Beane—Ordered dedimus issue to take deposition of Thomas Yerby.

--Winifred Doggett granted administration on estate of John Doggett decd., she being his widow; John Berryman Gent, James Brent, William Gibson, & Thomas Carter appointed to appraise estate.

--Jury's report about mill petitioned for by Charles Carter Esq returned, with assent of John Hutchings.

--Inventory of estate of William Sanders decd. returned.

--Thomas Lawson & William Yerby appointed to take list of tithables below Carter's great mill, Charles Bell Gent between Carters and Conways mills, Edwin Conway Gent in Wiccomoco Parish, Henry Towles Gent in Corotoman, James Ball Junr. upon Rappahannock, & Henry Tapscott Gent in the upper end of the county.

--James Brent appointed guardian to Nancy, Judith, & Molly Hill orphans of Martin Hill decd.

[Index 207] Lancaster OB 16:53a, May Court 1780

Indenture of bargain & sale from Richard Mitchell Junr. to Bartholomew Dameron acknowledged.

--John Berryman vs John Fleet—Case.

--Rawleigh Hazard vs Thomas Carter—Case; James Pollard security for Deft.

--John McAdam vs George Beane—Case; John Beane special bail for Deft.

--George Beane vs John McAdam—Case; William Brown Gent special bail for Deft.

--Thomas Yerby & Will. Parrott executors of Wm. Parrott vs William Davenport—Case.

--John James vs Bushrod Riveer-Detinue.

[Index 208] Lancaster OB 16:53b, May Court 1780

Elizabeth Mctyre vs John Hazard—Case.

--John Edwards vs William Doggett—Petition.

--William Doggett vs William Doggett—Petition.

--Spencer Currell vs Thomas Bridgford—Case.

--Edwin Gaskins vs Jonathan Pullen—Petition.

--Ordered Jonathan Pullen pay Henry Hurst for attendance as witness for sd Pullen vs Edwin Gaskins, and traveling 11 miles.

--Richard Stott vs Will. Griffin executor of T. B. Griffin decd.—Case.

--Richard Goodridge vs James Robinson—Case; Eleazer Robinson special bail for Deft; James Ball, Richd. Mitchell, William Davenport, & Moses Lunceford Gent were referees.

--Thomas Pollard vs Bailie George—Case.

--William Scofield vs Thomas Pollard—Case.

[Index 209] Lancaster OB 16:54a, May Court 1780

Thos. Pollard assignee of Maurice Wheeler vs William Boatman &c—Debt.

--Commonwealth vs James Robinson.

--Travers Lunceford vs Maurice Brent—Case.

--William Steptoe vs Thomas Pollard—Assault & Battery.

Court 19 May 1780, present justices James Ball, John Fleet, Richd. Mitchell, Thomas Lawson, John Berryman, & John Selden.

--William Steptoe vs Thomas Pollard—Assault & Battery.

--Craven Everett vs Ruth Everett administratrix of Thos. Everett decd.—Case; a jury came, with Thomas Carter foreman; Judgment for Plt.

[Index 210] Lancaster OB 16:54b, May Court 1780

Travers Lunceford vs Maurice Brent—Case.

--James Montague & wife vs William Hunt—Case; A jury came with Thomas Carter foreman; Judgment for Plt.

--John Taylor Gent Sheriff acknowledged bond for tax collection.

--James Muse vs John Kirk—Debt.

--Nicholas George assignee of Geo. Norris vs John Garlington—Debt.

[Index 211] Lancaster OB 16:55a, May Court 1780

William Batten vs John Bailey—Detinue; A jury came, with Thomas Brent foreman; Judgment was that the Deft did not detain the negroes Judy, Hannah, & Dick as the Plt had complained.
--Bill of sale from John Wormeley to John McTyre proved by John Miller.
--Richard Hall vs John Selden—Ejectment.
--Fleet vs N. Keen's executors—Dedimus to take deposition of Sarah Keen.

Court 15 June 1780, present justices Richd. Mitchell, Thomas Lawson, Henry Tapscott, John Berryman, & William Yerby.
--Mungo Harvey & wife vs Richard Ball—Chancery. Judgment for the Plt returned by referees Richd. Mitchell, Edwin Conway, & James Gordon.

[Index 212] Lancaster OB 16:55b, June Court 1780
Richard Ball vs Mungo Harvey—Injunction; Judgment for Plt returned by referees Richd. Mitchell, Edwin Conway, & James Gordon.
--Rawleigh Hazard granted license to keep ordinary at his house.
--Inventory of estate of George Payne decd. returned.
--Present James Ball & James Ball Junr.Gent.
--Ordered Thomas Cottrell pay 25 shillings for getting drunk & being a common swearer.
--Commonwealth vs John Armes—Indictment.
--Job Carter vs Jesse Crowther—Case.

[Index 213] Lancaster OB 16:56a, June Court 1780
Thomas Nugent vs John Dale—Case.
--Margaret Davis vs Edward Carter—Case.
--Coleman Doggett vs John McTyre—Trespass, Assault, & Battery.
--Giles Boggess vs Jesse Harrison—Case.
--John Edwards vs William Doggett—Petition.
--William Doggett Junr. vs William Doggett—Petition.
--Indenture of bargain & sale from George Kelly to John Parrott further proved by Thomas Ashburn, and the receipt thereon was acknowledged by Richd. E. Lee Gent.
--Indenture of bargain & sale from Bailie George & Judith his wife to Jesse George was acknowledged.
--Additional inventory with allotment of dower of the estate of John Nichols decd., returned.

[Index 214] Lancaster OB 16:56b, June Court 1780
Henry Carter vs Henry Davis—For sureties of peace; Ordered sd Davis post bond, with Rawleigh Cotes & Thomas Davis his securities.
--Report of settlement of the bounds of land between William Montague & Richard Ball was returned.
--Richard Goodridge vs James Robinson—Case. The referees Jas. Ball, Richd. Mitchell, William Davenport, & Moses Lunsford returned their report.
--The processioners of the precinct from White Stone to the Glebe & from thence to Mrs. Eustace's mill certified that Maurice Wheeler refused to suffer the line between him & Bailie George to be processioned; ordered William Brown Gent attend a jury to lay out the bounds in dispute.
--William Hunt vs James Montague—Petition.
--Thomas Pollard vs Bailie George—Case. A jury came, with Elias Edmonds foreman.

[Index 215] Lancaster OB 16:57a, June Court 1780
Court 16 June 1780, present justices James Ball, John Fleet, Henry Tapscott, John Berryman, William Yerby, & James Ball Junr.
--Thomas Pollard vs Bailie George—Case. Yesterday's jury, Elias Edmonds foreman, returned verdict for Plt.
--Commonwealth vs William Nicken—Indictment.
--Ordered Thomas Pollard pay William Griggs for his attendance as witness for him vs Bailie George.
--Ordered Thomas Pollard pay John Wormeley for his attendance as witness for him vs Bailie George.

--Ordered Thomas Pollard pay Jonathan Wilder for his attendance as witness for him vs Bailie George.
--Ordered Thomas Pollard pay Bushrod Riveer for his attendance as witness for him vs Bailie George.
--Ordered Thomas Pollard pay John Sullivant for his attendance as witness for him vs Bailie George.

[Index 216] Lancaster OB 16:57b, June Court 1780
Ordered Thos. Pollard pay John Clayton for his attendance as witness for him vs Bailie George.
--Ordered Thos. Pollard pay Joseph Hubbard for his attendance as witness for him vs Bailie George.
--Ordered Thos. Pollard pay Thomas Hubbard for his attendance as witness for him vs Bailie George.
--Ordered Baillie George pay Jonathan Pullen for his attendance as witness for him vs Thomas Pollard.
--Ordered Thomas Pollard pay James Kelly for his attendance as witness for him vs Bailie George.
--Thomas Pollard vs John Carter—Case.
--Sarah Wilder vs Charles Lee—Assault & Battery.
--William Biscoe vs Henry Fleet—Case.
--Sarah Hinton vs Henry Fleet—Case.
--Webb vs Webb—Ejectment.
--William Griggs vs Thomas Brent—Debt.

[Index 217] Lancaster OB 16:58a, June Court 1780
Ordered John Carter pay Edward Carter for his attendance as witness for him vs Thomas Pollard.
--Ordered John Carter pay Spencer Carter for his attendance as witness for him vs Thomas Pollard, and for traveling 40 miles each time from & to his place of residence.
--Ordered John Carter pay Thomas Carter for his attendance as witness for him vs Thomas Pollard.
--Richard Hill vs John Wormeley—Injunction.

Court 20 July 1780, present justices James Ball, John Fleet, Richd. Mitchell, Thomas Lawson, Edwin Conway, James Gordon, John Berryman, & Henry Lawson.
--Maurice Wheeler vs Bailie George—Procession.
--John Roberts appointed Surveyor of road from the lower church to Kilmarnock.

[Index 218] Lancaster OB 16:58b, July Court 1780
Present Henry Tapscott, William Yerby, James Ball Junr., & Charles Bell Gent.
--William Chilton vs Job Carter—Trespass, Assault, & Battery.
--Patrick Connolly vs John McTyre—Detinue.
--Johnson Riveer executor &c vs John Kirk—Case.
--Giles Boggess vs Jesse Harrison—Case.
--Elizabeth Stott vs James Tapscott—Petition.
--Thomas Carter vs Sally Yerby—Case.
--Sarah Wilder vs William Griggs—Case.

[Index 219] Lancaster OB 16:59a, July Court 1780
James Gordon Gent and Ann his wife to George Norris was acknowledged.
--Spencer Wood bound to William James until age 21 to learn the trade of a Weaver.
--James Brent acknowledged his bill of sale to George Brent.
--Joseph Sullivant appointed guardian to Cornelius, Thomas, and Joseph West, orphans of Thomas West decd.
--John James vs Bushrod Riveer—Detinue. A jury came, Elias Edmonds foreman; judgment against Deft for £540 and negro man James.
--Henry George acknowledged his deed of bargain & sale to Jesse George, also a bond from Henry for his wife's dower.
--David Boyd vs William Montague—Case.
--Thomas Cottrell vs Maurice Wheeler—Slander.

[Index 220] Lancaster OB 16:59b, July Court 1780

Maurice Wheeler vs Thomas Cottrell—Trespass, assault & battery. Isaac Degge, Thomas Carter, & William Gibson appointed referees.
--Thomas Nugent vs John Dale—Case. William Miskell & Charles McCarty Gent appointed referees.
--George Brent vs William Garlington—Trespass, assault, & battery. A jury came, William Tapscott foreman; judgment for Plt.
--Ordered Bushrod Riveer pay Lettice Wheeler for her attendance as witness in his case vs John James.
--Joseph Hubbard vs Maurice Wheeler—Debt.
--Elijah Percifull vs John Galloway &c—Debt. A jury came, Elias Edmonds foreman; Judgment for Plt.

[Index 221] Lancaster OB 16:60a, July Court 1780
Ordered George Brent pay Jesse Crowther for his attendance (and for travelling six miles to & from his residence) as witness in Brent's case vs William Garlington.
--Joseph Hubbard vs Maurice Wheeler—Debt.
--Ordered Maurice Wheeler pay William Angell for his attendance (and for travelling 15 miles to & from his residence) as witness in Wheeler's case vs Bailie George.
--Ordered Maurice Wheeler pay William Angell Junr. for his attendance as witness (and for travelling 13 miles to & from his residence) in Wheeler's case vs Bailie George.
--On motion of George Glascock, Rawleigh Downman, John Chinn, & William Sydnor Gent appointed to settle guardian's accounts of Katherine Brent with Joseph Shearman her guardian.
--George Norris vs Joseph Hubbard—Case.
--Edwin Kent & wife vs James Newby executor of Moses Chilton decd.—Case. James Ball Gent appointed referee.

[Index 222] Lancaster OB 16:60b, July Court 1780
Court 21 July 1780, present justices James Ball, John Fleet, Thomas Lawson, & Edwin Conway.
--Edwin Kent & wife Jemima vs James Newby executor of Moses Chilton decd.—Case. Jas. Ball (referee) returned his report; judgment for Deft.
--George Norris vs Joseph Hubbard—Case. A jury came, William Tapscott foreman; judgment for Plt.
--Elizabeth Griggs administratrix vs Thomas Brent—Injunction.
--Thomas Brent executor of Geo. Brent decd. vs Bailie George—Case.

[Index 223] Lancaster OB 16:61a, July Court 1780
Petition of Rachel Taylor administratrix of William Taylor decd. vs Phillip Brooks abates by death of one of the parties.
--John Brenon vs John Read—Case.
--John Wormeley vs Stephen Hull—Detinue.
--John Wormeley vs Stephen Hull—Case.
--Thomas Carter vs Benjamin Williams—Case.
--John Heath vs Thomas Crowther—Case.
--Northumberland Justices vs John Eustace—Debt.

[Index 224] Lancaster OB 16:61b, July Court 1780
Thomas Pollard vs Fortun. Sydnor administrator of Wm. King decd.—Debt.
--Thomas Pollard administrator of Samuel Angell decd. vs Fortune. Sydnor administrator of Wm. King decd.—Case.
--William Nutt vs Thomas Pollard &c—Debt.
--James Newby executor of Thos. Pollard decd. vs Henry Tapscott administrator of Alex. Scurlock decd.—Case.
--Robert Edmonds vs John Goodridge—Assault & battery. Abates by death of Plt.
--Henry Tapscott vs Lowry Oliver—Case. Abates by death of Deft.
--Henry Tapscott vs James Newby executor of Thos. Pollard decd.—Case.
--Henry Tapscott vs Elias Edmonds—Case.

[Index 225] Lancaster County OB 16:62a, Aug Court 1780

Court 17 Aug 1780, present justices James Ball, John Fleet, Thomas Lawson, Edwin Conway, Henry Towles, James Ball Junr., Henry Lawson, & Charles Bell.
--William Stonum of Richmond County continued as Inspector at Deep Creek warehouse.
--Johnson Riveer administrator of   [illegible] vs John Kirk—Case.
--William & John Brockenbrough vs Richard Mitchell Junr.—Sci. fa.
--Indenture of bargain & sale from James Tapscott & wife to Charles Bell Gent, acknowledged.
--Thomas Carter vs Sally Yerby—Case.
--George Brent vs William Garlington—Trespass, assault & battery. A jury came, William Griggs foreman; judgment for Plt.

[Index 226] Lancaster OB 16:62b, August Court 1780

Thomas Pinckard vs Robert C. Jacob—Case. A jury came, William Chowning foreman; Judgment for Deft.
--Inventory, and allotment of widow's dower of estate of John Doggett decd. was returned.
--Division of estate of George Flowers decd. returned.
--Indenture of bargain & sale from Richard Mitchell Junr. & wife to William Mitchell, acknowledged.
--Mary Lawson appointed guardian to John & Bailey Lawson orphans of William Lawson decd.
--Indenture of bargain & sale from Joseph McAdam to John Clayton was proved by Edwin Conway, William Brown Gent, & Thomas Pollard.
--Smith & Gatewood vs Thomas West—Debt.
--Henry Tapscott vs James Newby executor—Case.
--Henry Tapscott vs Elias Edmonds—Case.

[Index 227] Lancaster OB 16:63a, August Court 1780

James Newby executor of Thos. Pollard decd. vs Henry Tapscott executor—Case.
--Ordered Thomas Pinckard pay Cornelius Miller for his attendance (and for travelling 35 miles to & from his residence) as witness for Pinckard in his case vs Robert C. Jacob.
--John Fleet vs William Biscoe—Case.
--Giles Robinson vs Elijah Robinson—Detinue.
--Rawleigh Hazard vs Thomas Carter—Case.
--Maurice Wheeler vs Thomas Cottrell—Trespass assault & battery. Report of William Gibson, Thomas Carter, & Isaac Diggs (arbitrators) was returned; Ordered the Plt & Deft pay their own costs.
--Charles & Charlotte Phillipson bound to Thomas Carter.
--Ordered George Brent pay George Paterson for his attendance as witness (and for travelling 7 miles to & from his residence) in Brent's case vs William Garlington.

[Index 228] Lancaster OB 16:63b, August Court 1780

Ordered George Brent pay Josiah Gaskins for his attendance as witness (and for travelling 7 miles to & from his residence) in Brent's case vs William Garlington.
--Ordered William Garlington pay Isaac Hurst for his attendance as witness in Garlington's suit vs George Brent.
--Ordered that William Garlington pay William Kent for his attendance as witness (& for travelling 10 miles to & from his residence) for Garlington in his suit vs George Brent.
--James Flemming granted administration of estate of Mary Ann Christian decd.; Henry Towles Gent, Matthew Myars, Nicholas George, & William Chowning appointed appraisers.
--Thomas Pollard vs Rawleigh Shearman—Case.
--William Taylor's petition about a mill, continued.
--William Griggs vs Bridgar Haynie &c—Debt.
--Geo. Yerby executor of Eliza. Yerby vs Thomas Ellett—Case.

[Index 229] Lancaster OB 16:64a, August Court 1780

Ambrose Wake vs Henry Currell—Debt.
--Nicholas George vs John Taylor—Case.
--Joseph Batcheler vs Isaac Currell—Debt.

--Thomas Pollard vs John Goodridge—Trespass assault & battery.
--Jesse George vs John Thrall—Attachment.
--Commonwealth vs Rawleigh Hazard—Summons.
--James Wallace vs Elijah Percifull—Case.

[Index 230] Lancaster OB 16:64b, August Court 1780

Travers Lunceford vs Maurice Wheeler—Scandal.
--Jesse George vs John Clayton—Case.
--Maurice Wheeler vs Bailie George—Trespass assault & battery.
--Wm. & LeRoy Peachey administrators vs Phillip Smith administrator—Case.
--Will. & LeRoy Peachey administrators vs Henry Armistead—Case.
--Justices vs Judith Brent &c—Debt.

[Index 231] Lancaster OB 16:65a, August Court 1780

Vincent Brent vs Fortunatus Sydnor—Debt.
--Elizabeth Mctyre vs William Lewis—Case.
--Elisha Hall vs Elias Edmonds—Case.
--William Norris vs John Hutchings executor—Case.
--Jeduthen James vs James Ewell—Case.

[Index 232] Lancaster OB 16:65b, August Court 1780

Henry Tapscott Junr. vs Rawleigh Stott—Case.
--John Ramey vs Moncieure Collins—Case.
--William Boatman vs Thomas Hubbard—Case.
--Spencer George vs John Mctyre—Trepass assault & battery.
--Moses Sutton vs David Boyd—Chancery.
--John McTyre vs James Pinckard—Attachment.
--Moses Sutton vs John Webb—Attachment.
--William Dounting vs Redm Lunceford—Trespass assault & battery.

[Index 233] Lancaster OB 16:66a, August Court 1780

William Allason vs Robert Clark—Attachment.
--James Gordon vs George Carter—Case.
--Bushrod Riveer vs Bailie George—Case.

--Court 21 Sept 1780, present justices James Ball, John Fleet, Edwin Conway, James Ball Junr. & William Yerby.
--Thomas Carter vs Benjamin Williams—Case.
--On motion of William Davenport Gent, ordered a dedimus issue to take depositions of Ezekiel Lunceford (a Regular soldier), Richard Partridge (aged & infirm), & Robert Smee (aged & infirm) in Davenport's suit vs Thomas Yerby.

[Index 234] Lancaster OB 16:66b, Sept Court 1780

Thomas Nugent vs John Dale—Case.
--James Newby's account of his guardianship of Newman Chilton's estate, recorded.
--William Chowning produced account of his guardianship of William Chowning's estate.
--Indenture of bargain and sale from Thomas Pollard and Mary his wife to Rawleigh Hazard was acknowledged.
--Thomas Lawson Gent recommended to Governor as proper person to serve as Sheriff.
--Ordered Benjamin Williams pay Daniel Stringer for his attendance as witness (and traveling 20 miles to and from his residence) in his suit against Thomas Carter.
--Ordered Benjamin Williams pay George Williams for his attendance as witness (and for traveling 27 miles to and from his residence) in his suit against Thomas Carter.

--William Boatman was security for appearance of Jeremiah Ashburn in sd Ashburn's suit against Thomas Hunton and son.
--Vincent Brent vs John Edwards—Case.

[Index 235] Lancaster OB 16:67a, Oct Court 1780
Court 19 Oct 1780, present justices James Ball, Richard Mitchell, Edwin Conway, James Ball Jur., & William Yerby.
--On motion of James Brent, ordered Richard Mitchell, James Gordon, Henry Lawson Gent & William Gibson divide land of Hugh Brent Gent decd.; William Brown Gent ordered to attend as Surveyor.
--Richard Mitchell Gent appointed to take lists of tithables in place of Henry Tapscott Gent decd.
--William Sydnor produced his account of tobacco at D. Creek Warehouse.
--John Taylor Gent Sheriff, James Newby, & John Bailey his substitutes took oath prescribed by act of Assembly entitled "Act to proceed in a summary way."
--Henry Towles & Henry Lawson Gent appointed Commissioners of the Grain Tax.
--Petition of Henry George against George Yerby referred to William Yerby Gent, James Brent, Thomas Pollard, & William Gibson.
--John Heath vs Will. Schofield Jur. & Elijah Percifull—Detinue.

[Index 236] Lancaster OB 16:67b, Oct Court 1780
Thomas Hunton & son vs Jeremiah Ashburn—Case. William Boatman & James Kelly were special bail for Deft. Ordered dedimus issue to take deposition of Richard Kenny for the Plt.
--Thomas Carter vs Benjamin Williams—Case. Referred to James Ball, John Chinn, & James Gordon Gent.
--Jupiter vs Vulcan—Ejectment. John Hutchingson entered himself Deft.
--On motion of Thomas Haydon, ordered William Montague, Richard Ball, & John Taylor Gent divide estate of George Payne decd.

Court 9 Nov 1780, for trial of Charles and Tom, negro slaves belonging to Nicholas Currell Gent & James Currell, charged with stealing muslin the property of Sarah Hunton, present justices James Ball, Edwin Conway, Thomas Lawson, & Henry Lawson;

[Index 237] Lancaster OB 16:68a, Nov Court 1780
[cont'd] Tom was found not guilty; Charles was found guilty, ordered he be burned in the hand and receive 39 lashes on his back at the public whipping post.

Court 16 Nov 1780, present justices James Ball, Richd. Mitchell, Edwin Conway, James Ball Junr.
--Thomas Lawson Gent sworn as Sheriff.
--Grand jury came, to wit. Matthew Myars (foreman), Will. Martin, Will. Griggs, Jesse George, John Miller, John Carter, Henry George, John Bean, Meridith Mahanes, John Yerby, John Payne, Will. Warren, Richd. Goodridge, Thos. Dunaway, Ozwald Newby, Jesse Robinson, & Jesse Robinson Junr.
--Will of Isaac Mercer decd. presented by Mary his widow.
--James Wallace Ball appointed Surveyor of Road from Peter Conway's mill to Cundoff's old field, in place of John Boyd.
--James Newby, John Bailey, & John Newby sworn as Under Sheriffs; they, with Thos. Lawson Gent took oath prescribed by Assembly to "proceed in a summary way."

[Index 238] Lancaster OB 16:68b, Nov Court 1780
William Merideth returned account of tobacco at Dymer's warehouse.
--The county levy was laid. These men were mentioned by name and were allowed their accounts: David Boyd (Attorney for the Commonwealth); Michael Wilder (Constable); Joseph Dobs; James Newby; John Bailey.
--Thomas Carter vs Sally Yerby—Attachment. George Phillips was special bail for Deft.

Court 17 Nov 1780, present justices James Ball, Richd. Mitchell, Edwin Conway, James Ball Jur.

--John Taylor Gent was sworn as a Magestrate, and as Vestryman for Christ Church Parish.
--Grand jury offenders summoned to next court, except John Mctyre, who came into court and paid his fine.

[Index 239] Lancaster OB 16:69a, Nov Court 1780

On motion of Spencer George, ordered John Berryman, Thomas Lawson Gent, Harry Currell, & Thomas Carter divide estate of Walter James decd.
--Sarah James appointed guardian to orphans of Benjamin James decd.
--Winny Doggett appointed guardian to Maryann and George Doggett, orphans of John Doggett.

The county levy was laid. These men were paid [only those given by name shown here]: Job Carter (for his account), William Hunt[?] (for 2 sign posts), Thomas Dunaway (1 sign post), Will. Boatman ("refused by the country"), Thomas Garner (Constable), John Mctyre (for a law book), Thads. McCarty (account), Will. Warren (attendance as witness), Will. Boatman (for repairing jail), Cyrus Griffin Esq (for blank record book), John Bailey.

[Index 240] Lancaster OB 16:69b, Nov Court 1780

William Doggett appointed guardian to Lucy, John, & William Doggett orphans of John Doggett decd.

Court 17 Nov 1780 for trial of Will a negro slave belonging to John Tarpley Gent, also Sam and Daniel, two negro slaves belonging to Jas. Montague Gent of Middlesex County, charged with burglary of the house of Alice Smith on 13 Nov 1780, present justices James Ball, Richd. Mitchell, Edwin Conway, & James Ball Jur.; David Boyd was Attorney for the Commonwealth; The Defts pleaded not guilty; Sam and Daniel were found not guilty; Will was found guilty, and was sentenced to hanging; Sam and Daniel were then charged with felony, they pleaded not guilty, but were found guilty, Daniel was sentenced to 39 lashes and Sam was sentenced to be burned in the hand and received 39 lashes; Will was valued at £5000.

[Index 241] Lancaster Ob 16:70a, Dec Court 1780

Court 8 Dec 1780 for trial of Will, negro slave belonging to Thomas Griffin Peachey of Amelia County, charged with stealing one sheep, property of Col James Gordon of Christ Church Parish, present justices James Ball, John Taylor, John Berryman, William Yerby & James Ball Junr.; Will pleaded not guilty; he was found guilty, and sentenced to be burned in the hand and receive 25 lashes.

[Index 242] Lancaster OB 16:70b, Dec Court 1780

Court 21 Dec 1780, present justices James Ball, Richd. Mitchell, Edwin Conway, James Gordon, Henry Towles, John Berryman, William Yerby, Henry Lawson.
--Benjamin Garton & Roger Kelly exempted from levy, they being aged and infirm.
--Charles Rogers, Inspector, returned account of tobacco at Davis's and Lowry's warehouses.
--On motion of Elizabeth Hinton, Thomas Lawson, John Berryman, Henry Lawson Gent, and Lawson Hathaway appointed to divide estate of Richard Hinton decd.; and Thomas Hunton appointed guardian to Sarah, Elizabeth, Mary, Judith, Nancy, Richard, and Robert Hinton orphans of sd Richard Hinton decd.
--Thomas Lawson Gent acknowledged bond as Sheriff for collection of taxes.

[Index 243] Lancaster OB 16:71a, Dec Court 1780

Peter Conway, presented by grand jury for killing trees near the road, ordered he pay fine 20 shillings.
--Grand jury vs Eleazer Robinson is dismissed; same vs William Mitchell; same vs James Pullen; same vs Thomas Pinckard; same vs John Wormeley; same vs Thomas Brent.
--Grand jury vs Rawleigh Shearman for getting drunk, ordered he pay fine 5 shillings.
--Grand jury vs James Currell for swearin one profane oath, ordered he pay find 5 shillings.
--Grand jury vs Henry Fleet for being a common swearer, ordered he pay find 20 shillings.
--Thomas Pinckard Gent and Elmoure Doggett ordered to remove their fence that stands on the main road below Kilmarnock, each of them 15 feet.
--Indenture of bargain and sale from Moses George & Wilmoth his wife to William Chilton "the younger" was acknowledged.

[Index 244] Lancaster OB 16:71b, Jan Court 1781
Court 18 Jan 1781, present justices James Ball, James Gordon, Edwin Conway, John Berryman and Henry Lawson.
--On complaint of Sarah Bluford, formerly bound to Matthew Green til age 31, and now sold to Rawleigh Hazard, ordered that sd Hazard not remove sd Bluford out of the county.
--Indenture of bargain and sale from Richard Payne and Alice his wife to Joseph Sampson was further proved by John Davis.
--Indenture of bargain and sale from John Hall to Peter Conway was acknowledged.
--William Doggett, guardian to John Doggett's orphans, acknowledged his bond.
--William Kirk vs John Mctyre—Trespass, assault, & battery.
--Will of Isaac Mercer decd. presented by Mary Mercer the widow, and she was granted admin.
--Thomas Hunton & Co vs David Gallow—Case. Referees were James Gordon and James Tapscott Gent.

[Index 245] Lancaster OB 16:72a, Jan Court 1781
Henry Towles Gent, William Chowning, Matthew Myars, & Nicholas George appointed to appraise estate of Isaac Mercer decd.
--William Stonum, William Sydnor, Charles Rogers, & Joseph Shearman sworn as Inspectors at the county warehouses.
--William Merideth appointed Inspector at Dymers Warehouse.
--Richard Mitchell & James Ball Junr. Gent appointed to try the weights at Deep Creek Warehouse; and James Gordon & Edwin Conway Gent at Davis's Warehouse.

Court 15 February 1781, present justices James Ball, Richd. Mitchell, Jas. Gordon, Henry Towles and Henry Lawson.
--Indenture of lease and release from Peter Conway and Frances his wife to Robert Clark Jacob was acknowledged.
--Indenture of lease and release from Peter Conway and Frances his wife to Robert C. Jacob was acknowledged.
--Inventory and division of estate of Richard Hinton decd. was returned.
--On motion of George Edwards, an infirm person, ordered he was exempted from future levies.

[Index 246] Lancaster OB 16:72b, Feb Court 1781
On motion of Thomas Hammond, he was exempted from paying future levies during his inability.
--Present John Fleet, Edwin Conway, John Taylor, & William Yerby Gent Justices.
--On motion of William Riveer Junr., he was allowed to turn the main road upon the line between sd Riveer and William Riveer Senr.
--William Hunt vs John Selden—Trespass Assault & Battery.
--Bond for performance of covenants from Joseph McAdam to John Clayton was proved by witnesses.
--Ordered the Clerk certify to the Auditor that allowances had been made to James Ball Gent, Richd. Mitchell Gent, and Edwin Conway Gent as Commissioners of the Tax for the county.
--John Clayton vs Anthony George—Case.
--Will of Francis Webb decd. proved by William Webb, the executor named therein. Thomas Brent, Elijah Percifull, James Wallace, and William Galloway appointed appraisers.
--James Gordon Gent appointed guardian to orphans of Robert Henning decd., and James Tapscott, Robert C. Jacob, and William Montague appointed to settle the accounts with Edwin Conway Gent & Bridgar Haynie executors of sd decd., and John Taylor Gent the former guardian.
--Gawen Lowry appointed Inspector at Davis's Warehouse.
--Edwin Conway, John Taylor, & James Gordon Gent appointed to view repairs to the prison.

[Index 247] Lancaster OB 16:73a, Feb Court 1781
Thomas Hunton & Son vs Jeremiah Ashburn—Case. Referees were James Ball, Richard Mitchell, and James Gordon Gent.

Court 5 Feb 1781, pursuant to an Act of General Assembly for supplying army with clothes, provisions, and wagons, present justices James Ball, John Fleet, Richard Mitchell, Edwin Conway, John Taylor, James Gordon, Henry Towles, William Yerby, James Ball Junr., Henry Lawson, and John Selden, who contracted with John McTyre for a wagon with two horses, etc., and James Ball Gent appointed to purchase the other two horses for sd wagon.

Court 15 March 1781, present justices James Ball, Richard Mitchell, Edwin Conway, James Gordon, John Berryman, and James Ball Junr.
--William Brumley made oath that Samuel Brumley died intestate, sd William was granted administration.
--James Ball, Richd. Mitchell, James Ball Junr., Gent & William Sydnor appointed to appraise estate of Samuel Brumley decd.

[Index 248] Lancaster OB 16:73b, March Court 1781
On motion of William Hill orphan of John Hill decd., John Fleet, John Berryman, Henry Lawson Gent, and William Merideth appointed to allot sd William Hill one fifth part of the estate of Elizabeth Blackerby decd., who was former wife of sd John Hill.
--Henry George vs George Yerby—Petition.
--Inventory of estate of Isaac Mercer decd. was returned.
--Ordered the Sheriff pay Job Carter for prison charges.
--Inventory of estate of Francis Webb decd. was returned.
--Will of Thomas Carter decd. presented by Thomas Towles, executor therein named, and was proved by Edward Carter.
--On motion of Martin Norris who married a daughter of Isaac Mercer decd., Henry Towles Gent, Matthew Myars, William Chowning and Nicholas George were appointed to allot sd Norris his wife's part of her father's estate.
--James Gordon Gent, Elias Edmonds, John Yerby, and Coleman Doggett appointed to appraise estate of Thomas Carter decd.
--Ordered the Sheriff pay William Boatman for repairs done to the prison.

[Index 249] Lancaster OB 16:74a, March Court 1781
Joseph Hubbard vs Vachal Fandrie—Case.
--William Schofield vs Thomas Pollard—Case.
--John Kirk vs Samuel Denny—Case.
--Thomas Pollard vs Rawleigh Hazard—Case.
--William Chilton Junr. vs Job Carter—Trespass Assault & Battery.
--John Dye vs William Chilton Junr & John Hutchinson—Trespass.
--John Dye vs William Chilton Junr.—Case.
--Henry Towles, James Ball Junr., & James Tapscott Gent chosen Commissioners of the Tax for 1781.

[Index 250] Lancaster OB 16:74b, March Court 1781
Henry Tapscott vs James Newby Exor.—Case. Abates by death of Plt.
--Henry Tapscott vs Elias Edmonds—Case. Abates by death of Plt.
--Vincent Brent vs Fortunatus Sydnor—Debt. Abates by death of Deft.
--James Gordon Gent appointed Commissioner of Tax in place of James Ball Junr., who begs indulgence on account of his ill health.

Court 19 April 1781, present justices James Ball, Edwin Conway, Henry Towles, John Berryman, William Yerby, James Ball Junr., and Henry Lawson.
--Division of negros of Elizabeth Blackerby decd. was returned.
--Division of negros of Col Thomas B. Griffin decd. was returned.
--John Heath Junr., Gent, sworn as an Attorney.

[Index 251] Lancaster OB 16:75a, April Court 1781

Indenture of bargain and sale from Richard Chilton and wife [not named] to William Chilton Junr. was proved by Thads. McCarty and Vachal Fandrie.

--Division of land of Hugh Brent Gent decd. was returned.

--Present James Gordon Gent.

--On petition of Willoughby Rout, an aged and infirm person, ordered he be exempt from levy in future.

--On petition of Anthony Garton, an aged person, ordered he be exempt from levy in future.

--John Heath vs Elijah Percifull &c—Detinue. Ordered a dedimus issue to take depositions of William Galloway and Robert Short.

--Indenture of bargain & sale from Roger Kelly and wife [not named] to Jesse Crowder, acknowledged.

--Will of Henry Tapscott Gent presented by wife Mary Tapscott and Rawleigh Tapscott (the executors therein named), proved by Richard Mitchell Gent and Joseph Shearman; William Sydnor, John Chinn, Robert Chinn, and Thomas Stott appointed appraisers of the estate in Lancaster County, and Will. Stonum, John Pope, George Scurlock, and Jehu Pullen appointed appraisers of the estate in Richmond County.

[Index 252] Lancaster OB 16:75b, April Court 1781

Will of Rawleigh Downman Esq decd. presented by Richard Mitchell Gent and Rawleigh W. Downman (executors therein named), proved by Robert Chinn and William Sydnor; James Ball Junr. Gent, William Sydnor, Robert Chinn, and Thomas Stott appointed appraisers of the estate in Lancaster County; and Rawleigh Downman, John Glascock, George Glascock Junr., and Dominick Burnham appointed appraisers of the estate in Richmond County; and James Kenyon, Anthony Strother, Wm. Alexander, and John Mason appointed appraisers of the estate at the Little Falls; and John Mason, James Jefferies, John Humphrey, and Windsor Farrish in Stafford County; and Charles Martin, Daniel A. Wills, John Wheatley, and   in Fauquier County.

--William Davis orphan of Moses Davis bound to John Edwards.

--Betty King orphan of William King chose Isaac Digge her guardian; William Sydnor appointed guardian to Molly and Caty King, and Richard Mitchell Gent appointed guardian to John King, all orphans of sd William King.

--Edwin Conway, Charles Lee Gent, and Benjamin George appointed to settle accounts of orphans of William King decd. with the executors Anthony and Fortunatus Sydnor decd. their former guardians, and possess the present guardians with their estates.

[Index 253] Lancaster OB 16:76a, May Court 1781

Court 17 May 1781, present justices James Ball, Henry Towles, John Berryman, Henry Lawson.

--Henry Carter appointed Surveyor of Road from main road to Lowry's Warehouse, in place of John Harris.

--Rawleigh Tapscott appointed Surveyor of Road from Richard Mitchell's shop to Mr. Downman's lane, and down to William Sydnor's gate, in place of John Chilton.

--Thomas Flint appointed Surveyor of Road from county line to the crossroads between Mrs. Margaret and Mrs. Agatha Ball's mills, in place of John Atkinson [? blotted].

--Division of estate of Joseph Carter decd. returned.

--Robert Chinn foreman of grand jury; he and other jurors, to wit. Joseph Shearman and others returned with their presentments.

--Inventory of estate of Walter James decd. returned.

--Administration of estate of Bushrod Riveer decd. granted to Peter Riveer; Johnson Riveer, Richard Goodridge, Jesse Robinson Junr., and James Norris appointed appraisers.

[Index 254] Lancaster OB 16:76b, May Court 1781

Division of estate of Josiah Harris decd. returned.

--Moses Sutton vs David Boyd—Chancery.

--Jeduthan Davis orphan of Moses Davis decd. chose Jesse Crowder as his guardian; John Berryman Gent, James Brent, and Isaac Degge appointed to settle guardian's accounts of sd Davis with William Gibson his former guardian, and possess the present guardian with his estate.

--On petition of William Hubbard, an infirm person, ordered he be exempt from paying levy.

--Will of Richard Cundiff decd. was presented by Nathan Pullen executor therein named, and proved by William Edwards.

--Indenture of bargain and sale from Nathan Pullen and Elizabeth his wife to Jeduthan Moore was acknowledged.
--A writing purporting the settlement of the line between lands of Bailie George and Maurice Wheeler was proved by John Roberts and James Kelly.
--Inventory of estate of Henry Tapscott Gent decd. returned.

[Index 255] Lancaster OB 16:77a, May Court 1781
Indenture of bargain and sale from Richard Chilton and wife [not named] to William Chilton Junr. was further proved by Epaphroditus Lawson and recorded.
--Indenture of bargain and sale from Jesse Robinson Junr. to James Norris was proved and recorded.
--Will of Elmor Doggett decd. was presented by William Doggett Junr., and was proved by William West and William Gibson, and sd William Doggett Junr. was granted administration, William Gibson refusing to qualify as an executor; William Yerby Gent, James Brent, William Gibson, and William Merideth appointed appraisers.
--Maryann Doggett widow of Elmore Doggett decd. entered dissent to her husband's will; Edwin Conway, James Gordon, William Yerby Gent, and Benjamin George appointed to allot her dower.
--Matthew Myars vs Henry Towles—Case.
--Edward Carter vs Thomas Towles executor of Thomas Carter decd.—Case.
--Richard Mitchell Junr. vs William Rich—Petition.

[Index 256] Lancaster OB 16:77b, May Court 1781
John Fleet and William Yerby Gent appointed to take list of tithables below Carter's Mill, James Gordon Gent between said mill and Jacob's mill, Edwin Conway Gent in Wiccomoco Parish, Richard Mitchell and James Ball Junr. Gent above the courthouse in the upper part of the county.
--John Berryman vs John Fleet—Case.
--Richard Stott vs Will. Griffin executor of T. B. Griffin—Case.
--John McAdam vs George Beane—Case.
--George Beane vs John McAdam—Case.

[Index 257] Lancaster OB 16:78a, May Court 1781
[Part of this page is missing on the Family History Library microfilm. The Library of Virginia microfilm contains the full page.]
John Dye vs Will. Chilton Jr & John Huchinson---Trespass.
--John Dye vs William Chilton Jr---Case.
--Ordered Bushrod Riveer pay Travers Lunceford for eight days attendance as witness in sd Riveer's case against Bailie George.
Court 21 June 1781, present justices James Ball, Richd. Mitchell, Edwin Conway, Henry Towles, John Berryman, William Yerby, James Ball Junr., and Henry Lawson.
--Settlement of account of guardianship of Jeduthun Davis was returned.

[Index 258] Lancaster OB 16:78b, June Court 1781
Indenture of bargain and sale from James Gordon and Anne his wife to Thaddeus McCarty was acknowledged.
--Indenture of bargain and sale from Thaddeus McCarty and Mary his wife to James Gordon was acknowledged.
--John Chinn Gent qualified as executor of the will of Rawleigh Downman Esq decd.
--Elmore Doggett orphan of George Doggett decd. chose William Griggs as his guardian.
--Thomas Hunton and son vs Jeremiah Ashburn—Case.
--Inventory of estate of Elmore Doggett decd. returned.
--William Brown vs John Hutchinson—Sureties of the Peace.
--Thomas Ashburn vs William and Mary Sullivant—Sureties of the Peace.
--Ann Shearwood vs John Roberts—Sureties of the Peace.

[Index 259] Lancaster OB 16:79a, June Court 1781
Ordered Ann Shearwood pay David Garland for his attendance as witness in her suit against John Roberts.
--Rawleigh Hazard vs Robert Collins—Case.

--Joseph Shearman vs James Howard administrator of Lowry Oliver decd.—Case.
--Grand Jury vs John McTyre and John Thrall—Summons.
--Grand Jury vs William Mitchell—Summons.
--Grand Jury vs James Tapscott.
--James Pinckard, presented by grand jury, ordered he pay fine.
--Elias Edmonds appointed Surveyor of Road from Norris's mill to Mrs. Robb's gate, thence to the crossroads that divides sd Edwards, John Yerby, and Charles Bell Gent decd.
--Bailie George recommended to Governor as proper person to act as 1st Lieutenant, William Kirk as 2nd Lieutenant, and John Flowers as Ensign in Capt Gibson's company; Lott Palmer as 1st Lieutenant, Presly Saunders 2nd Lieutenant in Capt Richd. Selden's company, militia.

[Index 260] Lancaster OB 16:79b, June Court 1781
Edwin Conway, James Gordon, William Yerby Gent, and Benjamin George appointed to divide personal estate of Elmore Doggett decd.
--Richard Stott vs William Griffin executor of T.B.G. [Griffin]—Case; A jury came, with Spencer George foreman.
--John Berryman vs John Fleet—Case.
--John McAdam vs George Beane—Case; A jury came, with William Norris foreman.
--Matthew Myars vs Henry Towles—Case. Ed. Conway, John Taylor, and Jas. Gordon Gent were referees.

[Index 261] Lancaster OB 16:80a, June Court 1781
Ordered Richd. Stott pay Thomas Stott for his attendance as witness for sd. Richard in his suit vs William Griffin executor of T.B. Gfriffin decd.
--Ordered John McAdam pay Thomas Yerby for his attendance as witness in sd McAdam's suit against George Beane, and for traveling six miles to and from his place of residence.

Court 19 July 1781, present justices James Ball, Edwin Conway, Henry Towles, James Ball Junr., and John Selden.
--Will of Winifred Campbell decd. was presented by George Campbell executor therein named, and was proved by William Stonum and Betty Burn.
--Will of John Boyd decd. was presented by Thomas Garnet executor therein named, and was proved by Richard Ball and John Leland; Richard Ball, James W. Ball, Richard Selden, and Richard Cundiff appointed appraisers.

[Index 262] Lancaster OB 16:80b, June Court 1781
Thomas Potts appointed guardian to John and George Boyd orphans of John Boyd decd.
--Will of Charles Bell decd. was presented by Elizabeth Bell the widow, John Hull, and James Gordon Gent (executors therein named), and was proved by Edwin Conway Gent and Sarah C. Conway; Edwin Conway, James Tapscott, Elias Edmonds, and John Yerby appointed appraisers.
--The different inventories of estate of Rawleigh Downman Esq decd. were returned.
--A bond from James and Jesse Robinson to William Lattimore, that was acknowledged in May 1767 by said James and Jesse, but was not recorded, was now at request of Charles Lattimore (lawful representative of sd William Lattimore) recorded.
--Ordered Bailie George pay Travers Lunceford for his attendance as witness for sd George in his suit vs Maurice Wheeler.
--James Gordon Gent recommended to Governor as proper person to act as Colonel in county militia, in place of Edwin Conway Gent who resigned; and James Ball Junr. to succeed sd Gordon as Lieutenant Colonel.
--Thomas Pollard Gent sworn as Captain of a company of Cavalry in this county; Newton Brent as Lieutenant in sd company; and John Sullivant as Cornett in the same.

[Index 263] Lancaster OB 16:81a, June Court 1781
James W. Ball, James Ewell, and Richard Selden Gent recommended to Governor as proper person to be added to Commission of the Peace, in place of Richard Mitchell, Henry Tapscott, and Charles Bell Gent decd.

Court 16 Aug 1781, present justices James Ball, John Fleet, James Ball Junr., and Henry Lawson.

--Present justices Edwin Conway, John Taylor, James Gordon, Henry Towles, William Yerby, and John Selden Gent.
--William Brown Gent appointed Attorney for the Commonwealth in place of David Boyd Gent, deceased.
--Bill of sale from John Wormeley to William Brown was proved by Edwin Conway and James W. Ball.
--Henry Towles Gent recommended to Governor as proper person to act as Major in militia, in place of James Ball Junr.
--Indenture of bargain and sale from John Heath Senr to John Heath Junr was acknowledged.
--Thomas Lawson Gent Sheriff executed bond for collection of taxes.
--William Yerby Gent, James Brent, Benjamin George, and William Gibson appointed to allot to widow of Elmore Doggett decd. her part of his estate.

[Index 264] Lancaster OB 16:81b, August Court 1781
Indenture of bargain and sale from Rawleigh Hazard and Sarah his wife to Newton Brent was acknowledged.
--Indenture of bargain and sale from Rawleigh Hazard and Sarah his wife to Alexander Hunton and others was acknowledged.
--James Newby presented his account of Newman Chilton's estate.
--Elias Edmonds and John Yerby appointed, in place of Richard Mitchell and Charles Bell Gent decd., to settle accounts of the orphans of Thos. Pollard decd. agreeable to order of this court in Aug 1779.
--Articles of agreement between Fortunatus Sydnor decd. and William Brown were proved by George Phillips.
--Indenture of bargain and sale from Mungo Harvey and Priscilla his wife to John Selden was recorded.
--Upon complaint of Frances Hutchinson, wife of John Hutchinson, for ill treatment, ordered sd John post bond for £10,000; William Gibson and Jonathan Pullen were his securities.
--On petition of Betty Smith, whose husband Wm. Smith is in the service of the state, ordered the Treasurer pay her for the support of herself and three small children.

[Index 265] Lancaster OB 16:82a, Sept Court 1781
Court 20 Sept 1781, present justices James Ball, Edwin Conway, Henry Towles, William Yerby, and James Ball Junr.
--Division of estate of Elmoure Doggett decd. returned.
--On motion of William Griggs, who married the widow of Thos. Everitt, ordered James Gordon, Henry Towles Gent, James Tapscott, and William Brown allot to sd Griggs his wife's dower in the land of her decd. husband (by consent of the guardian to sd Everitt's orphan), and make return to next court (William Brown to attend as Surveyor).
--Isaac Degge appointed guardian to John King orphan of William King decd.; Edwin Conway, Chas. Lee Gent, and Benjamin George appointed to settle guardian's accounts of the orphans of sd William King with the executors of Anthony and Fortunatus Sydnor decd., their former guardians, and possess the current guardians with their several estates.
--Receipt from Richard Payne to Joseph Sampson for a tract of land was proved, ordered to lie for further proof.
--Report of settlement of administration of estate of James Kirk decd. was returned.
--Report of settlement of estate of Sarah Kirk decd. was returned.
--Report of settlement of guardian's accounts of Thomas Kirk decd. was returned.
--On petition of James Tapscott, Edwin Conway, Jas. Gordon, Henry Towles Gent, and John Wormeley were appointed to view road petitioned for by sd Tapscott.

[Index 266] Lancaster OB 16:82b, Sept Court 1781
Will of William Stott decd. was presented by William Sydnor (one of the executors therein named), and he was granted administration, and the codicil to the will was proved by James Newby; James Ball, James Ball Junr., Rawleigh Tapscott, and William Hunt were appointed appraisers.
--Will of Richard Mitchell decd. was presented by Robert and Richard Mitchell (executors therein named), and was proved by James Gordon, Henry Towles Gent, and William Sydnor, and the said executors were granted administration; Ann, the widow, renounced her rights; James Ball, Edwin Conway, James Ball Junr. Gent, and William Sydnor appointed to appraise the estate and allot the widow's dower, and divide the negroes.

--On motion of Agatha Ball, widow of Jesse Ball Gent decd., John Chinn, William Sydnor, Nathaniel Burwell, and John Bailey were appointed to allot her part of her husband's estate according to his will.
--James Ball and James Ball Junr. appointed guardians to the orphans of Jesse Ball Gent decd.
--On motion of John Clutton, Richard Goodridge, John Goodridge, Johnson Riveer, and Richard Cundiff (or any three of them) were appointed to view the road petitioned for by sd. Clutton.

[Index 267] Lancaster OB 16:83a, Sept Court 1781

Bushrod Riveer vs Bailie George—Case. Abates by death of Plt.
--David Galloway vs David Boyd—Chancery. Abates by death of Deft.
--James Newby executor of Thos. Pollard decd. vs Henry Tapscott administrator of Alexr. Scurlock—Case. Abates by death of Deft.
--Thomas Pollard vs Fortun. Sydnor administrator of Wm. King decd.—Debt. Abates by death of Deft.
--David Boyd vs Elihu Hall & wife—Chancery. Abates by death of Plt.
--Moses Sutton vs David Boyd—Chancer. Abates by death of Deft.
--Katherine McDonald vs John Selden administrator of Jas. Seldon decd.—Case.
--William Doggett Jun. vs Thomas Pinckard—Case. Abates by death of Deft.
--Angell's administrator vs Fortun. Sydnor administrator of Wm. King—Case. Abates by death of Deft.

[Index 268] Lancaster OB 16:83b, Oct Court 1781

Court 18 Oct 1781, present justices James Ball, Edwin Conway, William Yerby, Henry Lawson, and John Selden.
--James Wallace Ball Gent. sworn as Magistrate.
--Receipt from Richard Payne to Joseph Sampson for land agreeable to deed of bargain and sale, further proved by Mary Ann Cundiff, and recorded.
--Indenture of bargain and sale from John Selden to Richd. Selden, acknowledged.
--Bond for settlement of bounds of land between Bailie George and Maurice Wheeler was further proved by Thomas Hathaway, and recorded.
--Nicholas George appointed guardian to John Wood Davis orphan of William Davis decd.
--Articles of agreement between Fortunatus Sydnor decd. and William Brown Gent was further proved by Bailie George, and ordered to lie for further proof.
--John Taylor and John Selden Gent appointed Commissioners of the Grain Tax.
--Sheriff ordered to pay Cyrus Griffin Esq for a record book.
--Deed of trust from William Kent to Edwin Conway Gent in favor of sd Kent's wife was proved.
--John Heath vs Elijah Percifull &c—Detinue. Dedimus issued to take deposition of John Allen for the Deft.
--Charles Chilton, Charles Morhead, Horton Ransdell &c appointed to appraise estate of Edward Blakemore decd. in Fauquier County.

[Index 269] Lancaster OB 16:84a, Oct Court 1781

Account of tobacco at Deep Creek Warehouse returned by William Sydnor, Inspector.
--Inventory of estate of William Stott decd. returned.

Court 15 Nov 1781, present justices James Ball, Henry Towles, Henry Lawson, and James W. Ball.
--Administration of estate of Thomas Robb decd. granted to William Merideth; James Gordon Gent, Jno. Yerby, William Edwards, and James Pinckard appointed appraisers.
--Grand jury impannel'd: Joseph Shearman (foreman), Jesse Robinson, Ozwald Newby, John Chilton, Richd. Mitchell, William Warren, William Kent, Richd. Goodridge, Rawleigh Stott, John Hutchings, John Flowers, John Miller, John Bean, James Pinckard, Jesse George, Thomas Hubbard, and Moses George.

[Index 270] Lancaster OB 16:84b, Nov Court 1781

County levy laid. The following individuals' accounts were allowed [only those given by name presented here]: executors of David Boyd Gent decd., Attorney for the Commonwealth; Thomas George for an extraordinary levy; to John Rogers for same; Lott Palmer for his account; Abner Palmer for his account; Thomas Kern for his account, John Bailey for his account; Joseph Dobbs for repairs done to the prison; John Newby for his account; Charles

Dodson for his account; James Newby for his account; Thads. McCarty for his account; Spencer George for his account; Michael Wilder for his account.

--Indenture of bargain and sale from John Mohone and wife [not named] to Geo. Brent was proved.

--One. Harvey &c executors vs Thomas March—Case.

--On petition of Thomas Pollard for leave to build water grist mill on Carter's Creek, ordered the Sheriff summon a jury to view the land.

--Ordered the hands of Richard and James W. Ball be taken off the road of Mahon's Bridge, and attend the road from Jacob's mill to Cundiff's old field.

--John Davis appointed Surveyor or Road from James Tapscott's gate to Davis's Warehouse.

[Index 271] Lancaster OB 16:85a, Nov Court 1781

Robert Chinn appointed Surveyor of Road from Morathis Mill to Deep Bottom in place of Richard Mitchell Gent decd.

--Edwin Conway Gent recommended to Governor as proper to act as Colonel in place of Richd. Mitchell Gent decd.

--Robert Chinn, one of the executors of will of William Stott decd., qualified as administrator.

--Thomas Hathaway appointed Surveyor of Road from lower church to Shearman's Ferry in place of Henry Lawson Gent.

--Thomas Pollard presented a bill in payment of a judgment obtained by Newton and son against him in 1780.

--Account of tobacco in Davis's Warehouse presented by Chas. Rogers, Inspector.

Court 20 Dec 1781, present justices James Ball, Edwin Conway, James Gordon, Henry Towles, John Selden, and James W. Ball.

--James Ewell Gent sworn as Magistrate.

[Index 272] Lancaster OB 16:85b, Dec Court 1781

Indenture of bargain and sale from Rawleigh Hazard and Sarah his wife to Alexander Hunton was acknowledged.

--Bill of sale from Charles Rogers to Joseph Sydnor was proved.

--James Tapscott, Robert C. Jacob, and Matthew Myars recommend to Governor as proper persons to be added to Commission of the Peace; Richard Selden, who was lately recommended, refused to qualify.

--William Yopp, presented by grand jury for getting drunk, did not appear, and was fined.

--William Brown, presented by grand jury for getting drunk, did not appear, and was fined.

--These grand jury presentments were dismissed upon payment of costs: grand jury vs James Tapscott, John Wormeley, John Hill, Samuel Dunaway, James Pullen, Sarahan Dye, and Alice Smith.

--Indenture of bargain and sale from Rawh. Hazard and Sarah his wife to Newton Brent was acknowledged.

--Privy examination of Ann Selden, wife of John Selden Gent, relative to a deed of bargain and sale to Richd. Selden, was returned.

[Index 273] Lancaster OB 16:86a, December Court 1781

Division of estate of Richard Mitchell Gent was returned.

--Allotment of Mrs. Agatha Ball's part of estate of her decd. husband Colo. Jesse Ball, was returned.

--Administration of estate of Thomas Brent decd. granted to William Brent; Edwin Conway, James Gordon, James W. Ball Gent, and James Newby were appointed appraisers.

--Administration of estate of Joseph Sullivant decd. was granted to Vincent Brent; John Bean, Thomas Garner, Henry Carter, and Stephen Lock were appointed appraisers.

--Administration of estate of James Bush decd. granted to James Bush his son; James Newby, Ozwald Newby, Johnson Riveer, and Jesse Robinson were to appraise and divide the estate.

--Betty and Peter Bush orphans of James Bush decd. chose James Bush as their guardian.

--Commonwealth by Will. Luckham, Proprietor vs John Armes—Sureties of the Peace. John Arms ordered to post bond, with Henry Towles Gent his security; William Luckham ordered to post bond, with James Ewell Gent his security.

[Index 274] Lancaster OB 16:86b, Dec Court 1781

Elizabeth Hinton appointed guardian to Mary, Judith, Ann, Richard, and Robert Hinton orphans of Richard Hinton decd.
--Stephen Stott's orphans by Will. Sydnor and Robt. Chinn their next friends vs William Brent and wife—Detinue. Edwin Conway, James Gordon, and Henry Towles Gent were referees.
--John James orphan of Bartlet James decd. chose Lawson Hathaway as his guardian.

County levy was laid; Job Carter, James Carter, and John Pinckard were allowed their accounts.

[Index 275] Lancaster OB 16:87a, Dec Court 1781
Division of estate of Richard Mitchell Gent decd. was returned.
--Allotment of estate of Jesse Ball Gent decd. to Mrs. Agatha Ball his widow was returned.
--Administration of estate of Thomas Brent decd. granted to William Brent; Edwin Conway, James Gordon, James W. Ball Gent, and James Newby appointed appraisers.

Court, 7 Jan 1782, for examination of Thomas and Vincent Brent, charged with having robbed George Brent, present justices James Ball, Edwin Conway, John Taylor, James Gordon, and James Ball Junr.; Defts brought to the bar; witnesses were Ann Brent, Elijah Percifull, James Brent, and Coleman Doggett; Defts were found guilty, and they were referred to the next grand jury court; Defts posted bond; John Goodridge and Elijah Percifull were securities for Thomas Brent; Jedithen Brent, Daniel Kent, and Edwin Kent were securities for Vincent Brent.

[Index 276] Lancaster OB 16:87b, Jan Court 1782
Court 17 Jan 1782, present justices James Ball, Edwin Conway, William Yerby, Henry Lawson, and James W. Ball.
--On motion of Epaphroditus Lawson, Henry Lawson Gent, Lawson Hathaway, James Currell, and Thomas Hathaway were appointed to allot to sd Epaphroditus his part of his decd. father's negroes.
--Commonwealth by Geo. Brent, Prosecutor vs Vincent Brent—For sureties of the Peace. Ordered a scire facias issue against sd Vincent Brent and Jedithen Brent and ___ Sullivant, his securities.
--Will of Edney Tapscott decd. presented by Henry Tapscott (one of the executors therein named), who was granted administration; Edwin Conway Gent, William Brown, James Tapscott, and John Degge were appointed appraisers.
--On motion of Charles Purcell who married Juannah [thus], a daughter of John Yerby decd., ordered Elias Edmonds, William Gibson, Jonathan Pullen, and John Merideth allot to sd Charles his wife's part of her father's estate.
--Inventory of estate of Thomas Robb decd. returned.

[Index 277] Lancaster OB 16:88a, Jan Court 1782
Mary Yerby appointed guardian to Richard, James, and Jesse Yerby, orphans of John Yerby decd.; Elias Edmonds, William Gibson, Jonathan Pullen and John Merrideth appointed to allot sd Mary Yerby, the widow, her part in the estate of the decd.
--On motion of Lawson Hathaway, William Peachey, William Miskell, John Fauntleroy, and Charles McCarty Gent were appointed to appraise and divide estate of Elizabeth Yerby decd. in Richmond County; and James Brent, William Norris, John James, and James Pollard were appointed to appraise and divide estate of the sd decd. in Lancaster County.
--Ordered the wardens of Wiccomoco Parish bind the orphans of Thomas West decd., namely, Cornelius, Thomas, and Joseph West.
--Lease and bond from John Mahone to George Brent was proved by Robert Fergusson and William Merrideth.
--Benjamin George, James Brent, Thomas Pollard, and John Sullivant appointed to appraise and divide estate of Richd. Brent decd.
--Fanny Hill orphan of James Hill decd chose Thomas Hubbard as her guardian.
--Coleman Doggett appointed guardian to Brittain, Mildred, & Elizabeth Hill orphans of James Hill decd., James Gordon Gent, Thads. McCarty, John Miller, and Jedithen Pinckard appointed to allot to Thomas Hubbard Fanny Hill's part of her decd. father's estate.

[Index 278] Lancaster OB 16:88b, Feb Court 1782

Court, 21 Feb 1782, present justices James Ball, James Gordon, Henry Towles, William Yerby, Edwin Conway, and John Taylor.
--Allotment of Fanny Hill's part of estate of James Hill dec.d her father was returned.
--Report about road petitioned for by James Tapscott was returned.
--Catharine Tapscott orphan of Edney Tapscott decd. chose James Tapscott her guardian.
--Allotment of William Biscoe's part of estate of Edward Blakemore was returned.
--Report of allotment of Epaphroditus Lawson's part of the negroes of his decd. father's estate was returned.
--Appraisement & division of estate of Edward Blakemore decd. in Fauquier County returned, and allotment of negroes belonging to Elizabeth, Sarah, & Nancy Blakemore orphans of sd. decd. was ordered to remain in hand of the executors until sd orphans arrive to age.
--Indenture of bargain sale Corbin Griffin Esq to Nathaniel Burwell Esq proved.
--Inventory & division of estate of James Bush decd. returned.
--Division of estate of Richard Brent decd. returned.
--Division of estate of John Yerby decd., with allotment of widow's dower, returned.
--On motion of Eliza. Hill widow of James Hill decd., ordered James Gordon Gent, Thads. McCarty, John Miller, Jedithen Pinckard appointed to divide estate and allotment widow's dower.

[Index 279] Lancaster OB 16:89a, February Court 1782
Brittain Hill orphan of James Hill decd. chose John Clayton his guardian.
--Bill of sale George Brent to James Brent was proved.
--Bill of sale William Kent to George Brent was proved.
--Elias Edmonds appointed guardian to Mildred & Elizabeth Hill orphans of James Hill decd.
--On motion of John Degge, ordered Edwin Conway Gent, John Cundiff, William Schofield view road petitioned for by sd. Degge.
--Will of Thomas Brent decd. proved by Thomas Pollard, Jedithen Brent, & John Parrot, and administration granted to William Brent, and Elias Edmonds, James Pollard, John Miller, & Benjamin George appointed to appraise the estate and settle the former administration account.
--Will of William Griggs decd. presented and proved by Henry Lawson Gent one of the executors, and codicil to sd will proved by witnesses Rawleigh Shearman, William and Thomas Doggett, and Ruth Griggs widow of sd decd. renouinced her right & claim, and ordered Edwin Conway Gent, Bailie George, Lawson Hathaway, and John Parrott allot sd Ruth her part of sd estate.

[Index 280] Lancaster OB 16:89b, Feb Court 1782
Will of Coleman Doggett decd. was presented by executors James Tapscott & Elias Edmonds, and was proved by witnesses James Gordon Gent & Moses George, and administration was granted to sd executors, and ordered James Gordon, Thads. McCarty, John Yerby, and James Pinckard appraise estate.
--On motion of Charles Bean who married the widow of Thomas Edwards decd., ordered Edwin Conway Gent, James Tapscott, James Pinckard, & Elias Edmonds divide the estate and allot the widow's dower.
--Administration of estate of Henry George decd. granted to William Gibson & Bailie George, and ordered William Merrideth, James Pollard, William Mason, & John James appraise estate.
--Administration of estate of Thomas Jarrott decd. granted to Fanny Jarrott, and Ozwald Newby, Thomas Flint, Johnson Riveer, and Rawleigh Davenport appointed appraisers.
--Fanny Jarrott appointed guardian to Betty Jarrott orphan of Thomas Jarrott decd.
--Thomas Carter vs Sally Yerby—Case. Judgment confessed by William Boatman for Deft.
--Thomas Hammonds appointed guardian to his son Charles Hammonds.
--George Norris appointed guardian to Agatha Edwards orphan of Thomas Edwards, and ordered sd Norris be possessed with sd Agathy's part of the estate.

[Index 281] Lancaster OB 16:90a, Feb Court 1782
Ann Carter orphan of Josiah Carter decd. chose John Degge her guardian, and on motion of Thos. Mott who married Betsy the sister of sd Ann, ordered Edwin Conway, James Gordon Gent, George Norris, & Elias Edmonds divide land of the decd. between sd Ann and Thomas Mott, and William Brown to attend as Surveyor.

--Joseph Shearman Plt vs James Howard adminr. of Lowry Oliver decd—Case. Referees James Ball, James Gordon, Henry Towles Gent.

--Leave granted to James Gordon Gent to turn the road that leads by his house to Davis's Warehouse, on the north side of the plantation he lately purchased of Edward Carter.

--Certificates relative to a contract between William Griggs decd. and Jesse Wilder were certified by Henry Lawson Gent.

--Edwin Conway Gent, John Carter, Thomas Carter, & Benjamin George ordered to possess the church wardens of Wiccomoco Parish with the estate of Thomas & Joseph West orphans of Thos. West decd. which is in the hands of Vincent Brent, and sd wardens ordered to bind sd orphans.

--Ordered that William Brent pay William Yopp for attendance as witness in sd Brent's suit vs Vincent Brent.

--Cornelius West orphan of Thomas West decd. was bound to Richard Dye until age 21, to learn the trade of a Taylor.

[Index 282] Lancaster OB 16:90b, Feb Court 1782

Stott's orphans vs William Brent & wife—Detinue. Edwin Conway, James Gordon, and Henry Towles, having been chosen by William Sydnor & Robert Chinn, next friends to Saml. B. Stott & William Stott, orphans of Stephen Stott decd. and William Brent who intermarried with the widow of Stephen Stott decd. to determine a suit relative to the title of slaves Sarah, Adam, and Eve, were of opinion that sd slaves belonged to the estate of Stephen Stott decd.

Court, 12 March 1782, for ascertaining taxes and duties and for establishing a permanent revenue, present justices James Ball, Edwin Conway, John Taylor, James Gordon, Henry Towles, James Ball Jur., Henry Lawson, John Selden, and James W. Ball.

--Henry Towles, James Ball, and Henry Lawson Gent appointed Commissioners for Ascertaining Value of all Lands in the county, and John Taylor and Edwin Conway Gent are appointed to ascertain value of sd Commissioner's lands.

--John Taylor and John Selden Gent appointed Commissioners of the Specific Tax.

[Index 283] Lancaster OB 16:91a, March Court 1782

James Ball Jur. Gent appointed to receive list of tithables for Rappahannock Hundred; John Selden Gent appointed to received in Corotomon Hundred; James W. Ball in Forest Hundred; John Berryman Gent in Fleets Island Hundred, William Yerby Gent in Fleets Bay Hundred; Edwin Conway Gent in Curreso Hundred.

--Rawleigh Tapscott who acted as Deputy Commissioner under appointment of John Brown, Commissioner to receive a wagon and horses pursuant to an act of Assembly for supplying the army, having been accused of a breach of duty, produced a letter from Nat. Nason Quarter Master, which was recorded [the letter is given on page 91b]

[Index 284] Lancaster OB 16:92a, March 1782

Court, 21 March 1782, present justices James Ball, James Gordon, Henry Towles, Henry Lawson, James W. Ball.

--Inventory of estate of Charles Bell Gent decd. returned.

--Bill of sale from William Griggs to Jesse Wilder proved.

--Report of road petitioned for by John Degge was returned.

--Mary Doggett widow of Coleman Doggett decd. entered her dissent to her husband's will, ordered that James Gordon Gent, John Miller, John Yerby, James Pinckard allot her dower and divide estate.

--Molly Doggett orphan of Coleman Doggett decd. chose Thaddeus McCarter her guardian.

--Articles of agreement between Fortunatus Sydnor decd and William Brown was further proved by Benjamin George.

--Mary Doggett widow of Coleman Doggett decd appointed guardian to Dennis and Priscilla Doggett orphans of sd decd.

--Ezekiel Hudnall Plt vs Lott Palmer Deft—Debt.

[Index 285] Lancaster OB 16:92b, March Court 1782

Will of William Griggs decd further proved by Nicholas Currell Jur.

--The executors of William Griggs decd refusing to qualify, administration was granted to James Connolly, and Edwin Conway Gent, Bailie George, Lawson Hathaway, and John Parrott appointed appraisers.
--Administration on estate of John Stonum decd. granted to Thomas Stott, and James Newby, Rawleigh Tapscott, William Carpenter, and Richard Stott appointed appraisers.
--Division and plat of land of Josiah Carter decd. was returned.
--On motion of Thomas Hammonds, ordered James Tapscott Gent, Benjamin George, John Degge, and Merideth Mahanes possess sd Thomas with the estate of his son Charles Hammonds which is in hands of the executors of Edney Tapscott decd.
--On motion of George Edwards by William Brown attorney, ordered that John Carter, Thomas Carter, Stephen Lock, and James Simmons view a road petitioned for.
--James Wallace made oath that he attended seven days as witness for the Commonwealth vs Elijah Percifull, ordered sd Wallace be paid for his attendance.
--Joshua Palmer made oath that he attended five days as witness for the Commonwealth against Elijah Percifull, ordered he be paid for his attendance.

[Index 286] Lancaster OB 16:93a, March Court 1782
Inventory of estate of Joseph Sullivent decd was returned.
--William Doggett orphan of George Doggett decd chose Charles Lee his guardian.
--Thomas Doggett orphan of George Doggett decd chose James Pollard his guardian.

Court, 22 March 1782, present justices James Ball, Edwin Conway, James Gordon, Henry Towles, John Selden, James W. Ball, and James Ewill.
--Inventory, division, and account of estate of Thomas Brent decd. was returned.
--Upon complaint of William Brown Gent against Jedithen Brent for sureties of the peace, court ordered Brent post bond, with John Goodridge, Thomas Hubbard, and Thomas Pollard his securities.

[Index 287] Lancaster OB 16:93b, March Court 1782
Indenture of mortgage from Jedithen Brent to Thomas Griggs was proved.
--Indenture of bargain and sale from Thomas Griggs to Jedithen Brent was proved by Thomas Pollard and John Bean.
--Upon complaint of Elijah Weaver against Jesse Waddy for taking off and carrying away his son Spencer, ordered sd Waddy appear at next court.
--Upon complaint of James Hill, ordered Elizabeth Hill administratrix of James Hill decd be summoned to show why the guardianship account of sd Hill has not been settled.

Court, 22 April 1782, for trial of George a negro man slave belonging to Joseph Ball Downman Esq, charged with felony, present justices James Ball, Edwin Conway, James Gordon, Henry Towles, James W. Ball, John Selden, and James Ewell, he was found not guilty, but that he received 39 lashes.

[Index 288] Lancaster OB 16:94a, April Court 1782
Court, 18 April 1782, present justices James Ball, James Gordon, Henry Towles, William Yerby, James Ball Jur., Henry Lawson, and James W. Ball.
--Apprasement and division of estate of Coleman Doggett decd was returned.
--On motion of Sarah James, ordered her negro woman Cloe be exempted from taxes during the inability of sd negro.
--Lewis Stephens of Frederick County appointed joint guardian with James Gordon Gent to Lewis & Milly Henning orphans of Robt. Henning decd.
--Deed from Henry Tapscott and wife to Thomas Haydon was proved.
--Deed from Edward Carter and wife to James Gordon Gent was acknowledged.
--Inventory and division of estate of Samuel Brumley decd. was returned.
--John Purcell orphan of Thomas Purcell decd was, with assent of sd orphan, bound to George Standard for four years and eight months, to learn the trade of a Carpenter and House Joiner.

--Benjamin Cundiff Plt vs Moses Sebree Deft—Attachment.

[Index 289] Lancaster OB 16:94b, April Court 1782
Deed from Thomas Griggs to Jedithen Brent proved by witness Fanny Hill.
--Ezekiel Hudnall executor &c Plt vs George Phillips Deft—Debt.
--Inventory and division of estate of John Boyd decd was returned.
--On motion of Thomas George, an infirm person, ordered he be exempted from taxes.
--James Tapscott, Robert Clark Jacob, and Matthew Myars were sworn as justices.
--James Gordon took the oath as Colonel, James Ball Jr. as Lieut Colonel, and Henry Towles as Major in the militia.
--Division and allotment of dower of estate of Thomas Edwards decd was returned.
--Will of John Pearson decd was proved by Isaac Degge, who also refused to qualify as executor.
--Report about a mill petitioned for by Thomas Pollard was returned.
--The summons of Elijah Weaver against Jesse Waddy was dismissed.
--On motion of Betty Robinson by her brother Jesse Robinson, ordered negro woman named Cumbo be exempted from taxes.
--On motion of Jonathan Pullen, ordered James Pinckard, William Edwards, John Miller, and James Carter view road petitioned for by sd Pullen.

[Index 290] Lancaster OB 16:95a, April Court 1782
Court, 19 April 1782, present justices James Ball, James Bordon, Henry Towles, James Ball Jur., John Berryman, Henry Lawson, Robert C. Jacob, Matt. Myars.
--On motion of John Roberts ordered that Elmoure Doggett be summoned to answer sd Roberts' complaint.
--Bailie George took oath as First Lieutenant, William Kirk as Second Lieut, and John Flowers as Ensign in the 3rd company of militia.
--William Yerby Gent appointed to ascertain value of the Commissioners lands according to act of Assembly in case of absence or inability of either of the former Gent appointed for the purpose.
John Selden and Matthew Myars Gent appointed to try the weights at Davis's and James Ball and James Ball Jur Gent at Deep Creek Warehouse.
--A bond from Thomas Lawson Sheriff, for collection of taxes, was ordered to be lodged.

The court then proceeded to receive the different certificates and accounts for claims against the public agreeable to act of Assembly for adjusting claims for property impress'd or taken for publick service, to wit.

[Index 291] Lancaster OB 16:95b, April Court 1782
[the sums due to the claimants for the following public claims are omitted here]
--To John Chinn Gent for bay horse impressed by Nicholas Currell by order of Col William Griffin in Oct 1781; also for beef impressed by Rawh. Tapscott D.C. for John Brown in May 1781 and Oct 1781; also for 20 gallons brandy impressed by Saml. Guthrie by order of Col John Taylor in Sept 1781; also for bacon.
--To Rev Mr David Currie for a grey horse impressed by Nicholas Currell by order of Col William Griffin in Sept 1781; also for beef impressed by Rawh. Tapscott D.C. for John Brown in Oct 1781.
--To John Hill Carter Esq for two horses impressed by Nicholas Currell by order of Col William Griffin in Sept 1781; also for beef impressed by Rawh. Tapscott Dep Commissioner for John Brown in July 1781; also for mutton and lamb.
--To Col John Taylor for a horse impressed by Nicholas Currell by order of Col William Griffin in Sept 1781.
--To Robert Clark Jacob for horse impressed by Nicholas Currell by order of Col William Griffin in Oct 1781; also for beef impressed by Tim. Conner in June 1781; also for bacon in April 1781; also for ferriages for the militia on their march to Gloster in 1781.
--To John Wormeley for 1 horse impressed by George Guthrie in Aug 1781; also for beef impressed by Rawh. Tapscott D. Com. For John Brown in Oct 1781.
--To Elias Edmonds for a mare impressed by Nicholas Currell by order of Col William Griffin in Sept 1781; also for beef impressed by Rawh. Tapscott D. Com for John Brown in Oct 1781.

--To Capt James Ewell for gun detained by Gen Weedon at siege of York; also for beef impressed by Rawh. Tapscott D. Com. In Oct 1781; also for boat hire in carrying troops over Rappahk. River in March 1781; also for mutton and lamb in May & Sept 1781.
--To Nicholas George Commissary to the different guards in Lancaster Co, for beef impressed by Rawh. Tapscott D. Com. In June 1781; also for brandy in Oct 1780.

[Index 292] Lancaster OB 16:96a, April Court 1782

[the sums due to the claimants for the following public claims are omitted here]
To Jesse George D. Com. In Lancaster Co for beef in 1781
--To Capt Robert Chinn for gun lost in duty at siege of York in 1781; also for beef impressed by Rawh. Tapscott D. Com. In June 1781 and July 1781.
--To Job Carter, Gaoler, for imprisoning deserters and soldiers in 1781; also for keeping the county magazine.
--To estate of Rawh. Downman Es decd. for beef impressed by Rawh. Tapscott D. Com. June and Oct 1781; also for brandy impressed by Sam. Guthrie by order Col Taylor Sept 1781.
--To John Clayton for beef impressed by Rawh. Tapscott D.C. in June 1781; to Thomas Stott for same in May 1781; to John Miller for same in Oct 1781; to George Campbell for same in June 1781; to Richd. Goodridge for same in June 1781; to Col Edwin Conway for same in June and May 1781, and for necessaries furnished in 1780 & 1781.
--To Henry Lawson for beef impressed by Rawh. Tapscott D.C. in July 1781; to Mary Lawson for same in Oct 1781, and for brandy in Oct 1780.
--To Henry Currell for beef impressed by Rawh. Tapscott D.C. in Oct 1781; also for lamp impressed by Saml. Eddings Capt Art in Aug 1781.
--William Brent for beef impressed by Rawh. Tapscott D.C. in July 1781; also for use of his cart Oct 1780.
--James Wallace for beef impressed by Rawh. Tapscott D.C. in Oct 1781; Thomas Flint for same in July 1781; Thomas Lawson for same in July 1781, and for necessaries in Feb and March 1781.
--To Col John Fleet for beef impressed by Rawh. Tapscott D.C. in Aug 1781; also for necessaries Nov 1780.
--To Elizabeth Saunders for beef impressed by Rawh. Tapscott D.C. in Oct 1781; to Thomas Hubbard for the same in Oct 1781; to James Tapscott for the same in July 1781, and for bacon in Aug 1781.
--To Mungo Harvey for beef impressed by Rawh. Tapscott D.C. in July 1781.

[Index 293] Lancaster OB 16:96b, April Court 1782

[the sums due to the claimants for the following public claims are omitted here]
Nicholas Currell for beef impressed by Rawh. Tapscott D.C. in Oct 1780; also for necessaries in June & Aug 1781.
--To estate of Fortunatus Sydnor decd for beef impressed by Rawh. Tapscott in June 1781; to William Griggs for the same in Oct 1781, also for sundries etc for Sam. Eddings Capt Art in Aug 1781.
--To Joseph Shearman for beef impressed by Rawh. Tapscott D.C. in June 1781; to Elizabeth Mctyre for same in June 1781; to James Newby for same in Aug 1781.
--To John Clutton for beef taken by Thos. Walker for Northumberland militia in June 1781.
--To Robert Gilmoure for beef impressed by Richd. Easton in Nov 1781; also for bacon for use of the minute service under Col Peter P Thornton in July 1776; also for horse impressed by Chas. Lee by order of his Excellency Thos. Nelson in Oct 1781; also for beef impressed by Rawh. Tapscott D. Com. In Oct 1781.
--To Gorwin Lowry for ferriages over Corotoman River in 1781.
--To Elmoure Doggett for beef impressed by Rawh. Tapscott D.C. in June 1781; also for the same in July 1781; to James Wallace for the same in Oct 1781.
--To Mrs. Mary Tapscott for pasturage for beef cattle by R. Tapscott in June 1781; also for same in Oct 1781.
--To Edney Tapscott for beef impressed by R. Tapscott D. Com. In June 1781; to Matthew Myars for same in June 1781, also for mutton in July 1781.
--To Thomas Myars for mutton in July 1781; also for bacon and lamb in June 1781.
--To James Kirk's estate for beef impressed by Rawh. Tapscott D.C. in Oct 1781; to Edward Carter for some in Oct 1781, and for brandy impressed by P. Tillman by order Col John Taylor in Sept 1781.
--To William Brown for beef impressed by R. Tapscott D.C. in Oct 1781; to Joseph Norris for same in May 1781; to William Yopp for same in July 1781; to Sarah Bond for same in Oct 1781; to Jonathan Pullen for same in July 1781; to Ann Shearman for same in June 1781, and for peas in March 1781.

--To William Carpenter for beef impressed by R. Tapscott D.C. in June 1781; to Joshua Hubbard for same in July 1781.

[Index 294] Lancaster OB 16:97a, April Court 1782
[the sums due to the claimants for the following public claims are omitted here]
To Col James Gordon for beef impressed by Rawh. Tapscott D. Com. In Oct 1781; to Nathaniel Gordon for same in Oct 1781; to George Norris for same in Oct 1781; to Ann Stephens for same in Oct 1781; to estate of Charles Bell decd. for same in Oct 1781; to William Chilton for same in July 1781; to Coleman Doggett for same in Oct 1781; to William Schofield for same in Oct 1781, also for brandy in Oct 1781.
--To John Carter for beef impressed by R. Tapscott D. Com.
--To John Carter for beef impressed by R. Tapscott D. Com. in Oct 1781; also for bacon in Oct 1780.
--To Judith Yerby for beef impressed by R. Tapscott D. Com. in Oct 1781; to Stephen Chilton for same in Oct 1781; to John Davis for same; to John Cundiff for same; to John Bean for same; to William Edwards for same; to Joseph Dobbs for same; to Elizabeth Hill for same; to Harry Carter for same; to Abner Palmer for same; to Francis Robb for same; to Jedithun Pinckard for same; to Ellen Lizenby for same; to William Stott for same in May 1781, also for bacon.
--To William Sydnor for beef impressed by R. Tapscott D.C. in June 1781, also for mutton in July 1781, also for brandy impressed by Henry Pointer.
--To Col John Taylor for brandy in Sept 1781.
--To Moore Fauntleroy for beef impressed by R. Tapscott D.C. in June and July 1781; to Jonathan Wilder for same in July 1781; to William Warren for same in June and July 1781; to William Weblin for same in Oct 1781; to Mrs. Alice Smith for same in July 1781.

[Index 295] Lancaster OB 16:97b, April Court 1782
[the sums due to the claimants for the following public claims are omitted here]
To Mrs. Agatha Ball for beef impressed by Rawh. Tapscott D. Com. in Oct 1781; also for corn furnished troops on their march to York in Sept 1781.
--To Charles Rogers for beef impressed by R. Tapscott D.C. in Oct and June 1781, also for beef & mutton in Feb 1781.
--To James Simmonds for beef impressed by R. Tapscott D.C. in July 1781; to Thomas Robb for same in Dec 1781; to Benjamin George for same in July 1781; to Mary Haydon for same in July 1781; to William Martin for same in June 1781; to Thomas Carter for same in June 1781, and for necessaries in Nov 1780.
--To James Pinckard for beef impressed by R. Tapscott D.C. in Oct 1781; to William Chowning for same in July 1781, also for brandy in Oct 1780.
--To John Harris for beef impressed by R. Tapscott D.C. in Oct 1781; to John Chowning for same in July 1781, and for ferriages on Rappahannock in Sept and Oct 1781.
--To Henry Hinton for beef impressed by R. Tapscott, D.C. in Oct 1781; to James Brent for same, and for necessaries furnished the guards in1781.
--To Thomas Hunton for beef impressed by R. Tapscott, D.C. in June 1781, and for necessaries furnished the guards in June and July 1781.
--To William Dunaway for beef impressed by R. Tapscott, D.C. in June 1781; to John Longwith for same.
--To John Roberts for 301 pounds salted beef furnished the guards in March 1781, and for 314 pounds in Feb 1781.
--To William Merrideth for stalling two beaves in July 1781, and for mutton furnished the guards in Aug.
--To Samuel Yopp for 30 gallons brandy impressed by Paul Tilman by order of Col John Taylor in Sept 1781.
--To William Doggett for 206 pounds bacon furnished the guards in June 1781.
--To James Flemming for pork for the guards in July 1781.

[Index 296] Lancaster OB 16:98a, April Court 1782
--To Jemima Blakemore for necessaries furnished the guards in June 1781.
--To Elijah Percifull for certain services by order of the commanding officer in 1781.
--To William Boatman for necessaries furnished the guards in Nov 1780.

--To Henry Towles for 24 gallons brandy impressed by Saml. Guthrie by order Col Jno Taylor Sept 1781, and for 20 barrels corn in Oct 1780, and for sundries furnished the guards in June 1781.
--To Andrew Robertson for 27 gallons brandy in Oct 1780.
--To Thomas Lee for 162 gallons rum and brandy.
--To John Tarpley a pilot 7 days by Richd. Taylor in Oct 1780.
--To John Eustace for sundires furnished the guards in 1780.
--To Judith Brent for necessaries furnished the guards in July 1780, and bor beef impressed by Rawh. Tapscott, D. Com.
--To Col James Ball for 86 pounds bacon for use of the army in June 1781.
--To William Ball for beef impressed by R. Tapscott, D.C. in Oct.
--To Thads. McCarty for beef impressed by R. Tapscott, and for necessaries furnished the guards in Aug 1780.
--To Mrs Margaret Ball for beef impressed by R. Tapscott, D. Com. in July 1781.
--To Edwd. Blakemore for removing tobacco from the warehouse in 1781.
--To Jesse Chilton for beef impressed by R. Tapscott, D. Com. in Oct 1781.

Court, 16 May 1782, present justices James Ball, Henry Towles, William Yerby, John Berryman, Henry Lawson, and Matt. Myers.
--On motion of Henry Lawson Gent, ordered his negro Will be struck off the Commissioners List of taxes.
--On motion of Ann Stephens, ordered her negro Bob be struck off the list of taxes.
--On motion of James Ball Gent, ordered his negro Moses be struck off the list of taxes.

[Index 297] Lancaster OB 16:98b, May Court 1782

On motion of Matthew Myars Gent, ordered his negro Dick be struck off the list of taxes.
--On motion of Richard Mitchell, ordered his negro Dinah be struck off the list of taxes.
--Grand jury was sworn, William Warren foreman, and William Edwards, William Kirk, John Miller, John James, John Bean, James Pinckard, William Martin, John Carter, William Doggett, William Mason, Thomas Stott, Ozwald Newby, John Clutton, Rawh. Stott, Rawleigh Davenport, Joseph Stephens, John Goodridge, Jesse Robinson, Richd. Goodridge, Richd. Mitchell, and Jesse Robinson Jur.
--Commonwealth vs Thomas and Vincent Brent, Defts—Indictment.
--On motion of Jedithon Pinckard, ordered his negro George be struck off the list of taxes.
--On motion of John Degge, ordered John Cundiff, William Schofield, George Norris, and Thomas Brent allot to Nancy Carter orphan of Josiah Carter her part of her father's estate, and possess sd Degge her guardian with the same.
--On motion of Isaac Degge, ordered his negroes Lively and Dinah be struck of the list of taxes.
--On motion of Ann Shearman by Henry Lawson Gent her friend, ordered her negro [not named] be struck off the list of taxes
--Account of sale of Joseph Sullivant's estate presented by Vinct. Brent, administrator.

[Index 298] Lancaster OB 16:99a, May Court 1782

Sarah Pearson widow of John Pearson decd. qualified as executrix to her husband's will, and Henry Lawson Gent, William Martin, Harry Currell, and Lawson[?] Hathaway appointed appraisers.
--On complaint of William Angell against Abner Palmer for ill treatment of his sister Sarah Angell, court found that she was not ill treated and ordered her to return to her servitude.
--Will of John Mason decd presented by his widow Peggy Mason, who was granted probate thereon; Johnson Riveer, Jesse Robinson Jur., Joseph Norris, and William Riveer appointed appraisers.
--Certified that H. Towles and H. Lawson Gent, Commissioners of the Grain Tax in 1781, are allowed 3 pounds for their services.
--Viewer's report about road petitioned for by Jonathin Pullen, dismissed.
--On motion of James Ball Gent, ordered the road from Morattico Mill to Deep Bottom be turned by the mill of the sd Ball.

--Henry Lawson Gent appointed to take list of tithables below Mrs. Eustace's mill, William Yerby between sd mill and Carter's great mill, Robert C. Jacobs between Carter's mill and Jacob's mill, James Tapscott in Wiccomoco Parish, John Selden above Jacob's mill, James Ewell on Rappahannock River, and Matthew Myars Gent in Corotoman.

--John Roberts's motion to have a road through the land of George Yerby, rejected.

--John Steptoe, orphan of William Steptoe decd. chose Willm. Gibson as his guardian.

[Index 299] Lancaster OB 16:99b, May Court 1782
Inventory of estate of Bushrod Riveer decd. returned.

--Ann Chinn vs George Glascock Jur.—Petition.

--John Hazard vs George Davis—Assault & battery.

--Thomas Pollard vs William Schofield Jur.—Case.

--John Wormeley vs Jesse Harrison—Case.

--William Edwards vs Jedithen Pinckard—Detinue.

--Commonwealth vs Vincent Brent &c—Sci. fa.

--Simon Laughlin vs Elias Edmonds guardian to Lucy Denny—Case.

[Index 300] Lancaster OB 16:100a, May Court 1782
Ezekiel Hudnall vs James Ewell—Case.

--William Davenport vs William Parrott—Case.

--William Brown vs Jedithen Brent—Case.

--Maurice Wheeler vs James Connolly administrator of William Griggs decd.—Case.

--John Boswell vs James Connolly administrator of William Griggs decd.—Case.

--James Newby assignee of Burges Ball assignee of Peter Conway vs James Connolly administrator of William Griggs decd.—Debt.

--Jedithen Brent vs William Brown—Slander.

[Index 301] Lancaster OB 16:100b, May Court 1782
John Cundiff vs Benjamin Cundiff—Chancery.

--Thomas Bell vs Robert Jones—Slander.

--John James vs Peter Riveer administrator of Bushrod Riveer decd.—Chancery.

--Charles Bean vs John Hutchinson—Slander.

--Thomas Jones executor of William Tait decd. vs William Kent for Ann Taylor executrix of Isaac Taylor decd.—Sci. fa.

--Commonwealth vs Thomas & Vincent Brent—Indictment. A jury came, John Sullivant etc.

[Index 302] Lancaster OB 16:101a, May Court 1782
Court, 17 May 1782, present justices James Ball, Henry Towles, James Ball Jur., James W. Ball, James Tapscott, and Matt. Myars.

--Commonwealth vs Thos. & Vincent Brent—Indictment. A jury was sworn, to wit. John Sullivant, Joseph Kern, Edwd. Blakemore, William Chilton, John Roberts, George Carter, Rawh. Tapscott, William Carpenter, Lot Palmer, Newton Brent, William Mitchell, and Jedithen Moore, not guilty verdict.

--William Griggs vs Bridgar Haynie &c—Debt.

--Thomas Brent vs William Griggs—Chancery. Abates by death of the parties.

--Ordered Rawleigh Hazard be paid for his attendance at trial of Thomas & Vincent Brent, and for traveling nine miles from and to his residence.

--On complaint of Jemima Carter wife of Aaron Carter, ordered Rawleigh Tapscott retain the hire of a negro woman the property of sd Aaron Carter.

--James Ball Gent, Commissioner to ascertain value of lands, ordered he be for his services.

[Index 303] Lancaster OB 16:101b, May Court 1782
Henry Towles Gent, Commissioner for ascertaining value of lands, allowed for his services.

--Henry Lawson Gent, Commissioner for ascertaining value of lands, allowed for his services.

Court, 20 June 1782, present justices James Ball, John Fleet, Henry Towles, James Ball Jur., James Tapscott, and Matt. Myars.
--John Davis, Weaver, presented by grand jury for getting drunk, fined. .
--Thomas Cottrell, presented by grand jury for swearing two oaths, fined.
--Thomas Pinckard Jur., presented by grand jury for swearing two oaths, fined.
--Grand jury vs Job Carter, dismissed.
--Grand jury vs Newton Brent, dismissed.
--Grand jury vs Robert C. Jacob, dismissed.
--Grand jury vs Eleazer Robertson, dismissed, Deft dead.

[Index 304] Lancaster OB 16:102a, June Court 1782
John Selden Gent, presented by grand jury for swearing two oaths, fined.
--John Mctyre, presented by grand jury for getting drunk, fined.
--Mary Lewis, presented by grand jury for having a bastard child, fined.
--Justices William Yerby, Henry Lawson, and John Selden Gent present.
--Will of William Steptoe decd. proved by witness Will. Brown.
--Deed of trust from Will. Steptoe decd. to Edwin Conway Gent proved by witness Will. Brown.
--Sarah Pearson executrix of John Pearson decd. vs Jonathen Pearson—Chancery.
--William Sullivant vs James Connolly administrator—Petition.
--John Goodridge vs George Tillery—Petition.
--Rawleigh Tapscott granted administration on estate of Martha Carter decd.; William Sydnor, James Newby, Thomas Stott, and John Newby appointed appraisers.
--Eleazer Robinson being dead and buried, ordered "he be not only struck off the Commissioners list of taxes but erased out of the memory of man as having been a poor inoffensive being and a useless member of society, he wou'd fall to sleep while on duty of a jury.

[Index 305] Lancaster OB 16:102b, June Court 1782
Elizabeth Mctyre vs William Lewis—Case. A jury came, to wit. Joseph Stephens &c.
--Inventory of estate of John Stonum decd. returned.
--John Boyd orphan of John Boyd decd. bound to Rev Mr John Leland until age 21, to learn trade of a Shoemaker.
--Matthias Maughon vs John Maughon—Attachment.
--Ordered Elizabeth Mctyre pay Ozwald Newby for his
attendance as witness for her against William Lewis.
--Ordered Elizabeth Mctyre pay Samuel Dunaway for his attendance as witness for her against William Lewis.
--Ordered Elizabeth Mctyre pay William Montague for his attendance as witness for her against William Lewis.
--James Hill vs Elizabeth Hill administratrix &c—Summons. Ordered John Yerby, Elias Edmonds, and James Pinckard settle the guardianship accounts of James Hill decds with the Plt, and make report.

[Index 306] Lancaster OB 16:103a, June Court 1782
John James vs Peter Riveer administrator of Bushrod Riveer decd—Chancery. Ordered the Plt recover negros Charles and Jenny (and her increase).
--On motion of Thomas Hubbard, ordered John Yerby, Elias Edmonds, James Pinckard, and William Edwards settle accounts of Thomas Brent decd as executor of George Brent decd. with William Brent the administrator of sd Thomas Brent decd.

Court, 21 June 1782, present justices John Taylor, Henry Towles, John Selden, James Tapscott, and Robert C. Jacob.
--Ordered that dedimus issue to take deposition of Thomas Pollard in suit Charles Bean vs John Hutchinson.
--John Brenon vs John Reid.

--It appearing that John Taylor Gent late Sheriff had credited sundry persons with certificates for brandy for use of the army, and that he had not been allowed any settlement with the Auditors of Public Accounts, the claims were allowed as just claims, as follows:

[Index 307] Lancaster OB 16:103b, June Court 1782
[continued from above, these persons were issued certificates for brandy in Oct 1780, the amount of brandy and sums are omitted here] William Carpenter, William Stott, Spencer Brown, Joseph Wilkerson, Jesse Robinson, Bushrod Riveer, John Riveer, Thomas Dunaway, Thomas Pitman, Rev John Leland, Henry Tapscott's estate, Richd. Mitchell, Richd. Ball, George Cammell, Richd. Goodridge, Richd. Cundiff, John Boyd, James Riveer, William Riveer, Robert Chinn, John Clutton, Ozwald Newby, Jesse Robinson Jur., William Montague, Stephen Lock, Col Edwin Conway, James Newby, James Norris, Peter Conway, Col James Ball,

[Index 308] Lancaster OB 16:104a, June Court 1782
[continued from above, these persons were issued certificates for brandy in Oct 1780, the amount of brandy and sums are omitted here] Col James Gordon, Thomas Curtis, Maurice Wheeler, Newton Brent, Elizabeth James, Bailie George, Thomas Hunton, Betty Saunders, John Merideth, Joseph Hubbard, William Stephens, James Pollard, John Berryman, John Parrott, Henry Lawson, Mary Lawson, John Davis, Henry Currell, Isaac Currell, Thomas Lawson, William Mitchell, Charles Lee, Eleazer Robinson, Isaac Degge, John McLain[?], Nicholas Currell, Elizabeth Mctyre, James Currell Jur. , Rawh. Downman's estate, James Currell, John Chinn, Thomas Pinckard, Judith Brent, William Griggs, John & Thos. Carter, Martin George, Mrs. Alice Smith, William Mason, Charles Bell, Eliza. James Jur., James Brent, John Longwith, George Norris, Judith Yerby, William Gibson, John Maughon, Sarah James,

[Index 309] Lancaster OB 16:104b, June Court 1782
[continued from above, these persons were issued certificates for brandy in Oct 1780, the amount of brandy and sums are omitted here] James Simmonds, John Clayton, Harry Hinton, John James, Fortunatus Sydnor, Joseph Dobbs, James Wallace, Isaac Currell, Col John Taylor, William Schofield, George Carter, William Doggett, Thomas Brent, William Brown, William Kirk, William Lawson, Elijah Percifull, John Flowers, Charles Williams, Elijah Robinson, Coleman Doggett, Edny Tapscott, John Miller, Betty Hill, Lawson Hathaway, Thomas Hathaway, William George, Jesse George, Job Carter, Abner Palmer, Mary & Richd. Selden, John Selden, Rodham Lunceford, Willoughby Rout, John Sebrie, Robert Belvaird, Presly Neale, William Bean, Peter Riveer, John Payne, William Warren, Joseph Stephens, Eliza. Biscoe, John Bailey, Nicholas George, James Ewell, Edward Carter, William Sydnor, James Pullen, Doctr. Andrew Robertson, Thomas Flint, Johnson Riveer, Joseph Norris, John Norris, Peter Conway, John Goodridge,

[Index 310] Lancaster OB 16:105a, June Court 1782
[continued from above, these persons were issued certificates for brandy in Oct 1780, the amount of brandy and sums are omitted here]

ONLY HALF OF THIS PAGE WAS FILMED. THE IMAGE IS CUT OFF.

[Index 311] Lancaster OB 16:105b, July Court 1782
Court of Enquiry, 10 July 1782 for examination of Maurice Wheeler on suspicion of murdering Bailie George, present justices James Ball, Edwin Conway, James Gordon, Henry Towles, James Ball Jur., Henry Lawson, John Selden, James W. Ball, James Tapscott, Robt. C. Jacob, and Matt. Myars. He was found guilty and the case was referred to the General Court in Richmond. David Garland, John Edwards, Elizabeth Garland, Margaret Hill, Cloe Fairy, Thomas Carter, Michel [thus] Wilder, George Doggett, Job Carter, Martha Cottrell, and Judith George were witnesses.

[Index 312] Lancaster OB 16:106a, July Court 1782
Court, 10 July 1782, present justices James Ball, Henry Towles, William Yerby, James Ball Jur., and John Selden.

--Will of Robert Gilmour decd. presented by William Ball, John Dean and Mungo Harvey, executors therein named, and proved by Judith Galloway, and John Richardson; James Ball Jur., John Tarpley, William Sydnor, and James W. Ball Gent were appointed appraisers.
--Will of William Steptoe decd. further proved by oaths of witnesses Elmour Doggett and John Masden.
--Deed of gift from William Steptoe to Edwin Conway in trust for his wife Joannah was further proved by Elmour Doggett and John Masden.
--Lawson Wale orphan of George Wale decd. chose James Brent his guardian, and John Berryman, William Yerby Gent, Joseph Shearman, and William Gibson ordered to settle guardian account of sd orphan with Zachariah Barr his former guardian.
William Wiblin vs Tarpley Thomas—Petition.
--Thomas Ellett vs Mungo Harvey—Petition.

[Index 313] Lancaster OB 16:106b, July Court 1782
Hugh Kelly Plt vs Jonathan Pearson—Debt.
--Ordered Mungo Harvey pay Willoughby Rout for attendance as witness in his suit vs Thos. Elliott.
Present Edwin Conway, James Gordon, Henry Lawson, Jas. Tapscott, & Matt. Myars, justices.
--James Newby assignee of Burges Ball vs James Connolly administrator of Wm. Griggs decd.—Debt.
--On motion of Richard Selden for leave to build a water grist mill between his land and Everitt's land, ordered the Sheriff summon a jury to view said land.

[Index 314] Lancaster OB 16:107a, July Court 1782
Court 17 July 1782, present justices James Ball, Edwin Conway, James Gordon, Henry Towles, William Yerby, James Ball Jur., James W. Ball, and Matt. Myars.
--Inventory of estate of Thomas Jarrott decd. returned.
--Elisha Hall vs Elias Edmonds—Case.
--Spencer George vs John Mctyre—Trespass, assault, battery.
--John Dye vs William Chilton Jur.—Case. A jury came, to wit., Elias Edmonds &c.
--John Dye vs Wm. Chilton Jur. & John Hutchinson—A jury came, to wit., Elias Edmonds &c.

[Index 315] Lancaster OB 16:107b, July Court 1782
James Gordon Jur. vs George Carter—Case.
--John Ramey vs Monc. Collins—Case.
--On complaint of Peter Haw, infirm person, ordered the Collector remit him his bodily tax, and that he be exempted in future.
--John Carter vs Thomas Pollard &c—Chancery.
--John Garlington vs George Norris—Slander.
--Thomas Griggs vs Anthony Kirk &c—Chancery.
--Margaret Davis vs Edward Carter—Case.

[Index 316] Lancaster OB 16:108a, July Court 1782
Ordered John Dye pay Maryan Dye for her attendance as witness in his suit vs William Chilton.
--William Boatman vs Thomas Hubbard.
--Jury's report about a mill petitioned for by William Taylor is recorded.
--Richard Ball vs George Bean—Debt.
--On complaint of William Brown by Henry Towles Gent, ordered dedimus issue to take depositions of Lettice and Catherine Ball for the Complainant.

[Index 317] Lancaster OB 16:108b, Aug Court 1782
Court 15 Aug 1782, present justices James Ball, Edwin Conway, James Ball Jur., James W. Ball, and James Tapscott.
--Account of the profits of estate of King's orphans presented by Isaac Degge their guardian.
--Account of the profits of estate of Sarah Simmonds presented by Henry Lawson Gent her guardian.

--Account of the profits of estate of Newman Chilton presented by James Newby his guardian.
--Account of the profits of estate of Hill's orphans presented by James Brent their guardian.
--Account of the profits of estate of Kirk's orphans presented by Edward Carter their guardian.
Present justices James Gordon, Henry Towles, Henry Lawson, John Selden, Robt. C. Jacob, and Matt. Myars.
--On motion of Thomas Gaskins Gent, ordered Thomas Pinckard produce at next court the will of Thomas Pinckard Gent decd and that the witnesses be summoned.
--William Sullivant vs James Connolly administrator &c---Petition.
--William Lewis vs Johnson Riveer administrator &c---Case. Dismissed agreeable to instructions by Ozwald Newby.

[Index 318] Lancaster OB 16:109a, Aug Court 1782

Robert Coleman assignee of Thomas Rountree vs George Robertson & Sam. Denny---Sci. fa.
--Charles Webb assignee &c vs George Phillips & ___ Waddy---Debt. William Brown Gent special bail for Deft.
--John McAdam vs George Bean---Case.
--George Bean vs John McAdam---Case. A jury came, to wit., Thomas Flint &c.

[Index 319] Lancaster OB 16:109b, Aug Court 1782

Henry Tapscott vs Rawleigh Stott---Case. A jury came, to wit., John Parrot &c.
--Inventory of estate of John Mason decd. returned.
--William Barber Jur. vs Joseph Hubbard---Case. James Gordon Gent was appointed referee in place of Richard Mitchell Gent decd.
--Ordered Rawleigh Stott pay LeRoy Stott for his attendance as witness in his suit vs Henry Tapscott.
--Ordered Spencer George pay Thomas Garner for his attendance as witness in his suit vs John Mctyre.
--Complaint of Henry Towles Gent against William Brown Gent, dismissed.
--On motion of Thomas Ellett, ordered John Degge, Benja. George and One. Henry settle the account of John Doggett decd on the estate of Charles Lee decd.
--Jury's report about a mill petitioned for by Richard Selden was returned, & Rawh. Tapscott to attend as Surveyor.

[Index 320] Lancaster OB 16:110a, Aug Court 1782

Administration on estate of Thomas Smither decd. granted to Edwin and Daniel Kent; Benjamin George, John Clayton, William Doggett, and William Doggett Jur. appointed appraisers.
--Ordered John McAdam pay Thomas Yerby for his attendance as witness in his suit vs George Bean.
--Ordered John McAdam pay William Taylor Gent for his attendance as witness in his suit vs George Bean.
--Ordered John McAdam pay William Montague for his attendance as witness in his suit vs George Bean.
--Spencer M. Ball vs John Eustace---Trespass.
--Richard Ball vs George Bean---Debt. A jury came, to wit., John Parrott &c.
--John Hazard vs George Davis---Trespass, assault, battery.

[Index 321] Lancaster OB 16:110b, Aug Court 1782

Ordered George Bean pay John Wormeley for his attendance as witness in his suit vs Richard Ball.

Court, 16 Aug 1782, present justices James Ball, Henry Lawson, John Selden, James W. Ball, Robert C. Jacob, Matt. Myars, and James Ball Jur.
--Mary Lawson vs Charles Rogers &c---Chancery.
--Margaret Davis vs Edward Carter---Case. A jury came, to wit., William Martin &c.
--Samuel Yobb vs James Simmonds---Chancery.

[Index 322] Lancaster OB 16:111a, Aug Court 1782

Northumberland Justices vs John Eustace---Debt.
--Elizabeth Yerby's executors vs Thomas Ellett—Case.
--Thomas Pollard vs John Goodridge---Trespass, assault, battery.
--John Heath vs Thomas Crowther---Case.

--Jesse George vs John Thrall---Attachment.
--James Wallace vs Elijah Percifell---Case.
--Jesse George vs John Clayton---Case.
--Richard Ball vs George Bean---Debt.
--Flood's administrators vs Smith's administrators---Case.
--William Dounton vs Rodham Lunceford---Assault & battery.
--Jupiter vs Vulcan---Ejectment.
--John Garlington vs George Norris---Slander.
--William Boatman vs Thomas Hubbard---Case.

[Index 323] Lancaster OB 16:111b, Aug Court 1782
Ordered Richard Ball pay Margarett Alford for her attendance as witness in his suit vs George Bean.
--Ordered Richard Ball pay Franky Robinson for her attendance as witness in his suit vs George Bean.
--George Yerby vs Judith Brent---Case.
--Thomas Pollard vs Rawleigh Shearman---Case.
--Flood's administrators vs Henry Armistead.
--William Norris vs Horton's executors---Case.
--Thomas Pollard vs Bailie George---Slander. Abates by death of Deft.
--Jeduthen James vs James Ewell---Case.
--John Mctyre vs James Pinckard---Attachment.
--John Boswell vs William Griggs---Case. Abates by death of Deft.

[Index 324] Lancaster OB 16:112a, Aug Court 1782
Thomas Hunton vs Benja. Garton Jur.---Case.
--Moses Sutton vs John Webb Jur.---Attachment.
--William Alleson vs Robert Clerk [thus]---Attachment.
--Francis Bond &c vs William Lewis---Detinue.
--Jonathan Pullen vs James Pinckard---Case.
--Spencer Currell vs William Hinton---Assault & battery.
--William Schofield vs Thomas Pollard administrator &c---Sci. facias.

[Index 325 Lancaster OB 16:112b, August Court 1782
Ordered Edward Carter pay Henry Davis for his attendance as witness in his suit vs Margaret Davis.
--Ordered Margaret Davis pay John Wilkerson for his attendance as witness in her suit vs Edward Carter.
--Thomas Pollard vs Bailie George---Case. Abates by death of Deft.

Court, 19 September 1782, present justices James Ball, Henry Towles, James Ball Jur., William Yerby, and Henry Lawson.
--Inventory of Thomas Smither decd. returned.
--Indenture of bargain & sale from James Williams to Richd. Mitchell proved.
--Present James Gordon, Robt. C. Jacob, and Matt. Myers Gent.
--Commonwealth vs Henry Fleet---Recognizance.
--Presly and Sally White orphans of Abraham White decd. chose Presly Saunders their guardian, and sd Saunders is appointed guardian to Fanny White.
--Will of Thomas Pinckard Gent decd. proved by Jane Swan alias Nutt.

[Index 326] Lancaster OB 16:113a, Sept Court 1782
Indenture of bargain & sale from Valentine Bell to Thomas Bell proved.
--James Gordon and John Berryman Gent recommended to Benjamin Harrison Esq Governor as proper persons to execute office of High Sheriff.
--William Blackerby vs Johnson Riveer executors---Case.
--Thomas Mash vs William Dunaway---Assault & battery.

--LeRoy Peachey vs John Selden administrator &c---Petition.
--Surveyor's return of land petitioned for by Richard Selden for building a mill, recorded.
--Spencer Currell vs William Hinton---Assault & battery.
--Robt. Coleman assignee of Thos. Rountree vs George Robertson---Alias sci. facias. Judgment against Deft and Samuel Denny his security.

[Index 327] Lancaster OB 16:113b, Sept Court 1782
Robert Carter Esq vs Presly Cockrell—Case.
--Onesephorus Henry vs Jesse Waddy---Trover. Referees James Ball, John Fleet and Henry Towles Gent.
--Richard Davis vs John Degge---Petition.
--Ordered Richd. Davis pay John Hornsby for his attendance as witness in his suit vs John Degge, and for traveling six miles to and from his residence.
--Ordered Richd. Davis pay Ellis Lunceford for his attendance as witness in his suit vs John Degge, and for traveling nine miles to and from his residence.
--Commonwealth vs Elijah Percifull---Indictment. Dismissed due to the death of Thomas Brent the complainant.
--Good Title vs Thrustout---Ejectment. Judgment against the Deft and Jonathan Pullen the tenant in possession.

[Index 328] Lancaster OB 16:114a, Sept Court 1782
James Moore and comp. vs John Kirk---Debt.
--Thomas Pollard vs John Goodrige &c---Assault & battery. A jury came, to wit., John Parrott &c.
--Settlement of administration account of John Doggett decd. on estate of Charles Lee decd. was recorded.
--John Garlington vs George Norris---Slander.
--Joseph Hubbard vs Vachal Fandrie---Case. Referees John Fleet, William Yerby Gent.
--William Sydnor appointed guardian to John Smith orphan of Burges Smith Gent decd.
--On petition of Alice Smith relict of Burges Smith Gent decd., ordered James Ball Gent and Mungo Harvey allot her dower in land of her decd. husband.

[Index 329] Lancaster OB 16:114b, Sept Court 1782
Court, 20 Sept 1782, present justices James Ball, James Gordon, Henry Towles, John Selden, James Tapscott, Robt. C. Jacob.
--William Sydnor recommended to Gov Benjamin Harrison as proper person to execute office of Inspector of Tobacco at D. Creek Warehouse, and Rawleigh Tapscott assistant, Gowen Lowry and Charles Rogers at Davis's, and John Davis assistant.
--Thomas Pollard vs John Goodridge &c—Assault and battery. A jury sworn, to wit., John Parrott &c., and returned verdict against George Goodridge, John Goodridge, Richard Goodridge, LeRoy Pope, Richd. Pitman, and Ambrose Pitman.
--Present justices Edwin Conway and John Taylor Gent.
--Northumberland Justices vs John Eustace---Debt.
--James Wallace vs Elijah Percifull---Case.
--Jesse George vs John Clayton---Case.
--Thomas Pollard vs Rawleigh Shearman---Case.
--William Norris vs Ellenor Horton's executor---Case.
--Jedithen James vs James Ewell---Case.

[Index 330] Lancaster OB 16:115a, Sept Court 1782
Francis Bond &c vs William Lewis---Detinue
--Jonathen Pullen vs James Pinckard---Case.
--William Schofield vs Thomas Pollard---Sci. facias.
--Mary Lawson vs Charles Rogers &c---Chancery.
--Thomas West vs Henry Fleet—Assault and battery.
--Charles Lee executor &c vs Elisha Hall—Case.
--Onesephorous Harvey vs Jesse Waddy---Trover. Referees Jas. Ball, John Fleet, Henry Towles.

--Rawleigh Shearman vs William Griggs---Case. Abates by death of Deft.
--Thomas Pollard released the Defts John and Richd. Goodridge, Richd. and Ambrose Pitman of damages agreable to verdict in a suit Pollard vs Goodridge &c.
--Sarah Hammonds vs Peter Poole---Case.
--Rawleigh Hazard vs John Parrott---Case.

[Index 331] Lancaster OB 16:115b, Sept Court 1782

Elizabeth Mctyre vs John Hazard---Case.
--Job Carter vs Jesse Crowther---Case.
--Coleman Doggett vs John Mctyre---Assault & battery. Abates by death of Plt.
--Patrick Connolly vs John Mctyre---Detinue.
--Thomas Pollard vs Rawleigh Hazard---Case.
--Sarah Wilder vs William Griggs---Abates by death of Deft.
--Thomas Carter vs Benjamin Williams.
--William Schofield vs Thomas Pollard---Case.

[Index 332] Lancaster OB 16:116a, Sept Court 1782

John Wormeley vs Jesse Harrison---Case.
--William Edwards vs Judithen Pinckard---Detinue.
--Commonwealth vs Vincent Brent &c---Sci facias.
--Simon Laughlin vs Elias Edmonds guardian to Lucy Denny---Case.
--On motion of Lawson Hathaway, ordered Edwin Conway, James Gordon, and James Tapscott Gent settle guardianship accounts of Spencer George with the estate of John James orphan of Bartlet James decd.
--On motion Thaddeus McCarty, present Clerk, leave given him to remove the records to his plantation on Morattico in Richmond County.
--On motion of Thads. McCarty, present Clerk, ordered Edwin Conway, James Gordon, and James Tapscott Gent examine the state of the records.
--On motion of Edwin Conway Gent, time allowed him to finish building his grist mill.

[Index 333] Lancaster OB 16:116b, Oct Court 1782

Court, 17 October 1782, present justices James Ball, Henry Lawson, James W. Ball, Matt. Myars.
--Inventory of estate of Henry George decd. returned.
--On motion of Mary Carter relict of John Carter decd., administration granted to her on his estate; Henry Lawson Gent, John Bean, Presly Saunders, and Benjamin George appointed to appraise the estate and allot her dower.
--Present justices William Yerby, James Ball Jur., and John Selden Gent.
--Power of attorney from Charles Hunt of Augusta County to Thaddeus McCarty was proved by James Ball and James Ball Jur.
--Indenture of bargain and sale from Jesse Harrison and his wife [not named] to Thads. McCarty was proved.
--On motion of Judith George relict of Bailie George decd., Jesse George, and Nicholas George, administration granted them on estate of the decd.; William Yerby Gent, William Gibson, Lawson Hathaway, and James Pollard appointed appraisers.
--Richard Yerby orphan of John Yerby decd. chose William Yerby his guardian, and sd William also appointed guardian to Jesse Yerby orphan of sd decd.

[Index 334] Lancaster OB 16:117a, Oct Court 1782

James Yerby orphan of John Yerby decd. chose John Hutchings his guardian.
--Elias Edmonds, John Yerby, William Gibson, Jonathan Pullen appointed to possess the guardians to the orphans of John Yerby decd. with their estates; on motion of William Yerby Gent, ordered he make sale of negro Isaac belonging to sd. Estate.
--James Gordon Gent produced commission from Gov Benjamin Harrison appointing him Sheriff, and took the oath.

--On motion of James Gordon Sheriff, John Bailey & John Newby sworn as his substitutes.

--The court valued a horse belonging to Col James Gordon, impressed by Nicholas Currell by order of Col William Griffin.

--Deed of gift from Presly Cockrell to Elizabeth Tillery was proved.

--Present justices Henry Towles, James Ewell.

--John Eustace vs John Parrott---Debt.

--Mary Newsom vs Daniel George—Assault & battery.

[Index 335] Lancaster OB 16:117b, Oct Court 1782

William Hunt vs Robt. & Richd. Mitchell executors of Richd. Mitchell decd.---Case.

--Olivers administrators vs James Selden's administrator---Case.

--Samuel Yobb vs James Simmonds---Attachment.

--John Eustace vs Thomas Carter---Petition.

--John Thrall vs John Hutchings---Petition.

--William Sydnor, Inspector, swore to the outstanding tobacco at D. Creek Warehouse.

--Charles Rogers, Inspector, swore to the outstanding tobacco at Davis's Warehouse.

--William Barber Jur. vs Joseph Hubbard---Case.

--Hugh Kelly vs Jonathan Pearson---Attachment.

[Index 336] Lancaster OB 16:118a, Oct Court 1782

Bill of sale Edward Carter to Ann Carter was proved by Edward Carter Jur.

--Lease from John Sullivant to William Allen was acknowledged.

--Indenture of lease and release from Nicholas Payne to Nicholas George was acknowledged.

--Inventory of estate of William Griggs decd. with allotment of dower was returned.

--Settlement of accounts of orphans of William King decd. with the executors of Anthony and Fortunatus Sydnor decd. their former guardians was returned.

--William Sullivant vs James Connolly administrator &c---Petition.

--Jesse George vs John Clayton---Case.

--Northumberland Justices vs John Eustace---Debt.

--John Garlington vs George Norris---Slander. A jury came, to wit., Elias Edmonds &c

--Yarrot Hulet and Jesse Robinson Jur., summoned as jurymen and failing to appear, were fined.

[Index 337] Lancaster OB 16:118b, Oct Court 1782

Nicholas George vs James Ewell---Petition.

--William Norris vs John Hutchings exr. E. Horton---Case. A jury came, to wit., John Chowning &c.

--Settlement of Zachariah Barr's guardianship of estate of Lawson Wale, returned.

--Joseph Shearman vs Olivers admors., Jesse Howard---Case. Report of arbitrators James Ball and Henry Towles Gent was returned.

--Francis Bond &c vs William Lewis---Detinue. A jury came, to wit., Rawleigh Tapscott &c.

Court, 18 Oct 1782, present justices James Ball, Hen. Towles, James Ball Jur., Hen. Lawson, and James W. Ball.

--William Norris vs Horton's executors (Jno. Hutchings)---Case.

[Index 338] Lancaster OB 16:119a, Oct Court 1782

Francis Bond &c vs William Lewis---Detinue. Jury [not named] found for Plt, also for five hundred pounds on negro Moses

--Fortunatus Sydnor &c vs Francis Bond &c---Chancery. Ordered dedimus issue to take depositions of Gowen Lowry and Edward Carter.

--John Mctyre appointed Surveyor of Road over Matrons Bridge.

--Edward Blakemore appointed Surveyor of Road from the post near Nicholas George's to the church.

--James Ball and James Ball Jur. appointed to try the weights at D. Creek and James Ewell and Matt. Myars Gent at Davis's Warehouses.

[Index 339] Lancaster OB 16:119b, Oct Court 1782
On motion of William Chilton, ordered Elias Edmonds, Thomas Hubbard, John Miller, and Edwin Kent divide estate of John Parquet decd.
--Jonathan Pullen vs James Pinckard---Case.
--Ordered Jonathen Pullen pay Rawleigh Hazard for his attendance as witness in Pullen's case vs James Pinckard, and for traveling 8 miles to and from his residence.
--Ordered Jonathen Pullen pay David Garland for his attendance as witness in Pullen's case vs James Pinckard.
--Sarah Hamonds [thus] vs Peter Poole—Dedimus issued to take deposition of Thomas West.
--Rawh. Hazard vs John Parrott—Case.
--Elizabeth McTyre vs John Hard---Case.
--William Edwards vs Jedithen Pinckard---Detinue.
--George Davis Jur. appointed Surveyor of Road from the church to Mrs Aga. Ball's mill.

[Index 340] Lancaster OB 16:120a, Nov Court 1782
Court 4 Nov 1782 for trial of Harry and Charles negro slaves of Mrs Margaret Ball, charged with burning down her house on night of 23 Oct last and stealing articles therefrom, present justices James Ball, John Berryman, William Yerby, James Ball Jur., Henry Lawson, James W. Ball, and Matt. Myars; William Brown was attorney for the state; Defts pleaded not guilty, they were found not guilty of burning the house, but Harry was found guilty of stealing, and ordered he be burnt in the hand.

Court, 21 Nov 1782, present justices James Ball, John Berryman, James Ball Jur., James W. Ball, and Matt. Myars.
--Division of estate of John Parquet decd. was returned.

[Index 341] Lancaster OB 16:120b, Nov Court 1782
William Cornelious orphan of William Cornelious decd. was bound to William Wiblin.
--Receipt from Edward Carter to James Gordon Gent for a purchase of land was acknowledged.
--Allotment of Nancy Carter's part of the estate of her father Josiah Carter decd was returned.
--Grand jury was sworn, Lawson Hathaway was foreman.
--James Ball Gent, William Montague, Andrew Robertson appointed to settle estate of Robert Mctyre decd. with executor William Yerby.
--Power of attorney Thomas Hill to William Hill was proved.
--Power of attorney William Everitt and John Hill to William Hill (with a certificate from Clerk of Mecklenburg County NC) was recorded.
--John Fleet, John Berryman, Henry Lawson Gent, and and William Merideth appointed to divide estate of Eliza. Blackerby decd and possess William Hill with the parts of William Everitt, John Hill, and Thomas Hill.

[Index 342] Lancaster OB 16:121a, Nov Court 1782
[county levy cont'd, the following were allowed their accounts, only entries with names shown here, amounts are not included] To William Brown Gent Commonwealth's Attorney; to John Newby his account; to John Bailey his account; to William Arms, Constable; to James Newby, Constable; to Mrs Ann Shearman for one levy extra paid; to Job Carter his account; to same per order from the guards over Maurice Wheeler; to same for former allowance not paid about a negro prisoner belonging to Thos. G. Peachey Esq; to James Carter, James Newby Jur., Ozwald Newby Jur., John Webb, Nicholas George Jur., and Abner Palmer, who were guards over Wheeler; to Michael Wilder, Constable; to David Garland and his wife for attendance one day vs Wheeler; to William George Senr. for attendance vs same; to Thads. McCarter, his account; to Rawh. Hazard for attendance one day vs Thos. & Vincent Brent.
--Charles Hubbard and Robert Pollard refusing to serve as guards when summoned, fined 100 pounds of tobacco.

[Index 343] Lancaster OB 16:121b, Nov Court 1782
Inventory of estate of Martha Carter decd was returned.

Court, 19 December 1782, present justices James Ball, John Berryman, William Yerby, James Ball Junr., John Selden, Matt. Myars.

--Deed Thads. McCarty and wife Mary to Robert Walker was acknowledged.

--Settlement of William Yerby's executorship of estate of Robert Mctyre decd was returned.

--Grand jury presentment vs John Mctyre for swearing four oaths, he was fined.

--Grand jury presentment vs Thomas Pitman for getting drunk, he was fined.

--Grand jury presentment vs Alice Smith for concealing all her tithables, dismissed.

--Grand jury presentment vs William West Jur. for swearing four oaths, he was fined.

[Index 344] Lancaster OB 16:122a, Dec Court 1782

Grand jury presentment vs Thomas Cottrell for swearing four oaths, he was fined.

--Grand jury presentment vs Jedithen Brent for swearing four oaths, he was fined.

--Grand jury presentment vs William Tapscott for swearing one oath, he was fined.

--Grand jury presentment vs Alexander Davis for a common swearer, he was fined.

--Grand jury presentment vs William Brown for getting drunk, he was fined.

--Grand jury vs Job Carter---Summons.

--Helen Gilmour, widow of Robert Gilmour decd, renounced by deed any benefit she may claim by her husband's will, deed proved by James W. Ball Gent.

--John Fleet vs William Burkan &c---Case.

--John Fleet vs William Burkan &c---Case.

[Index 345] Lancaster OB 16:122b, Dec Court 1782

Margarett Ball vs James W. Ball---For sureties of the peace.

--Joseph Hubbard vs Rawleigh Shearman---Case.

--Isaac Smith vs Moses Hester & John Heath Junr.---Debt; William Brown Gent was special bail for Deft Heath.

--John Berryman vs Joseph Kern---Case.

--Francis Bond &c vs William Lewis---Case.

--William Ball vs John Wormeley---Petition.

--Will of Dameron decd was proved by Lott Palmer & John Palmer.

[Index 346] Lancaster OB 16:123a, Dec Court 1782

Ozwald Newby vs John Taylor---Debt.—James Ewell Gent was special bail for the Deft.

--John Doggett appointed guardian to Dennis Doggett orphan of Coleman Doggett decd.

--James Gordon Gent, John Yerby, James Pinckard, and John Miller appointed to settle guardianship accounts of Dennis Doggett with Molly Doggett, als. [alias?] Mctyre, his former guardian, and possess the present guardian with his estate.

--Newman Chilton orphan of Moses Chilton decd chose Elias Edmonds his guardian.

--Edwin Conway, John Taylor, James Gordon, and James Tapscott Gent appointed to settle guardianship accounts of Newman Chilton with James Newby his former guardian, and possess his present guardian with his estate.

--On motion of Thomas Mott who married Winnifred Doggett widow of John Doggett decd, "which said Doggett was Sarah Lee's security for the guardianship of her children and Thomas Ellett who has since intermarried with the said Lee," ordered he give counter security for the sd. Guardianship, with Rawleigh Coats his security.

[Index 347] Lancaster OB 16:123b, Jan Court 1783

Court, 16 January 1783, present justices James Ball, Henry Towles, James Ball Jur., Henry Lawson, James W. Ball, Matt. Myars.

--Relinquishment of Mrs Helen Gilmour further proved by James Ball Gent.

--The allotment of land to Mrs. Alice Smith widow of Col Burges Smith decd. was returned.

--Commission for privy examination of Judith Chilton wife of Richard Chilton concerning their deed to William Chilton Junr. was returned.

--Job Carter granted license to keep tavern at his house.

--On motion of James Wallace, ordered his suit vs Elijah Persifull be reinstated.

--Mortgage from John Wormeley to John Hunton was acknowledged.

--Rawleigh Hazard's motion to keep a tavern at the courthouse, the court is divided.

--James W. Ball, James Tapscott, Elias Edmonds, and John Yerby appointed to divide the estate of Robert Henning decd., and possess Charles Lee (who married Mildred Henning) and James Gordon (guardian to Lewis Henning) with their parts.

--Joannah Steptoe widow of William Steptoe decd renounced all right and benefit from her husband's will.

[Index 348] Lancaster OB 16:124a, Jan Court 1783

Lindsay Thelkin orphan of John Thelkin chose George Carter his guardian, and sd Carter is appointed guardian to Patty Thelkin orphan of sd decd.

--Indenture of release Maurice Wheeler to Thomas Pollard was proved by James Newby and William Gibson.

--On motion of Thomas Carter, ordered his suit vs Benjamin Williams be reinstated.

--On motion of Elias Edmonds (joint security with John Goodridge for James Connolly's administration on estate of William Griggs decd.), for counter security from sd Connolly, sd Connolly relinquished administration, and sd administration was granted to sd Edmonds., with John Goodridge security.

--On motion of Elizabeth Mctyre, her suit vs John Hazard was reinstated.

--Present Edwin Conway and James Ewell Gent.

--John Goodridge appointed guardian to William Doggett orphan of Coleman Doggett decd.

--Edwin Conway Gent was sworn as Coroner.

[Index 349] Lancaster OB 16:124b, Jan Court 1783

The following claims against the public were allowed: Thads. McCarty, per certificate from Richd. Young for freight of brandy; James Tapscott for beef impressed by R. Tapscott, D.C. for J. Brown.

--Edwin Conway, James Gordon Gent, John Yerby, and John Miller appointed to settle guardian accounts of Will. Doggett orphan of Coleman Doggett decd. and possess John Goodridge his present guardian with his estate.

--William Yerby Gent, James Pollard, Lawson Hathaway, William Gibson, & John Parrott appointed to settle administration accounts of estate of Will. Griggs decd. with James Connolly the former administrator.

Court, 20 February 1783, present justices James Ball, Henry Towles, John Berryman, James Ball Jur., Henry Lawson.

--Deed of gift Vincent Brent to his son was acknowledged.

--Jonathen Williams orphan of John Williams decd. was bound to Thomas Bivins, to learn the trade of a Plaisterer.

--Will of Eleazer Robinson decd presented by Epaphroditus Robinson, who was granted administration.

[Index 350] Lancaster OB 16:125a, Feb Court 1783

Ozwald Newby, Giles Robinson, Jesse Robinson, and Jesse Robinson Jur. appointed to appraise estate of Eleazer Robinson decd.

--William Doggett orphan of George Doggett decd was bound to Willm. Lawson, to learn the trade of Shop Joiner.

--Jonathen Pullen vs George Standard—Petition.

--Settlement of accounts of estate of William Doggett orphan of Coleman Doggett decd was returned.

--Charles Lee acknowledged a bond for his guardianship of William Doggett orphan of George Doggett decd.

--Settlement of the guardianship accounts of the administrators of James Hill decd of the estate of James Hill was returned.

--Present justices Will. Yerby, Jas. W. Ball, Robt. C. Jacobs, & Matt. Myars.

--John Fleet vs John James---Sci. Facias.

--John Fleet vs Anthony George—Sci. Facias.

--Thomas Pollard vs Judith George &c administrators of Bailie George decd.---Sci. Facias.

[Index 351] Lancaster OB 16:125b, Feb Court 1783

Rawleigh Hazard vs Charles Purcell---Case.

--George Norris vs Charles Bean---Debt.

--James W. Ball vs Charles Bean---Debt.

--Thomas Garner vs George Phillips---Debt; William Kent was special bail for Deft.

--John Angell vs Robert C. Jacob [thus]---Case.

--Josiah Gaskins granted administration on estate of John Dameron decd.

[Index 352] Lancaster OB 16:126a, Feb Court 1783

Settlement of James Newby's guardianship account of Newman Chilton's estate was returned.

--Division of the negroes of Robert Hening decd. was returned.

--Settlement of Spencer George's guardianship accounts of John James's estate was returned.

--Rawleigh Hazard's petition to keep a tavern at the courthouse, again rejected.

--Daniel Muse granted administration on estate of Presly Cockrell decd., with James Tapscott his security; Robert Walker, Spencer George, Moses George, and Edward Blakemore appointed to appraise the estate.

--Elizabeth Mctyre vs John Hazard---Case; Referees were James W. Ball Gent, Andrew Robertson, and Thomas Flint.

--Inventory of estate of Robert Gilmour decd. was returned.

[Index 353] Lancaster OB 16:126b, Feb Court 1783

Job Carter vs Nathaniel Logain---Attachment.

--Following persons appointed to receive a list of the inhabitants within the county, agreeable to act of Assembly: Henry Towles & Matt. Myars Gent in Corotoman Dist, James Ball Jur. and John Selden Gent for Rappahk., James W. Ball and Robert C. Jacob Gent for the Forest, Edwin Conway and James Tapscott Gent for Currero, John Berryman and William Yerby Gent for Fleet's Bay, and John Fleet and Henry Lawson Gent for Fleet's Island.

--Thomas Carter granted administration on estate of William Steptoe decd., with the will annexed; William Yerby Gent, James Brent, Newton Brent, and John Flowers were appointed appraisers.

--Injunction granted Edward Carter vs Margrt. Davis.

--Rawleigh Downman vs William Palmer---Injunction.

--Elijah Percifull vs James Ledford---Sci. Facias.

--Division of the negroes of Elizabeth Blackerby decd. was returned.

[Index 354] Lancaster OB 16:127a, Feb Court 1783

Sarah Hammonds vs Peter Poole---Case.

--Edward Carter vs Margaret Davis---Chancery.

--Thomas Hunton vs Benjamin Garton---Case.

--The following appointed to receive lists of taxable property in the county: James Ewell in Corotoman, James Ball Jur. for Rappahk., Robt. C. Jacob for the Forest, James Tapscott for Currero, William Yerby for Fleet's Bay, and Henry Lawson for Fleet's Island.

--James Brent appointed Surveyor of Road from Mrs. Eustace's little mill to Kilmarnock.

[Index 355] Lancaster OB 16:127b, Feb Court 1783

Order Peter Poole pay Charles Lee Gent for his attendance as witness in Poole's suit vs Sarah Hammonds, and for traveling eight miles to and from his residence.

--Ordered Peter Poole pay John Sydnor for his attendance as witness in Poole's suit vs Sarah Hammonds, and for traveling seven miles to and from his residence.

--Ordered Peter Poole pay William Haydon for his attendance as witness in Poole's suit vs Sarah Hammonds.

--Ordered Sarah Hammonds pay Thomas Haydon for his attendance as witness in Hammonds's suit vs Peter Poole, and for traveling seven miles to and from his residence.

--Ordered Sarah Hammonds pay William Davis for his attendance as witness in Hammonds's suit vs Peter Poole, and for traveling nine miles to and from his residence.

--Ordered Sarah Hammonds pay Lucy Hammonds for her attendance as witness in Sarah's suit vs Peter Poole.

[Index 356] Lancaster OB 16:128a, April Court 1783

Special Court, 17 April 1783, pursuant to act of Assembly for ascertaining losses sustained from the depredations of the enemy, present James Ball & others; The following were allowed their claims [sums not shown here].
--Mungo Harvey for 2 negroes Will and Kitt.
--John Payne for one negro James.
--John Selden for one negro Daniel Butler.

Special Court, 16 May 1783 in pursuance of the aforesaid act of Assembly, present James Ball &c; These were allowed their claims [sums not shown here]: John Eustace for household furniture etc., also a negro man from 20 to 26 years of age.

[Index 357] Lancaster OB 16:128b, March Court 1783
Special Court, 21 March 1783, pursuant to act of Assembly for ascertaining losses sustained from depredations of the enemy, present justices James Ball, Henry Towles, John Fleet, William Yerby, Henry Lawson, and James Tapscott. The following were allowed their claims [no sums shown here].
--Mary Lawson, for one negro man Joshua, proved by oath of Henry Lawson.
--George Currell, for one negro man Oliver, proved by Henry Lawson.
--Rawleigh Shearman, for one negro man James, proved by Henry Lawson.
--Thomas Hunton, for two negroes Jack and Daniel, proved by John Fleet & Hen. Lawson.
--William Martin, for one negro Abraham proved by Thomas Carter.
--John Fleet, for two negroes Ambrose & Willoughby, proved by Thomas Hunton.
--Jemima Blakemore, for one negro man Will, proved by Jonathen Denison.
--Rodham Lunceford, for one negro man Moses, and other losses.
--Joseph Carter decd. est., for two negroes Argulus & Tom, proved by Rodm. Lunceford.
--Isaac Degge, for three negroes Spencer, Solomon, and Tom, proved by Thos. Carter.
--William Hinton, for salt kettles, proved by Thomas Hunton.
--Thomas Myars, for one negro man Dennis, proved by Matthew Myars.

[Index 358] Lancaster OB 16:129a, March Court 1783
[Special Court to ascertain losses sustained from the British, continued]
--Matthew Myars, for one negro Dick, and other losses.
--Thomas Carter, for one auger.
--George Yerby, for one negro man Nace, proved by Eppa. Stott.
--John Longweth, for one negro man Ben.
--Charles Carter Esq, for sixteen negroes John, Abraham, Alexander, Billy, Lewis, Young, Tom, Daniel, Siah, Billy, Ben, Talbert, James, Adam, Daniel, David, and other losses.
--Thaddeus McCarty, for two negroes Sam and Will, and other losses.
--Richard Selden, for tobacco, proved by Wm. Pitman.
--James Tapscott, for three negroes Aaron, Isaac, and Humphrey, and other losses.
--Elmoure Doggett, for one negro man Dick, proved by Thomas Pollard.
--George Brent, for one schooner boat.
--Robert C. Jacob, for tobacco, proved by G. Brent.
--James Brent, for one negro Mesheck, and other losses, proved by Geo. Brent.

[Index 359] Lancaster OB 16:129b, March Court 1783
[Special Court to ascertain losses sustained from the British, continued]
--Judith George, for gun and sword, etc.
--William Chowning, for two guns, etc.
--Thomas Ingram, for one gun, etc.
--Mrs. Alice Smith, for six negroes Tom, Jo [thus], Gunner, Sarah, and two small negroes, proved by John Bailey.
--Charles Lee, for one negro Daniel, and other losses, proved by Richard Lee.
--Mrs. Elizabeth Beale, for one negro man Jo [thus], and other losses, proved by Richd. Lee.
--Robert Gilmour decd. est., for two negroes Moses and James.

--Doctr. William Ball, for three negroes Frank, Will, and Tom, proved by Henry Towles.
--Thomas Pollard, for foresail and halliards of a sloop.

[End]

Lancaster County Order Book 17

[Index 360] Lancaster OB 17:1, March Court 1783
Court, 20 March 1783, present justices James Ball, Henry Towles, James Ball Jur., Henry Lawson and James Tapscott.
--Inventory of estate of John Carter decd. was returned.
--Deed John Eustice and wife Alice to Newton Brent was proved.
--Helen Gilmour appointed guardian to John Morton Gilmour and Robert Galloway Gilmour, orphans of Robert Gilmour decd.
--On motion of William Doggett Jur., ordered his two negroes Anthony and Jenny be exempted from tax.
--On motion of Elizabeth Hinton, ordered her negro Jerry be exempted from tax.
--On motion of Mary Carter widow of John Carter decd, ordered her negro Mima be exempted from tax.
--On motion of William Brent Jur., ordered his negro Keeler be exempted from tax.
--On motion of Richard Selden, ordered his two negroes Rachel and Pendar be exempted from tax.
--On motion of George Norris, ordered his negro Will be exempted from tax.
--On motion of William Chowning, ordered negro wench Winny belonging to Caterin[?] Chowning orphan of Geo. Chowning decd. be exempted from tax.
--On motion of Rawleigh Shearman, ordered his negro Hannah be exempted from tax.
--On motion of William Hinton, ordered his negro Lyddai [thus] be exempted from tax.

[Index 361] Lancaster OB 17:2a, March Court 1783
Deed William Robinson and wife [not named] to William Mason was acknowledged.
--The following certificates were received by the court as just claims against the public, vizt. [sums not given here]: To Thads. McCarty, assigned to Charles McCarty, for frieight, etc.; To Thomas Pollard for beef impressed by Rawh. Tapscott, D.C.
--Present justices Edwin Conway, William Yerby, and Matt. Myars.
--Edward Carter vs Margaret Davis---Injunction.
--Peter Poole's motion for errors in arrest of judgment at suit of Sarah Hammonds, rejected.
--James W. Ball vs Charles Bean---Attachment; George Norris was garnishee.
--Craven Everitt vs Ruth Griggs---Trespass.
--Craven Everitt vs Ruth Griggs---Case.

[Index 362] Lancaster OB 17:2b, March Court 1783
Vincent Brent vs Thomas Pinckard &c---Debt.
--John Degge vs Thomas Brent.
--Thomas Pollard assignee of Maurice Wheeler vs William Boatman & Jesse George---Sci. fa.
--John Craine vs Edward Carter---Petition.
--Rhoda James vs George Bean---Petition.
--John Fleet vs Anthony George---Sci. fa.
--Robert Gilmour's executors vs Willoughby Routt---Petition.
--Willoughby Routt vs Mungo Harvey---Petition.
--Edward Carter vs Jesse Harrison---Petition.
--John Mctyre vs John Selden administrator of Jas. Selden---Case.

[Index 363] Lancaster OB 17:3a, March Court 1783
On motion of John Taylor Gent, his negroes Harry, Beck, and Sarah exempted from tax.
--John Thrall vs John Hutchings---Petition.
--Charles Bean vs John Hutchinson.
--William Sullivant vs William Griggs's administrators---Petition.
--Ordered Griggs's administrators pay Richard Lee for his attendance as witness in their suit vs Will. Sullivant.
--James Newby, Ozwald Newby, Jesse Robinson, and Giles Robinson appointed to appraise the estate of Eleazer Robinson decd.
--Hugh Kelly vs Jonathen Pearson---Attachment; Henry Lawson Gent Coroner levied the attachment on a negro girl Daphne the property of the Deft.

[Index 364] Lancaster OB 17:3b, March Court 1783
Jesse George vs John Clayton---Assault and Battery; a jury came, to wit., Elias Edmonds &c, and they found for the Plt.
--Thomas Pollard vs Bailie George's administrators---Sci facias.

Court, 21 March 1783, present justices James Ball, John Fleet, Henry Towles, William Yerby, Henry Lawson, and James Tapscott.
--David Galloway Jur. granted administration on estate of Robert Gilmour decd.
--On motion of William Montague, ordered his negro Moll be exempted from tax.

[Index 365] Lancaster OB 17:4a, April Court 1783
Court, 17 April 1783, present justices James Ball, John Fleet, Edwin Conway, Henry Towles, John Berryman, Robt. C. Jacob.
--Will of Thomas Flint decd. presented by James Ball Jur. and James W. Ball, and they were granted administration; Johnson Riveer, Ozwald Newby, Joseph Wilkerson, and John Clutton were appointed appraisers.
--James Brent took oath as Vestryman for Christ Church Parish.
--Inventory of estate of William Steptoe decd. was returned.
--Inventory of estate of John Pearson decd. was returned.
--Charles Hubbard granted administration on estate of Joshua Hubbard decd.; George Norris, James Pinckard, John Miller, and Jeduthun Pinckard appointed appraisers.
--William Hubbard orphan of Joshua Hubbard decd. chose Charles Hubbard his guardian, and said Charles is appointed guardian to George, Ephraim, and Amia Hubbard orphans of sd Joshua.
--Amos Hubbard orphan of Joseph Hubbard decd. chose Thomas Hubbard his guardian, and Edwin Conway Gent, Saml. Yopp, James Pinckard, & Willm. Edwards appointed to divide estate of Joseph Hubbard decd. according to his will.

[Index 366] Lancaster OB 17:4b, April Court 1783
James Ball and Edwin Conway Gent appointed Commissioners of the Tax.
--On motion of John James, ordered his negro Sarah be exempted from tax.
--James Gordon and John Berryman Gent were recommended to the Governor as proper persons to execute the office of High Sheriffs.
--On motion of Rawleigh Coats who became counter security for Thos. Ellett who married Sarah Lee who was guardian to her children, ordered that unless Ellett give further security that sd Rawleigh be possessed with the estate of sd orphans.
--Ruth Griggs appointed guardian to Charles and John Denny Everitt orphans of Thomas Everitt decd.
--John Taylor, James Gordon, James Tapscott, and Robert C. Jacob appointed to settle the guardianship accounts of the orphans of Thomas Everitt decd. and possess the present guardian with their estate which was in the hands of Col Edwin Conway their former guardian.
--Ordered John Dye be tax exempt.
--Report possessing the administrators of William Griggs decd with his estate was returned.
--Mungo Harvey vs John Selden---Case; Referees were James Ball, Henry Towles Gent, & William Sydnor.

--Division of Eleazer Robinson's estate was returned.

--Catharine McDaniel was allowed tobacco for attendance as witness for Mrs. Margaret Ball in her complaint vs. James W. Ball for sureties of the peace.

[Index 367] Lancaster OB 17:5a, May Court 1783

Court, 15 May 1783, present justices James Ball, John Berryman, Henry Lawson, James W. Ball, and Matt. Myars.

--Instrument from Charles Carter Esq of Corotomon purporting the give of negro girl Jenny to Thomas Edwards orphan of Richard Edwards Gent decd. was proved by John Eustace and Nicholas Currell Jur.

--Joseph Hubbard vs Vachal Fandrie---Case.

--Grand jury was sworn, with William Warren foreman.

--James Ball and Edwin Conway Gent were sworn Commissioners of the Tax.

--Present justices John Fleet, Edwin Conway, William Yerby, John Selden, James Tapscott, and Robert C. Jacob.

--Peter Poole vs Sarah Hammonds---Chancery.

[Index 368] Lancaster OB 17:5b, May Court 1783

Will of George Edwards decd. was presented by Mary Edwards, and was proved by Edwin Conway Gent and Merideth Mahanes, and said Mary was granted administration; Benjamin George, Thomas Carter, Merideth Mahanes, and John Bean were appointed appraisers.

--Robert Carter vs Presly Cockrill---Case; Abates by death of Deft.

--Sarah Chinn orphan of Thomas Chinn decd. chose Robert Chinn her guardian.

--Joseph Shearman vs Mungo Harvey---Petition.

[Index 369] Lancaster OB 17:6a, May Court 1783

William Doggett appointed Surveyor of Road from the fork of the road by John Longwiths to Mrs. Carter's little mill in place of Jonathen Pullen.

--Rawleigh Tapscott sworn as Assistant Inspector at Deep Creek Warehouse.

--On motion of John Mason, ordered Edwin Conway, William Yerby Gent, Thomas Pollard, and John Yerby settled the guardianship accounts of Coleman Doggett decd. of the estate of Lucy Mason decd. with the executors of sd Doggett.

--Male tithables of Mrs. Ann Chinn ordered to attend the Surveyor of the Road from Morattico Mill to Deep Bottom.

--Inventory of estate of John Dameron decd. was returned.

John Heath vs Thomas Ellett---Debt.

--William Barber vs Spencer George---Petition.

--Baldwin Bean vs John Heath---Debt.

--James Currell Jur. vs Ruth Griggs & Ed. Conway---Debt; Elijah Percifull was special bail for the Deft.

[Index 370] Lancaster OB 17:6b, May Court 1783

William Brent vs Judith Sulivant---Case.

--Sarah Pearson vs Jonathen Pearson---Attachment; Henry Lawson Gent Coroner returned that he had levied the attachment on a negro girl Daphny, also property in the hands of Thomas Bridgford.

--Job Carter vs Nathaniel Logain---Attachment; James Gordon Gent was garnishee.

--Judgment granted to Joseph Hubbard vs Harry Currell.

--Petition of George Goodridge vs John Wormeley.

--Judgment granted Moses Hester vs Thomas Carter.

--Petition of James Hill vs Jedithen Pinckard.

--John Crowther vs Merideth Mahanes &c---Assault and Battery.

[Index 371] Lancaster OB 17:7a, May Court 1783

James Hill vs Elizabeth Hill administratrix &c---Case.

--Robert Carter Esq vs Daniel Muse administrator P. Cockrell---Case.

--Daniel McCarty administrator &c vs James Tapscott---Debt.

--Spencer George vs Thomas Hunton &c---Sci facias.

--Nicholas George vs John Hornsby---Case; George Bean was special bail for the Deft.
--Thomas Scurlock &c vs Henry Tapscott's executors---Chancery.
--Nathaniel Burwell vs William Rains---Debt.
--Henry Tapscott's executors vs Robert Jones---Trespass.

[Index 372] Lancaster OB 17:7b, May Court 1783

Reuben Couts vs John Taylor---Debt.
--John Watkins vs John Taylor---Debt.
--Parke Godall vs John Taylor---Debt.
--James Tapscott, James W. Ball, and James Ewell Gent appointed to settle the executorship accounts of Robert Henning decd.
--Privy examination of Winifred Tapscott wife of Henry Tapscott regarding her dower in a tract conveyed to Thomas Haydon was returned.
--Sydnor &c vs Sharp's executors---Chancery; Referees were James Gordon Gent and Doctr. William Ball.
--Jedithen James vs James Ewell---Case; a jury came, to wit., Rawleigh W. Downman &c.

[Index 373] Lancaster OB 17:8a, May Court 1783

Jedithen Moore appointed Surveyor of Road from Jacob's mill to Cundiff's old field.
--Flood's administrators vs Smith's administrators---Case; a jury came, to wit., Moses George &c, and they found for the Plts.
--On motion of Richard Ball by his attorney, execution issued against George Bean.

Court, 16 May 1783, present justices James Ball, James W. Ball, James Ewell, James Tapscott, Robert C. Jacob, and Matt. Myars.
--Jedithen James vs James Ewell---Case.

[Index 374] Lancaster Ob 17:8b, May Court 1783

William Edwards vs Jedithen Pinckard---Detinue; a jury came, to wit., Rawleigh W. Downman &c, and they found for the Plt, and the Plt to recover negro boy Burges.
--John Mctyre vs John Selden administrator &c---Case; Dedimus issued to take deposition of Mrs. Mildred Selden.
--Patrick Connolly vs John Mctyre---Detinue; a jury came, to wit., James Pollard &c, and they found for the Plt.
--Ordered Jedithen Pinckard pay Jonathen Pullen for his attendance as witness in Pinckard's suit vs William Edwards.
--Ordered William Edwards pay Milly Carter for her attendance as witness in Edwards's suit vs Jedithen Pinckard.

[Index 375] Lancaster OB 17:9a, May Court 1783

Ordered William Edwards pay Fanny Hill for her attendance as witness in Edwards's suit vs Jedithen Pinckard.
--Ordered William Edwards pay Saryann Galloway for her attendance as witness in Edwards's suit vs Jedithen Pinckard.
--Ordered William Edwards pay Polly Coffee for her attendance as witness in Edwards's suit vs Jedithen Pinckard.
--Ordered Jedithen Pinckard pay Nancy Jones for her attendance as witness in Pinckard's suit vs William Edwards.
--James Wallace vs Elijah Percifull.
--Simon Laughlin vs Elias Edmonds.
--Ordered John Mctyre pay Ozwald Newby Jur. for his attendance as witness in Mctyre's suit vs Patrick Connolly.
--Giles Boggess vs Jesse Harrison---Case.
--John Heath vs William Schofield &c---Detinue.
--Commonwealth vs Vincent Brent &c---Sci. facias.

[Index 376] Lancaster OB 17:9b, May Court 1783

Ezekiel Hudnall vs James Ewell---Case.
--William Davenport vs William Parrott---Case.
--On motion of Joseph Kern, his negro Amey exempted from tax.

--Maurice Wheeler vs James Connolly administrator of Wm. Griggs decd.---Abates by death of Plt, "he is hanged publickly for murder."
--John Boswell vs James Connolly adminirator &c---Case.
--John Cundiff vs Benjamin Cundiff---Chancery.
--John Wormeley vs Jesse Harrison---Case.

[Index 377] Lancaster OB 17:10a, May Court 1783
Rachel Hill administratrix &c vs William Hinton---Case.
Commonwealth vs John Armes---Indictment.
--Thomas Bell vs Robert Jones---Case.
--Thomas Jones executor of Wm. Suit vs William Kent & wife executors of Wm. Taylor---Sci. facias.

The court received the following certificates: To William Brown for beef impressed by Rawh. Tapscott D. Com.; Col John Fleet's and Elijah Percifull's certificates transmitted.

[Index 378] Lancaster OB 17:10b, June Court 1783
Court, 19 June 1783, present justices James Ball, John Fleet, Edwin Conway, John Berryman, and Hen. Lawson.
--Judgment granted James Connolly administrator &c of William Griggs decd. vs William James & Thomas Carter, and the judgment was assigned to James Newby.
--James Connolly administrator &c of Wm. Griggs decd. vs Isaac Currell & John Parrott---Petition.
--James Connolly administrator &c of Wm. Griggs decd. vs Thomas Lee & James Currell Jur.---Petition; Judggment for Plt, which was assigned to James Newby.
--James Hill vs Jedithen Pinckard---Petition.
--William Doggett vs John Smalwood---Petition.
--Charles Hubbard administrator &c of Joshua Hubbard decd. vs William Schofield---Petition.
--Joseph Hubbard vs John Baldwin & Geo. Doggett---Petition.

[Index 379] Lancaster OB 17:11a, June Court 1783
Joseph Hubbard vs John James---Petition; Referees were Willm. Lawson and Jonathen Wilder.
--Thaddeus McCarty vs Jedithen Pinckard---Debt; James Pinckard was special bail for the Deft.
--Thaddeus McCarty vs John Hutchings---Debt; William Norris was special bail for Deft.
--Thaddeus McCarty vs Robert Walker---Debt.
--Thaddeus McCarty vs Joseph Kern---Debt.
--John Fleet vs William Buchan & wife---Slander.
--John Fleet vs William Buchan & wife---Case.

[Index 380] OB 17:11b, June Court 1783
Joseph Kern vs Anthony George & John James---Debt.
--Rawleigh Hazard vs William Doggett Jur.---Case.
--Rawleigh Hazard vs William Doggett's administrators &c---Case.
--James Pinckard vs Jonathen Pullen---Case.
--Ordered James Hill pay Jedithen James for his attendance as witness for James in his suit vs Jedithen Pinckard.
--John Hutchings vs Joseph Hubbard---Debt; John Mctyre was special bail for the Deft.

[Index 381] Lancaster OB 17:12a, June Court 1783
James Connolly administrator &c of William Griggs decd. vs Thomas Cottrell & ___---Debt; Jonathen Pullen was special bail for the Deft Cottrell.
--Samuel Yopp vs Charles Bean & Thos. Hubbard---Debt.
--Elias Edmonds vs Rawleigh Hazard---Case; John Mctyre was special bail for Deft.
--James Mott vs Thomas Carter---Case.
--Rawleigh Hazard vs Job Carter---Assault & Battery.
--Rawleigh Hazard vs Moses Hester---Case.

[Index 382] Lancaster OB 17:12b, June Court 1783
Josiah Gaskins vs Robert Pitman & ___ Pitman---Debt; John Angell was special bail for the Defts.
--William Davenport vs William Parrott---Case; Referees were James Ball, Edwin Conway Gent & Onesiphorous Henry.
--William Carpenter vs Henry Tapscott---Case.
--Joseph Shearman vs Mungo Harvey---Case.
--Edward Carter vs John Hazard---Case.
--George Davis Jur. vs Henry Davis---Assault & Battery.
--George Davis Jur. vs Wm. Dunaway &c---Assault & Battery.
--Henry Davis vs Geo. Davis &c---Assault & Battery.
--Thomas Ellett vs Alice Smith---Case.

[Index 383] Lancaster OB 17:13a, June Court 1783
Division of the negroes of the estate of John Doggett decd. was presented.
--Grand jury presentment vs John Mctyre for swearing three oaths, he was fined.
--Grand jury presentment vs Mary Chilton for having a bastard child, she was fined.
--Grand jury presentment vs Mildred Galloway for having a bastard child, she was fined.
--Grand jury presentment vs Thomas Pinckard for swearing twenty oaths, he was fined.
--Grand jury presentment vs Isaac Currell for swearing eight oaths, he was fined.
--Grand jury presentment vs Alexander Davis for swearing four oaths, he was fined.
--Grand jury presentment vs Thomas Cottrell for swearing five oaths, he was fined.
--Grand jury presentment vs Charles Purcell for getting drunk, he was fined.
--Grand jury presentment vs William West for getting drunk, he was fined.
--Grand jury presentment vs Robert Crowther for swearing five oaths, he was fined.

[Index 384] Lancaster OB 17:13b, June Court 1783
The following grand jury presentments were dismissed: vs Robert C. Jacob; vs Samuel Dunaway; vs William Mctyre; vs Robert Clarke; vs William Brown; vs John Davis; vs Newton Brent; vs Jesse Wilder; vs James Brent; vs Thomas Pollard; vs Thomas Lawson Jur.; vs John Lawson; vs William Doggett; vs John Mason; vs Jonathen Pullen.
--Inventory of estate of George Edwards was returned.
--Rawleigh Downman vs William Palmer---Injunction.
--Peter Pool vs Sarah Hammonds---Injunction.
--Deed of surrender from Ann Brent to her son William Brent was proved.
--Deed Thomas Hammond &c to William Norris &c was proved.

[Index 385] Lancaster OB 17:14a, June Court 1783
Ordered John Mctyre pay Moses George for his attendance as witness in George's suit vs Patrick Connolly.
--James Carter appointed Surveyor of Highway from Davis's Warehouse to the main road by the courthouse.
--William Schofield Jur. appointed Surveyor of Highway from the lower church to Carter's new mill, "or little mill."
--Thomas Carter vs Benjamin Williams---Dedimus issued to take deposition of Daniel Stringer, an aged person.
--James Newby, William Warren, and John Bailey appointed to settle the guardianship accounts of the orphans of Charles Lee decd. with Thomas Ellett their former guardian and possess Rawleigh Coats (who was security for sd Ellett) with the estate of said orphans.

Court, 20 June 1783, present justices James Ball, Edwin Conway, John Taylor, William Yerby, James W. Ball, and James Ewell.
--On motion of Col LeRoy Peachey, who was empowered by the administrators of Col Burges Smith decd. to transact business of the estate of the decd, ordered that his account relative thereto be referred to Col James Ball for examination.

[Index 386] Lancaster OB 17:14b, June Court 1783

Thomas Pollard vs Judith George &c administratrix of Bailie George decd.---Sci facias.

--Jedithen James vs James Ewell---Case; a jury came, to wit., Elias Edmonds &c, and they found for the Plt.

--William Schofield vs Thomas Pollard administrator of Saml. Angell decd.---Sci. facias; a jury came, to wit., John Chowning &c., and they found for the Plt.

--Ordered Benjamin Williams pay Daniel Stringer for his attendance as witness in Williams's suit vs Thomas Carter, and for traveling 25 miles to and from his residence.

[Index 387] Lancaster OB 17:15a, June Court 1783

Ordered Thomas Pollard (administrator of Samuel Angell decd.) pay Mungo Harvey for his attendance as witness in Pollard's suit vs William Schofield.

--John Cundiff vs Benjamin Cundiff---Chancery.

--Ordered William Schofield pay John Angell for his attendance as witness in Schofield's suit vs Thos. Pollard, administrator.

--William Brown vs Jedithen Brent.

--Jedithen Brent vs William Brown.

--Simon Laughlin vs Elias Edmonds.

--Thomas Bell vs Robert Jones.

--Mary Lawson vs Judith Brent &c---Chancery; Dedimus issued to take deposition of Catherine Carter.

--Charles Webb assignee &c vs George Phillips &c---Debt.

--William Blackerby vs Johnson Riveer executor of Wm. Blackerby decd.---Case.

[Index 388] Lancaster OB 17:15b, June Court 1783

Newman Chilton by Jas. Newby his guardian vs Jonathen Pullen---Ejectment.

--John Eustace vs John Parrott---Debt.

--William Hunt vs Robt. & Richd. Mitchell executors &c of Richard Mitchell decd.---Case.

--James Howard administrator &c of Lowry Oliver decd. vs John Selden administrator &c of James Selden decd.---Case.

---Joseph Hubbard vs Rawleigh Shearman---Case.

--Isaac Smith vs Moses Hester---Debt.

[Index 389] Lancaster OB 17:16a, June Court 1783

John Berryman vs Joseph Kern---Case.

--Francis Bond by Elias Edmonds vs William Lewis.

--Ordered Robert Jones pay William Mctyre for his attendance as witness in Jones's suit vs Thomas Bell.

--Ordered Robert Jones pay Robert Angell for his attendance as witness in Jones's trial vs Thomas Bell.

--Ordered Robert Jones pay Richard B. Sugges for his attendance as witness in Jones's trial vs Thomas Bell.

--Ordered Jedithen James pay John Chowning for his attendance as witness in James's trial vs James Ewell.

July Court 1783

--John Eustace vs John Parrott---Debt.

[Index 390] Lancaster OB 17:16b, July Court 1783

Court, 5 July 1783, for trial of Lewis a negro man slave the property of Mrs. Mary Tapscott, charged with felony, present justices James Ball, James Ball Jur., James W. Ball, and Robert C. Jacob; Willian Brown was prosecutor for the Commonwealth; the Deft was charged with, on the night of 28 June, stealing ten Spanish milled dollars from Sawny a negro man in the service of Francis Humphrey Christian; the Deft pleaded not guilty; neither the witnesses nor the prosecutor appeared, therefore the Deft was discharged.

Court, 17 July 1783, present justice James Ball, John Berryman, James Ball Jur., James W. Ball, James Tapscott, Robt. C. Jacob.

--John Webb who was formerly bound to Tarpley Thomas, was with consent of sd Thomas now bound to William Everitt to learn the trade of a Taylor.

--Inventory etc of estate of Joshua Hubbard decd. was returned.

[Index 391] Lancaster OB 17:17a, July Court 1783
Deed of gift William Martin to his daughter Elizabeth Martin Gilbert was proved by Harry Currell and Gilbert Currell.
--The following Gent appointed to take list of tithables between ages 16-21: Henry Lawson in Fleet's Island, William Yerby in Fleet's Bay, James Tapscott in Cororo, Robert C. Jacob in the Forest, James Ball Jur. in Rappahk. District, and James Ewell Gent in Corotomon.
--John Eustace vs Robert Roebuck---Petition.
--William Griggs's administrators vs Thomas Bridgford---Petition.
--William Griggs's administrators vs Henry Hinton &c---Petition.
--William Grigg's administrators vs William Hinton &c---Petition.
--William Griggs's administrators vs Henry Lightburn---Petition.
--William Griggs's administrators vs Joshua Spilman---Petition.
--William Griggs's administrators vs William Sullivant &c---Petition.
--John Brown vs Henry Lightburn---Petition.
--Leannah Hutchings vs Joseph Hubbard---Petition.

[Index 392] Lancaster OB 17:17b, July Court 1783
Burges Longwith vs William Schofield Jur.---Petition.
John Davis vs Henry George's administrators---Petition.
--Burges Smith's administrators vs Jesse Robinson &c---Petition.
--Deed Thomas Hammonds, Sarah Hammonds & Ann Hammonds to William Norris and others was proved on 19 June by Jas. Hammonds and John Hammonds, and further proved at July Court by Ezekiel Tapscott.
--Report of settlement of Coleman Doggett's guardianship account of estate of Lucy Mason decd. was returned.
--Administration on estate of Lucy Mason decd. granted to John Mason.
--Hopkins Harding vs George Norris---Debt. William Brown was special bail for Deft.
--William Grigs's administrators vs William Cornelious &c---Debt.
--William Parrott vs John Gordon & Thos. Edwards---Debt. William Brown & LeRoy Peachey Gent were special bail for Deft.
--Thomas Hudnall assignee of Wm. Garner vs McAdam Gaskins & Edwin Conway---Debt. William Brown Gent was special bail for Defts.

[Index 393] Lancaster OB 17:18a, July Court 1783
Joseph Hubbard vs Rawleigh Shearman---Case.
--Thomas Ellett vs Joseph Kern---Case.
--Thomas Ellett vs Thomas Glascock---Case.
--Charles Barns vs James Tapscott---Case.
--Aaron Dameron vs Travers Lunceford---Assault & Battery.
--William Griggs's administrators vs John James & Wm. Hinton---Debt. Michael Wilder was special bail for Deft.
--William Griggs's administrators vs Maurice Wheeler & John James---Debt. Abates as to Wheeler, he being dead, and Michael Wilder was special bail for James.

[Index 394] Lancaster OB 17:18b, July Court 1783
Thos. Coleman assignee of James Connolly vs Ruth Griggs & James Currell Jur.---Debt. Peter Conway was special bail for Deft Griggs.
--Ruth Griggs vs Isaac Currell---Case. Thomas Hathaway was special bail for Deft.
--Indenture from Martin Norris & wife Nancy, William Garner and wife Ellen to William George was acknowledged.
--Vincent Brent assignee of Daniel Kent vs William Lee---Debt.
--Robert C. Jacob assignee of Peter Conway vs William Lee---Debt.
--Robert C. Jacob vs Peter Conway---Case.

[Index 395] Lancaster OB 17:19a, July Court 1783
William Griggs's administrators vs Ruth Griggs & Michael Wilder---Debt. Peter Conway was special bail for Deft.
--Hopkins Harding assignee &c vs Lot Palmer &c---Debt.
--Jonathan Wilder vs William Schofield---Case.
--Robert Jones Jur. vs Jesse Kelly---Assault & Battery.
--Ruth Griggs vs Elias Edmonds---Case.
--Mortgage from Charles Bean to George Norris was proved by Edwin Conway Gent & John Cundiff.
--Robert Pitman vs Jeduthun Pitman---Case.

[Index 396] Lancaster OB 17:19b, July Court 1780
Robert Pitman vs Henry Hazard---Case.
--Burges Smith's administrators vs James Ewell & John Taylor---Debt. Edwin Conway Gent was special bail for Deft Taylor.
--Thads. McCarty attorney for Chas. Hunt vs John Mctyre---Case.
--Goodtitle vs Holdfast---Ejectment. Margaret Ball entered as Deft.
--Leannah Hutchings vs Anthony George &c---Debt.
--John Mctyre vs John Doggett---Chancery.

[Index 397] Lancaster OB 17:20a, July Court 1780
William Griggs's administrators vs John Parrott & James Currell Jur.---Debt.
--James Ball assignee &c vs Peter Conway---Debt. Henry Towles Gent, William Montague & William Sydnor were referees.
--William Griggs's administrators vs Isaac Currell---Petition.
--Col James Ball's report relating to administration account of Col Burges Smith decd. was returned.
--Joseph Hubbard vs John James---Petition.
--Thomas Carter vs Benjamin Williams---Case.

[Index 398] Lancaster OB 17:20b, July Court 1780
Joseph Hubbard vs John Smalwood---Case.
--Ordered Thomas Carter pay Anthony George for his attendance as witness in Carter's suit vs Benjamin Williams.
--Justices of Northumberland Co for Thomas Carter & others vs John Eustace---Debt.
--Ordered Thomas Carter pay Aaron Dameron for attendance as witness for Carter against Benjamin Williams.
--Ordered William Garlington pay Thomas Gaskins Gent for attendance as witness in Garlington's suit vs George Brent, and for traveling 8 miles to and from his residence.
--Ordered the Northumberland Justices pay Ezekiel Haydon for attendance as witness in their suit vs John Eustace, and for traveling six miles to and from his residence.
--Ordered the Northumberland Justices by Thomas Carter &c pay William Schofield for attendance as witness in their suit vs John Eustace.
--Ordered the Northumberland Justices pay William Chilton for attendance as witness in their suit vs John Eustace.
--John Boswell vs William Grigg's administrators---Case.

[Index 399] Lancaster OB 17:21a, July Court 1783
Court, 19 July 1783, present justices James Ball, John Berryman, Henry Towles, and Robt. C. Jacob.
--Joseph Carter recommended to the Governor as an Assistant Inspector of tobacco at Davis's warehouse.
--Thomas Hubbard, James Pinckard, William Gibson, John Carpenter, William Hunt, William Kirk fined 100 pounds tobacco each for not attending as jurymen.
--John Boswell vs William Griggs's administrators---Case.

[Index 400] Lancaster OB 17:21b, July Court 1783
Northumberland Justices for Thos. Carter &c vs John Eustace---Debt.
--Simon Laughlin vs Elias Edmonds for Lucy Denny---Case.

--Ordered John Boswell pay Thomas Carter for attendance as witness in Boswell's suit vs Will. Griggs's administrators, and for traveling six miles to and from his residence.

--Ordered Will. Griggs's administrators pay Elizabeth Carter for attendance as witness in their suit vs John Boswell, and for traveling six miles to and from her residence.

[Index 401] Lancaster OB 17:22a, July Court 1783

Ordered John Boswell pay Thomas Pollard for attendance as witness in Boswell's suit vs Will. Grigg's administrators.

--Ordered John Boswell pay Simon Laughlin for attendance as witness in Boswell's suit vs Will. Griggs's administrators, and for traveling twenty miles from and to his residence.

--Rawleigh Hazard vs John Parrott---Case. Referees were Henry Towles, William Yerby, James Tapscott Gent.

--Thomas Pollard vs Rawleigh Hazard---Case. Referees were Henry Towles, William Yerby, James Tapscott Gent.

--Thomas Pollard vs Rawleigh Shearman---Case. Referees were Henry Towles, William Yerby, James Tapscott Gent.

--William Schofield vs Thomas Pollard.

--John Heath vs William Schofield Jur. &c.

--John Cundiff vs Benjamin Cundiff---Chancery.

--Commonwealth vs Vincent Brent &c---Sci. fa.

--Ezekiel Hudnall vs James Ewell.

[Index 402] Lancaster OB 17:22b, July Court 1783

Ordered Robert Jones pay Andrew Robertson for attendance as witness in his suit vs Thomas Bell.

--William Davenport vs William Parrott &c.

--John Wormeley vs Jesse Harrison.

--Rachel Hill administratrix vs William Hinton.

--Thomas Jones executor of William Tait decd. vs William Kent &c executors of Wm. Taylor decd.—Sci. facias.

--Thomas Pollard vs Bailie George's administrators.

--Charles Webb assignee &c vs George Phillips &c---Debt.

--William Hunt vs Richd. Mitchell's executors.

--Francis Bond vs William Lewis---Case.

[Index 403] Lancaster OB 17:23a, July Court 1783

Ordered the Justices of Northumberland on behalf of Thomas Carter &c pay Spencer Currell for attendance as witness in their suit vs John Eustace.

--Ordered the Justices of Northumberland for Thos. Carter &c pay Harry Currell for attendance as witness in their suit vs John Eustace.

--Sarah Pearson administratrix vs Jonathen Pearson---Chancery.

--William Blackerby vs Johnson Riveer executor of Wm. Blackerby decd.---Case.

--Oliver's administrators vs Selden's administrators---Case.

--Grand Jury vs Job Carter---Summons.

--Isaac Smith vs Moses Hester & John Heath Jur.---Debt.

--John Berryman vs Joseph Kern---Case.

[Index 404] Lancaster OB 17:23b, July Court 1783

Commonwealth vs John Arms---Indictment

---Ozwald Newby vs John Taylor---Debt.

--Rawleigh Hazard vs Charles Purcell---Case.

--John Degge vs Thomas Brent---Trespass.

--John Mctyre vs Selden's administrators---Case.

[Index 405] Lancaster OB 17:24a, August Court 1783

Court, 21 August 1783, present justices James Ball, Edwin Conway, John Berryman, Henry Lawson.

--Joseph Carter produced qualified as Assistant Inspector of at Davis's Warehouse.
--On motion of William Gibson, William Kirk, Thomas Hubbard, James Pinckard, William Hunt, and John Carpenter, fined at last court for not appearing as jurymen, they were discharged from the fine.
--Charles Lee produced his account of estate of William Doggett, recorded.
--John Flowers produced his account of estate of John Flowers, recorded.
--Nicholas George presented his public claim as Commissary to the guards at Chowning's and Fowler's Point, one month's service.
--On motion of Charles Carter Esq to rebuild his mill known as "the great Mill," ordered the Sheriff summon a jury to view the lands on both sides of the Run.

[Index 406] Lancaster OB 17:24b, August Court 1783
Settlement of estate of John Yerby decd. was returned.
--On complaint of William Chilton the elder against his son Wm. Chilton Jur. for sureties of the peace, ordered sd Chilton Jur. post bond, with John Davis and William Chilton Joiner his securities.
--Commonwealth vs William Angell---Complaint. Ordered Angell post bond, with William Norris and John Angell his security.
--Commonwealth vs John Wilkerson---Complaint. Ordered Wilkerson post bond, with John Arms and Tarpley Thomas his securities.
--Certified that William Newby Bailey is heir at law to Edward Bailey who was in the service of the state and since dead.
--John Carter orphan of John Carter decd. chose Michael Wilder as his guardian.
--John Berryman and Henry Lawson Gent appointed to settle estate of John Carter decds. now in hands of Peter Garton and possess Michael Wilder with it.
--Petition of Samuel Yopp Jur. vs William Angell, dismissed.
--Thomas Pollard vs William Schofield.

[Index 407] Lancaster OB 17:25a, August Court 1783
Thomas Pollard, administrator vs William Schofield---Chancery.
--Settlement of guardianship of orphans of Thomas Everitt decd. was recorded.
--William Brent administrator of Thos. Brent decd. vs Thomas Pollard &c.
--Thomas Brent vs Alice Smith---Petition.
--Alexander Hunton vs John Payne---Petition.
--Alexander Hunton vs Rawleigh Brown---Petition.
--Alexander Hunton vs Thomas Bevans---Petition.
--William Brent administrator of Thos. Brent decd. vs William Kent &c.
--Peter Goard vs John Tarpley---Petition.
--James Tapscott vs George Ingram---Petition.

[Index 408] Lancaster OB 17:25b, August Court 1783
Will of Thomas Pinckard Gent decd. further proved by Samuel S. McCroskey and Ellyson Armistead, and administration was granted to Thomas Pinckard Jur. one of the executors therein named. John Berryman, William Yerby, and Henry Lawson Gent were appointed appraisers.
--Account of sales of estate of William Griggs decd. was recorded.
--Ordered Thomas Brent pay Thomas Dye for attendance as witness in Brent's suit vs Mrs. Alice Smith. James Ball, Edwin Conway, James W. Ball, and Henry Lawson Gent.
--Ordered the Commonwealth pay William Luckham for attendance as witness for it vs John Arms.
--Ordered the Commonwealth pay William Smith for attendance as witness for it vs John Arms.
--Samuel Yopp vs James Simmonds---Chancery.

[Index 409] Lancaster OB 17:26a, August Court 1783
James Tapscott vs George Ingram---Petition. Dedimus issued to take depositions of James Ball of Northumberland and Nathaniel West Dandridge Gent.

--Elizabeth Mctyre vs John Hazard---Case.

Court, 22 Aug 1783, present justices James Ball, Edwin Conway, Henry Towles, John Berryman, William Yerby, James Ball Jur., Henry Lawson, Robt. C. Jacob.
--Certified that John Newby is heir to LeRoy Newby decd. who was in the service of this state and since dead.
--John Cundiff vs Benjamin Cundiff—Chancery. Referees were Edwin Conway and William Nutt Gent.
--Simon Laughlin vs Wm. Briggs's administrators—Petition.
--Archibald Ritchie vs Newton Brent—Petition.

[Index 410] Lancaster OB 17:26b, August Court 1783
On motion of John Dye by his attorney, ordered execution issue against John Hutchingson and William Kirk upon bond entered into by sd Hutchinson and Kirk for part of the estate of the sd Hutchinson taken in execution to satisfy judgment obtained against said Hutchinson by said Dye and restored with costs.
--William Miskell vs Nathaniel Burwell—Case.
--Thomas Garnett vs Nathaniel Burwell—Case.
--William Montague vs John Selden—Case.
--Henry Hinton vs John Taylor—Debt.
--Matthew Miars assignee vs Robert Mctyre—Debt.
--John Fleet vs Martin Shearman—Discontinued.

[Index 411] Lancaster OB 17:27a, August Court 1783
Henry Barns vs Rodham Lunceford &c—Debt; James Gordon Gent was special bail for Deft.
--James Muse & Co vs Josiah Greenwood & Robt. Mctyre---Sci. facias.
--Rawleigh Hazard vs Charles Purcell—Debt.
--James Newby vs Henry Hurst—Assault and Battery.
--Alexander Davis vs Vincent & Jed. Brent—Assault and Battery.
--John Parrott v James Pollard & Jesse Wilder—Case.

[Index 412] Lancaster OB 17:27b, August Court 1783
William Lawson vs John Berryman—Case.
--Lott Adams vs Jesse Crowther—Case.
--Rawleigh Shearman vs Joseph Hubbard—Case.
--William Montague vs John Heath Jur.—Case.
--Thomas West vs John Parrott—Slander.
--John Mctyre & wife guardians &c vs Jedithen Pinckard & T. Hubbard—Debt.
--William McClanneham Exor. &c vs Peter Conway—Debt.
--James Currell vs John Berryman—Case.

[Index 413] Lancaster OB 17:28a, August Court 1783
Burges Smith's administrators vs John Wormeley—Case.
--James Jones assignee &c vs John Wormeley—Debt. Vincent Brent and William Kirk were special bail for Deft.
--William Griggs's administrators vs Wm. Cornelious & Isaac Currell—Debt. James Pollard was special bail for Deft Currell.
--William Carter vs Jedithen Brent—Assault and Battery.
--Joseph Hubbard vs John Smalwood—Attachment. Thomas Pollard was special bail for Deft.
--Goodright vs Holdfast—Ejectment; James Pollard was admitted Deft instead of the said Holdfast.

[Index 414] Lancaster OB 17:28b, August Court 1783
Goodright vs Badtitle—Ejectment; James Pollard was admitted Deft instead of the said Badtitle.
--Deed of gift from James Brent to his niece Elizabeth Maxwell was acknowledged.
--Indenture of bargain and sale from John Wormeley and Ann his wife to James Gordon was acknowledged, and was recorded along with the commission for the privy examination of said Ann.

--Mary Lawson vs Charles Rogers & others—Chancery.
--John Wormeley vs Jesse Harrison—Case.
--John Heath vs William Schofield and others—Detinue; James Ball, Edwin Conway, and James Gordon Gent were referees.
--William Schofield vs Thomas Pollard—Case.

[Index 415] Lancaster OB 17:29a, August Court 1783

William Ball, James Brent, and Rawleigh Tapscott were recommended to the Governor as proper person to be added to the Commission of the Peace.
--Rachel Hill administratrix &c vs William Hinton—Case.
--Thomas Pollard vs Bailey George's administrators—Sci facias.
--William Hunt vs Richard Mitchell's executors—Case.
--Newman Chilton vs Jonathan Pullen—Ejectment.
--Ordered Jonathen Pullen pay Moses George for attendance four days as witness in Pullen's suit vs Newman Chilton.
--Ordered Newman Chilton pay Joseph Dobbs for his attendance as witness in Chilton's suit vs Jonathen Pullen.
--Ordered Newman Chilton pay William Chilton, Joiner, for his attendance as witness in sd Newman Chilton's suit against Jonathen Pullen.

[Index 416] Lancaster OB 17:29b, August Court 1783

John Degge vs Thomas Brent—Trespass.
--Ordered Newman Chilton pay James Newby for attendance as witness in Chilton's suit against Jonathen Pullen.
--On motion of John Fleet Gent by his attorney, ordered subpoena issue against Bridgar Haynie who is executor of Margaret Boyd decd., who was administratrix with the will annexed of David Boyd decd., who was executor of Newton Keene Gent decd., to revive the suit in Lancaster Court Fleet & wife against Newton Keen's executors.
--On motion of John Goodridge who was security for Mary Doggett's guardianship of Dennis and Priscilla Doggett orphans of Coleman Doggett decd., ordered that John Mctyre who intermarried with said Mary be summoned to give counter security for the performance of said Mary his wife.
--Ordered John Degge pay John Sullivant for his attendance as witness in Degge's suit against Thomas Brent.
--Ordered John Degge pay Jedithen Brent for his attendance as witness in Degge's suit against Thomas Brent.
--Ordered Jonathen Pullen pay James Carter for his attendance as witness in Pullen's suit against Newman Chilton.
--Ordered Jonathen Pullen pay William Edwards for his attendance as witness in Pullen's suit vs Newman Chilton.

[Index 417] Lancaster OB 17:30a, August Court 1783

Ordered John Degge pay Onesephorous Harvey for his attendance as witness in Degge's suit against Thomas Brent, and for traveling nine miles to and from his residence.
--Ordered John Degge pay Thomas Hunt for his attendance as witness in Degge's suit against Thomas Brent.

Court of Oyer and Terminer, 21 Aug 1783, for trial of Charles a negro slave belonging to Thomas Hathaway, charged with felony, present justices Edwin Conway, Henry Towles, William Herby, James Ball Jur., Henry Lawson, Robt. C. Jacob; The prisoner was led to the bar and pleaded not guilty; he was found guilty but within benefit of clergy, for which ordered he be burnt in the hand and receive on his bare back thirty nine lashes at the public whipping post.

[Index 418] Lancaster OB 17:30b, Sept Court 1783

Court, 18 September 1783, present justices James Ball, Edwin Conway, John Berryman, Henry Towles, Henry Lawson, James Tapscott.
--Sarah Mitchell orphan of William Mitchell decd. chose Thos. Mitchell her guardian.
--William Warren and Ozwald Newby appointed to settle the accounts of Thomas Flint decd. of his guardianship of the estate of Thomas and Sarah Mitchell orphans of William Mitchell decd. with the executors of the said Thomas Flint decd. and possess said Thomas Mitchell with his & Sarah's part thereof.

--Henry Towles, James Ball Jur. Gent, William Sydnor, and Rawleigh Tapscott appointed to settle James Newby's executorship accounts of the estate of Moses Chilton decd.

--Bill of sale from Spencer Hinton to James Harris was proved by the witnesses.

--Report and settlement of estate of John Carter decd. was returned.

--On petition of Charles Carter Esq for leave to build a water grist mill on the Great Mill Run where his former mill stood, and praying for an acre of land to be laid off, ordered the Sheriff summon a jury to view the land on both sides in the same or the next county, after having first laid off the said acre petitioned for on the land belonging to the orphans of William King decd.

--On motion of John Heath Jur. for a removal of the records into the County of Lancaster, they being at present by order of the court at the Clerk's house in Richmond County, tho' nearly on the line between the said counties of Richmond and Lancaster, ordered the records be removed within six months.

[Index 419] Lancaster OB 17:31a, Sept Court 1783

On motion of Richard Ball by his attorney against the Sheriff of Northumberland County for not settling the execution of a bond against George Bean, judgment granted sd Ball against the said Sheriff.

--Joseph Hubbard vs John Mctyre—Petition.

--Alexander Hunton vs Presly Cockrell—Petition.

--Epaphroditus Robinson vs Spencer Brown—Petition.

--Spencer Brown vs Epaphroditus Robinson—Petition.

--Archibald Ritchie vs Spencer Brown—Petition.

--Thomas Stott vs Jesse Gaskins & George Glascock Jur.—Petition.

--Samuel Menzes administrator of George Menzes decd. vs Jesse Gaskins—Petition.

--William Sydnor inspector of Deep Creek Warehouse returned his account of tobacco.

--Samuel Yopp Jur. appointed guardian to Priscilla Doggett orphan of Coleman Doggett decd.

--On motion of Rhoda James by her attorney, ordered execution issue against George Bean and Craven Everitt upon a bond entered into by said Bean and Everitt for part of the estate of said Bean taken in execution to satisfy a judgment obtained by said James against said Bean.

[Index 420] Lancaster OB 17:31b, September Court 1783

Joseph Kern vs George Carter &c---Petition.

--Joseph Kern vs John Parrott &c—Petition.

--Joseph Kern vs William James—Petition.

--Joseph Kern vs Rawleigh Shearman &c—Petition.

--Joseph Kern vs Thos. West & Thos. Pollard—Petition.

--Joseph Kern vs John Baldwin &c—Petition.

--Joseph Kern vs Anthony George—Petition.

--Edwin Kent vs William Chilton, Joiner—Petition.

--Thomas Webb vs William Schofield Jur.—Petition.

--Rawleigh Downman's executors vs Joseph Hubbard—Petition.

--Spencer George administrator of Eliza. James decd. vs Newton Brent—Petition.

--Thomas Stott vs William Angell & Robt. Mctyre—Debt.

[Index 421] Lancaster OB 17:32a, Sept Court 1783

Henry Fleet vs Richard Selden.

--William Newby vs John Mctyre.

--John Turbervile vs John Connolly—Debt.

--John Turbervile vs John Connolly—Debt.

--Inventory and appraisement of estate of Presly Cockrell decd. was returned.

--Mungo Harvey vs James Newby executor of Moses Chilton decd.—Debt; Newman Chilton the son and heir to said Chilton decd. confessed judgment for the debt and costs.

--Callender &c vs Job Carter—Debt.

--Callender &c vs Newton Brent—Debt. Henry Lawson Gent was special bail for the Deft.

--Joseph Kern vs Nicholas Currell Jur. &c—Debt.

[Index 422] Lancaster OB 17:32b, Sept Court 1783
Joseph Kern vs John Thrall & Hen. Lawson—Debt; Lawson Hathaway was special bail for the Deft.
--William Griggs's administrators vs James Faires—Debt; William Gibson and Jonathen Pullen were special bail for the said Faires.
--William Griggs's administrators vs George Carter & Thos. Carter—Debt.
--Downman's executors vs John Heath Jur. & John Selden—Debt; Edwin Conway Gent was special bail for the Deft.
--John Bean vs William Brown—Debt.
--On motion of Thomas Pollard by his attorney, ordered execution issue against George Goodridge, LeRoy Pope and _____ upon a bond entered into by said Goddridge [thus] &c for part of the estate of said Goodridge & Pope taken in execution to satisfy Thomas Pollard's judgment obtained against sd Goodridge and Pope and restored with costs.

[Index 423] Lancaster OB 17:33a, Sept Court 1783
Elizabeth Hinton vs John Smalwood—Case; Thomas Pollard was security for Deft.
--James Craine vs Vincent Brent—Debt; Thomas Pollard was special bail for the Deft.
--John Edwards vs John Hutchenson—Assault and Battery.
--Scurlock &c vs Tapscott's executors—Chancery; Ordered dedimus issue to take deposition of William Stonum of Richmond County.
--Ezekiel Hudnall vs James Ewell—Ordered dedimus issue to take deposition of Capt Richard Selden.
--William Brown recommended to the Masters of William & Mary College as a proper person to act as Surveyor for Lancaster County.
--Ezekiel Hudnall vs James Ewell—Ordered that dedimus issue to take deposition of James Ledford of Northumberland County.
--Ordered that the Clerk certify to the Auditors of the state that Nancy Dye is heir at law to Jonathen Dye who died in the Continental Service at the Battle at German Town.

[Index 424] Lancaster OB 17:33b, Sept Court 1783
The Will of William Hubbard decd. was presented by his widow Elizabeth Hubbard, executrix therein named, and was proved by Charles Hubbard and by him to have seen Joshua Hubbard decd. attest the same, and was admitted to record, and said Elizabeth was granted probate thereof; Edwin Conway Gent., John Cundiff, William Schofield, and George Norris were appraisers.
--Richard Ball vs Margarett Ball—Ejectment; Abates by death of the Deft.
--James Tapscott vs George Ingram—Petition; Ordered dedimus issue to take deposition of Archibald Payne of Goochland County.
--Edwin Conway, James W. Ball, and James Tapscott Gent ordered to possess Samuel Yopp Jur., with the estate of Priscilla Doggett orphan of Coleman Doggett decd. now in the hands of John Mctyre.

Court, 19 September 1783, present justices Edwin Conway, Henry Towles, John Selden, James Tapscott.

[Index 425] Lancaster OB 17:34a, Sept Court 1783
James Craine vs Vincent Brent—Debt.
--Order Richard Ball pay Ozwald Newby for attendance as witness in Ball's suit against Margaret Ball.
--On motion of James W. Ball Gent, ordered that George Norris be summoned to show cause why execution should not issued against the mortgaged goods of Charles Bean in his hands, agreeable to a former order of the court.

[Index 426] Lancaster OB 17:34b, Oct Court 1783
Court, 16 October 1783, present justices James Ball, Edwin Conway, John Berryman, William Yerby, James Ball Jur., Henry Lawson, and Robt. C. Jacob.
--On motion of Henry Lawson Gent, administration granted him on estate of "one" John Rains decd.; James Brent, Thomas Pollard, William Norris, and George Carter were appraisers.

--Gawin Lowry and Charles Rogers appointed Inspectors, and Joseph Carter and John Davis Assistant Inspectors, of tobacco at Davis's Warehouse; William Sydnor was appointed Inspector and Rawleigh Tapscott assistant at Deep Creek Warehouse.

--Charles Rogers, one of the Inspectors at Davis's Warehouse, rendered his account of tobacco.

--Indenture of bargain and sale from John Parrott and ___ his wife to Robert Clark Jacob was acknowledged.

--Frances H. Christian vs Joseph Stephens—Petition.

--Rawleigh Downman Executor &c vs John Hazard—Petition.

--Frances H. Christian vs Sarah Bond—Petition.

--William Glascock Jur. vs John Mctyre—Petition.

[Index 427] Lancaster OB 17:35a, Oct Court 1783
Archibald Ritchie vs Rawleigh Brown—Petition.

--Downman's executors vs John Crowther &c—Petition.

--Samuel Yopp vs Thomas Brent—Petition.

--Griggs's administrators vs John Clemmens & Michael Wilder—Petition.

--William Brown vs Ann Shearman—Petition; Judgment confessed by Henry Lawson Gent for the Deft.

--Jesse Wilder vs William Boatman—Petition.

--Mungo Harvey vs John Selden & James Ewell—Debt.

--George Glascock Jur. vs John Mctyre—Case.

--John Cundiff vs Benjamin Cundiff—Chancery; James Ball Gent added to the former referees in this suit.

[Index 428] Lancaster OB 17:35b, Oct Court 1783
Frances H. Christian vs Agatha Ball—Case; Judgment confessed by James Tapscott Gent for the Deft.

--Robinson vs Andrew Robertson—Ejectment.

--Downman's executors vs John Wormeley &c—Debt.

--Joseph Kern vs Thomas Cockrell &c—Debt.

--Grigg's administrators vs John Clemmons & George Brent—Debt; Deft Clemmons was returned "not to be found."

[Index 429] Lancaster OB 17:36a, Oct Court 1783
James Craine vs Vincent Brent—Debt; Thomas Hubbard and Jedithen Brent were special bail for the Deft.

--William Yerby vs Vincent Brent &c—Debt.

--Thomas Stott vs John Pullen &c—Debt.

--Burges Longwith vs Thomas Brent—Assault and Battery.

--William Schofield Jur. vs John Smalwood &c—Debt.

--John Smalwood vs Henry Fleet—Case.

[Index 430] Lancaster OB 17:36b, Oct Court 1783
James W. Ball vs George Norris—Summons.

--Thomas Webb vs Wm. Schofield Jur.—Petition.

--Alexander Hunton vs Presly Cockrell—Petition.

--Settlement of the administration accounts of Thomas Brent decd. of the estate of George Brent decd. was returned.

--Ordered Epaphroditus Robinson pay Jesse Robinson Jur. for attendance as witness in sd Epaphroditus's suit vs Spencer Brown.

--Will of Lazarous George decd. was presented by Benjamin George one of the executors therein named, and being proved by Sarah Ann Walker and Winifred Walker two of the witnesses, was recorded.

--On motion of Easter Newsom, James Ball, James W. Ball Gent & Ozwald Newby were appointed to divide the land and personal estate of George Newsom decd. which is now in the hands of Spencer Brown between the said Easter Newsom and Rachel Brown the wife of said Spencer Brown, and possess each party with their parts thereof.

--Will of Mrs. Margarett Ball decd. was presented by William Ball and Mungo Harvey executors therein named, and was proved by the witnesses, and probate was granted to said executors, and a codicil was offered by the said

executors which was rejected; William Montague, John Leland, James Tapscott, and Robert C. Jacob appointed appraisers in Lancaster County, and _____ were appointed appraisers in Westmoreland County.
--Ordered Thomas Pollard pay Daniel Carter as a witness from Essex County in Pollard's suit against Rawleigh Shearman, and for traveling 24 miles eight days to and from his place of residence, and for ferriages.

[Index 431] Lancaster OB 17:37a, Oct Court 1783
James Tapscott vs George Ingram---Petition; set for trial 1 March next.
--John Fleet, John Berryman Gent, Thomas Carter, and William Lawson appointed to settle guardianship accounts of John James of the estate of Fanny James.
--Ordered James Tapscott Gent pay David Martin for attendance in Tapscott's suit against George Ingram, and for traveling 110 miles to and from his place of residence, also for his ferriages.
--Ordered James Tapscott Gent pay David Mims for attendance as witness in Tapscott's suit against George Ingram, and for traveling 110 miles to and from his place of residence.
--James Ball and James W. Ball Gent appointed to try the weights at Deep Creek Warehouse; Edwin Conway and James Tapscott Gent at Davis's Warehouse.
--Ordered John Mctyre pay Ozwald Newby for attendance as witness in Mctyre's suit against William Glascock Jur.
--Mungo Harvey vs John Selden—Case; The award of James Ball, William Sydnor and Henry Towles Gent was returned, and judgment ordered for the Plt.

[Index 432] Lancaster OB 17:37b, Oct Court 1783
Court, 17 October 1783, present justices James Ball, Edwin Conway, John Berryman, James W. Ball, and James Ewell.
--Charles Lee executor of John E. Beale decd. vs Elisha Hall—Case.
--Charles Lee executor &c vs Elisha Hall—Case; a jury came, to wit., Elias Edmonds &c
--Callender &c vs Job Carter—Debt.

[Index 433] Lancaster OB 17:38a, Dec Court 1783
Court, 18 December 1783, present justices Edwin Conway, William Yerby, James Tapscott, and Matt. Myars.
--Ordered Edwin Conway, James Tapscott Gent, John Bean, and John Cundiff settle administration accounts of the estate of Thomas Brent decd. and divide the balance of said estate among the concerned parties.
--John Cundiff vs Benjamin Cundiff—Chancery; Ordered that as Milly Cundiff in the bill of complaint died intestate, thereupon her two negroes Duke and Milly became the sole property of the said Benjamin her heir at law, and having examined his administration account of the said intestate's estate, the court finds he has paid the Complainant and his other brother and sister their full proportion of the personal estate of the said decd., but on his consenting to divide the whole estate of the said deceased (including the said two negroes) between all his brothers and sisters equally on the Complainant's dismissing said suit and paying all costs, court finds that a balance was due the Complainant of twelve pounds, [signed] 22 Novr. 1783, Jas. Ball, William Nutt.

[Index 434] Lancaster OB 17:38b, Dec Court 1783
Privy examination of Franky Parrott wife of John Parrott respecting their deed of bargain and sale to Robert Clark Jacob was returned.
--Inventory and appraisement of estate of Thomas Flint decd. was returned.
--Joseph Carter orphan of Joseph Carter decd. chose Matthew Myars Gent his guardian.
--On motion of James Hill by his attorney, ordered a new execution issue against Jeduthun Pinckard upon a bond entered into by said Pinckard for part of the estate of sd. Pinckard taken in execution to satisfy a judgment obtained by sd Hill against sd Pinckard and restored with costs.
--Ordered William Yerby Gent, James Brent, Benjamin George, and Thomas Pollard settle the administration account of the estate of Elmour Doggett decd.
--Indenture of bargain and sale from Robert Clark Jacob and his wife [not named] to Kendall Lee was acknowledged.
--Deed of gift from William Brent to his son Jeduthun Brent was proved by one witness, and ordered to lie for further proof.

[Index 435] Lancaster OB 17:39a, Jan Court 1784
Court, 3 January 1784, for examination of John Sullivant who stands charged with having murdered John Taylor Gent on 28 December last, present justices James Ball, John Fleet, Edwin Conway, John Berryman, Henry Towles, William Yerby, James Ball Jur., Henry Lawson, John Selden, James W. Ball, James Tapscott, and Matt. Myars; the said Sullivant appearing at the bar, he pleaded not guilty; the court were of opinion that he was guilty and that he be sent for trial at the next General Court in Richmond; James Ewell Gent, Thomas Hubbard, and Thomas Brent to appear as witnesses in behalf of the Commonwealth.

[End]

Index

Numbers refer to the index number, <u>not to the page number</u>. Women are indexed twice, once by surname, and secondly by first name *in italics*. Spelling variants for surnames and given names have been reduced to one or two variants, insofar as possible, for indexing purposes. Place names are <u>underlined</u>.

Dogge(t)t, Elmor(e) 41 (+), 45, 48, 64, 136, 145, 174, 177, 255 (+), 243, 258 (+), 260, 263, 265, 290, 293, 312 (+), 358, 434

Dogget, Elmore Jr 100

Dogge(t)t, George 239, 258, 286 (+), 311, 350 (+), 378

Dogget, James 127

Dogget, Jeremiah 9, 44

Dogge(t)t, John 35 (+), 41 (+), 42 (+), 45, 48, 56, 136, 206, 226, 239-40, 244, 319, 328, 346 (+), 383, 396

Doggett, Lucy 240

Doggett, Mary 284 (+), 416

Doggett, Maryann 239, 255

Dogge(t)t, Molly 44, 284, 346

Doggett, Priscilla 284, 416, 419, 424

Dogget, Reuben 9 (+), 54 (+)

Dogget, Spencer 20, 33, 79, 81, 84, 94, 98, 127

Doggett, Thomas 279, 286

Dogge(t)t, William 56, 60, 64, 79, 150, 173, 177, 191, 194, 208 (+), 213 (+), 240 (+), 244, 279, 286, 295, 297, 309, 320, 348, 349, 350 (+), 369, 378, 380, 384, 405

Doggett, William Jr 133, 213, 255 (+), 267, 320, 360, 380

Doggett, Winifred 206, 346

Doggett, Winny 239

Dolly [no last name] 204

Dolly Davis 157

Dounting, William 232

Dounton, William 322

Downing, Thomas 52

Downling, William 102

Downman 26, 253, 422, 427-8

Downman, Joseph Ball 287

Downman, Rawleigh (Raleigh) 43, 93, 204, 221, 252 (+), 258, 262, 292, 308, 353, 384, 420, 426

Downman, Rawleigh W. 252, 372, 374

Downman, Robert Porteus 128

Downman, R. P. 195

Dunaway, Elizabeth 27

Dunaway, Samuel 61, 72, 94, 115, 121, 157, 177, 179, 272, 305 (+), 384

Dunaway, Susanna 150

Dunaway, Thomas 8, 73, 150, 186, 204, 237, 239, 307

Dunaway, William 295, 326, 382

Dye, John 249 (+), 257 (+), 314 (+), 316, 366, 410

Dye, Jonathan 423

Dye, Maryan 316

Dye, Nancy 423

Dye, Richard 281

Dye, Sarahan 272

Dye, Thomas 408

Dymer 12

Dymer, William 103, 105

Easter Newsom 430

Easton, Richard 293

Eddings, Samuel 292-3

Edmonds, Elias 12, 13 (+), 15, 18-20, 23-4, 30-31, 34, 46, 53, 55, 58, 63 (+), 66-7, 83, 88, 91, 97, 100, 126-7, 141, 143 (+), 157, 166, 171-2, 185, 188, 214-15, 219-20, 224, 226, 231, 248, 250, 259, 262, 264, 276-7, 279 (+), 280 (+), 281, 291, 299, 305-6, 314 (+), 332, 334, 336, 339, 346-8, 364, 375, 381, 386-7, 389, 395, 400, 432

Edmonds, John 141

Edmonds, Robert 100, 224

Edmonds, William 24

Edwards, Agatha 280

Edwards, Betty 205

Edwards, Charles 28

Edwards, George 20, 34, 123, 143, 181, 195, 245, 285, 368, 384

Edwards, John 61, 168, 173, 178, 187 (+), 191, 194, 208, 213, 234, 252, 311, 423

Edwards, Judith 83

Edwards, Mary 368

Edwards, Richard 34, 367

Edwards, Sally 74

Edwards, Thomas 40, 53, 83 (+), 127, 205, 280 (+), 289, 367, 392

Edwards, William 34, 66, 78 (+), 254, 269, 289, 294, 297, 299, 306, 332, 339, 365, 374 (+), 375 (+), 416

Eidson, John 108

Elenor Payne 169

Eliza James 147

Eliza Percifull 63

Elizabeth Beale 359

Elizabeth Bell 262

Elizabeth Biscoe 309

Elizabeth Blackerby 248, 250, 341, 353

Elizabeth Blakemore 278

Elizabeth Brady 76-7, 87

Elizabeth Carter 34, 400

Elizabeth Clayton 76

Elizabeth Dunaway 27

Elizabeth Flood 51 (+), 52, 57

Elizabeth Garland 311

Elizabeth Griggs 18, 102, 122

Elizabeth Hill 185, 277-9, 287, 294, 305, 371

Elizabeth Hinton 182, 198, 242 (+), 274, 360, 423

Elizabeth Hubbard 27, 424

Elizabeth James 64, 71 (+), 164 (+), 308, 420

Elizabeth James Jr 308

Elizabeth Jones 137

Elizabeth King 25, 177

Elizabeth Lawson 63 (+), 131

Elizabeth Martin 81

Elizabeth Martin Gilbert 391

Elizabeth Maxwell 414

Elizabeth McGrigor 122

Elizabeth McTyre 90, 208, 231, 293, 305 (+), 308, 331, 339, 348, 352, 409

Elizabeth Pope 88

Elizabeth Pullen 254

Elizabeth Purkins 147

Elizabeth Reid 24

Elizabeth Riveer 14

Elizabeth Roberts 189

George, Benjamin 20, 56, 147, 163 (+), 167, 182, 195, 252, 255, 260, 263, 265, 277, 279, 281, 284-5, 295, 319-20, 333, 368, 430, 434

George, Daniel 13, 24, 30, 33, 62, 334

George, Enoch 77, 82 (+)

George, Harry 79, 98

George, Henry 16, 20, 134, 174, 219, 235, 237, 248, 280, 333, 392

George, Jesse 4-5, 23, 78, 84, 86, 98, 123, 170, 213, 219, 229-30, 237, 269, 292, 309, 322 (+), 329, 333, 336, 362, 364

George, Judith 213, 311, 333, 350, 359, 386

George, Lazarus 43, 78, 430

George, Martin 4, 32, 45-6, 70, 308

George, Mary 82

George, Moses 81, 243, 269, 280, 352, 373, 385, 415

George, Nicholas 20, 26, 28, 30 (+), 33 (+), 45, 62, 69, 80, 81 (+), 121, 123, 136, 172-3, 183, 193, 210, 228-9, 245, 248, 268, 291, 309, 333, 336-8, 371, 405

George, Nicholas Jr 342

George, Nicholas Lawson 82 (+)

George, Spencer 20, 28, 31 (+), 33, 35, 38, 60, 71, 77, 94, 101, 127, 130 (+), 143-4, 194, 232, 239, 260, 270, 314, 319, 332, 352 (+), 369, 371, 420

George, Thomas 91, 126, 130 (+), 145, 270, 289

George, William 13, 21 (+), 309, 394

George, William Sr 342

George, Wilmoth 243

Gibbons, John 23

Gibbs, Charles 35

Gibbs, James 35

Gibson 259

Gibson, William 29, 32 (+), 33, 35 (+), 36-7, 39, 41 (+), 45, 48,

53, 55 (+), 60, 63-5, 70-71, 77, 91, 126, 130-31, 135-6, 143, 155, 156 (+), 163 (+), 164, 167, 175, 206 (+), 220, 227, 235 (+), 254, 255 (+), 263-4, 276-7, 280, 298, 308, 312, 333-4, 348-9, 399, 405, 422

Gilbert 31

Gilbert, Elizabeth Martin 391

Gilmour, Helen 344, 347, 360

Gilmour, John Morton 360

Gilmour, Robert {Gilmore] 20 (+), 23-4, 49, 52, 77, 83, 181, 198-9, 204, 293, 312, 344, 352, 359-60, 362, 364

Gilmour, Robert Galloway 360

Glascock, George 99, 221

Glascock, George Jr 252, 299, 417, 427

Glascock, John 252

Glascock, Judith 93

Glascock, Richard 83, 199

Glascock, Thomas 393

Glascock, William 93

Glascock, William Jr 93, 99, 426, 431

Goard, Peter 407

Godall, Parke 372

<u>Goochland County 424</u>

Goodridge, George 94, 329, 370, 422

Goodridge, John 16, 55, 75 (+), 83, 100, 153, 157, 224, 229, 266, 275, 286, 297, 304, 309, 322, 328, 329 (+), 330, 348 (+), 349, 416

Goodridge, Richard 7-8, 20, 102, 142, 178, 185, 189-91, 196, 208, 214 (+), 237, 253, 266, 269, 292, 297, 307, 329-30

Gordon, Ann 11, 219, 258

Gordon, James 4, 6 (+), 7, 11, 13, 15, 19-20, 21 (+), 24, 28-9, 34, 37 (+), 39, 50-51, 52 (+), 56, 61 (+), 66 (+), 67-9, (+), 77, 82, 115, 116 (+), 117, 118 (+), 119-20, 121 (+), 123, 125 (+), 126, 130

(+), 131 (+), 132, 134-7, 146, 148, 151, 153-4, 156, 160, 162 (+), 164-5, 167, 169, 171 (+), 172 (+), 175, 179 (+), 184, 185 (+), 186, 188-90, 194 (+), 211-12, 217, 219, 233, 235-6, 241-2, 244 (+), 245 (+), 246 (+), 247 (+), 248, 250-51, 255-6, 258 (+), 260 (+), 262 (+), 263, 265 (+), 266, 269, 271, 273-4, 275 (+), 277, 278 (+), 280 (+), 281 (+), 282 (+), 284 (+), 286-7, 288 (+), 289, 294, 308, 311, 313-14, 317, 319, 325-6, 329, 332 (+), 334 (+), 341, 346 (+), 347, 349, 366 (+), 370, 372, 411, 414 (+)

Gordon, James Jr 102, 126, 315

Gordon, John 159, 392

Gordon, Nathaniel 294

Gordon, Robert 12

Graham, William 36, 172

Green, Matthew 244

Greenwood, Josiah 411

Griffin, Corbin 184, 278

Griffin, Cyrus 40, 52, 53 (+), 57, 239, 368

Griffin, LeRoy 56

Griffin, T. B. 160   (+), 167, 170, 208, 256, 260-61

Griffin, Thomas B. 4, 17, 28, 37 (+), 39-40, 46, 52, 56, 61 (+), 69 (+), 88 (+), 90, 98, 124 (+), 136, 149, 156, 250

Griffin, William 69, 124, 167, 170, 208, 256, 260, 261, 291 (+), 334

Griggs 427-8

Griggs, Elizabeth 18, 102, 222

Griggs, John 18-19, 33

Griggs, Judith 197

Griggs, Lee 18 (+), 19 (+), 23 (+)

Griggs, Ruth 279, 361 (+), 366, 369, 394 (+), 395 (+)

Griggs, Sarah 135, 142

Griggs, Thomas 97, 135, 142, 287 (+), 289, 315

Kirk, James Jr 10, 15, 30-31, 34, 138

Kirk, John 72, 99, 123, 129, 210, 218, 225, 249, 328

Kirk, Mary 40-41, 170

Kirk, Sarah 27, 66 (+), 133, 172, 265

Kirk, Thomas 66 (+), 171-2, 265

Kirk, William 37, 60, 156 (+), 175, 244, 259, 290, 297, 309, 399, 405, 410, 413

Landing, Taylor's 12 (+)

Lane, Downman's 26

Langsdale, John 144

Lattimore, Charles 262

Lattimore, William 262

Laughlin, Simon 147, 151, 158, 200, 299, 332, 375, 387, 400-401, 409

Lawrence, William Jr 88

Laws, Amny 174, 182-3

Lawson 12

Lawson, Ann 63

Lawson, Bailey 226

Lawson, Elizabeth 63 (+), 131

Lawson, Epaphroditus 76 (+), 82, 255, 276, 278

Lawson, Eppa 47

Lawson, H. 298

Lawson, Harry 4, 11

Lawson, Henry 13, 14 (+), 19, 23, 26, 43, 46, 63, 71, 73, 76-7, 82, 121, 125 (+), 337, 408, 135, 142, 145, 154 (+), 157 (+), 158, 161, 162 (+), 163, 165, 169 (+), 172, 174 (+), 175, 178, 182, 184, 185 (+), 186, 192, 196, 217, 225, 235 (+), 236, 242 (+), 244-5, 247-8, 250, 253, 257, 263, 268-9, 271, 276 (+), 279, 281, 282 (+), 284, 288, 290, 292, 296 (+), 297, 298 (+), 303-4, 308, 311, 313, 317 (+), 321, 325, 333 (+), 340-41, 347, 349, 353-4, 357 (+), 360, 363-4, 367, 370, 378, 391, 405-6, 408-9, 417-18, 421-2, 426 (+), 427, 435

Lawson, John 226, 384

Lawson, Lettice 175

Lawson, Mary 76, 158, 226, 292, 308, 321, 330, 357, 387, 414

Lawson, Thomas 5-6, 11 (+), 12-14, 23, 24 (+), 28-9, 30 (+), 35, 37, 39, 41 (+), 42, 45, 48, 50, 53, 58, 61, 63 (+), 64 (+), 67-9, 70 (+), 76, 77 (+), 115-16, 119, 122-3, 127, 131, 134, 137, 159, 162-3, 172, 174, 175 (+), 178, 181-2, 187, 192, 204 (+), 206, 209, 211, 217, 222, 225, 234, 236, 237 (+), 239, 242 (+), 263, 290, 292, 308

Lawson, Thomas Jr 384

Lawson, William 19, 24, 26, 34, 63, 135, 175, 186, 226, 309, 350, 379, 412, 431

Lawson, William Jr 49, 158

Leach, Anthony 84 (+)

Leach, Margaret 84

Leach, Mary 84

Leanna Cornelius 127, 131

Leanna(h) Hutchings 41, 44, 130 (+), 135 (+), 136 (+), 391, 396

Leannah Overstreet 152

Ledford, James 36, 171, 173, 353, 423

Lee, Charles 19, 35, 41, 48, 59 (+), 73 (+), 88, 129, 131, 134, 167, 201, 216, 252, 265, 293, 308, 319, 328, 330, 347, 350, 355, 359, 385, 405, 432 (+)

Lee, Kendall 434

Lee, Molly 57

Lee, R. E. 73

Lee, Richard 127, 359 (+), 363

Lee, Richard E. 9, 28, 49, 51, 70-71, 76 (+), 81, 88, 100, 126, 131, 135 (+), 139-40, 151, 177, 192, 195, 213

Lee, Sarah 42, 346, 366

Lee, Susannah 42

Lee, Thomas 296, 378

Lee, William 394 (+)

Lee, Winny 42

Leland, John 52, 57, 92, 95, 172, 174 (+), 182, 183, 261, 305, 307, 430

Lettice Ball 316

Lettice Carter 22

Lettice Lawson 175

Lettice Wheeler 220

Lewis, Mary 304

Lewis, William 90, 129, 139, 231, 305 (+), 317, 324, 330, 337-8, 345, 389, 402

Lightburn, Henry 391 (+)

Lizenby, Ellen 294

Lock, Richard 66, 70, 141

Lock, Stephen 141, 195, 273, 285, 307

Lock, Winifred 141

Logain, Nathaniel 353, 370

Longwith, Burges 392, 429

Longwith/Longweth, John 17, 164, 295, 308, 358, 369

Lowry, Gavin/Gawin, etc. 28, 33-4, 38, 67, 155 (+), 246, 293, 329, 338, 426

Luckham, William 66, 199, 273 (+), 408

Lucy Chilton 77 (+)

Lucy Denny 299, 332, 400

Lucy Doggett 240

Lucy Hammonds 355

Lucy Hinton 187

Lucy Mason 61, 369, 392 (+)

Lucy Montague 174

Lucy Webb 12

Lucyann Wood 164

Lunceford, Ellis 327

Lunceford, Ezekiel 233

Lunceford, Moses 169, 195, 208

Lunceford, Redm. 232

Lunceford, Rodham 125, 309, 322, 357 (+), 411

Lunceford/Lunsford, Travers 22, 84-5, 96, 140, 159, 195, 199 (+), 209-10, 230, 257, 262, 393

Lunsford, Moses 214

Lunsford, Rhodam 28, 67, 102